Charles-Joseph, Prince de Ligne

Selected Letters

**Translated / Edited
by
Basil Guy**

Apocryphile Press
1700 Shattuck Ave #81
Berkeley, CA 94709
www.apocryphile.org

© Copyright 2017 by Basil Guy

Printed in the United States of America
ISBN 978-1-944769-91-8

All rights reserved. No part of this book may be reproduced, stored in a retrieval system, or transmitted in any form or by any means—electronic, mechanical, photocopy, recording, or otherwise—without written permission of the author and publisher, except for brief quotations in printed reviews. Printed in the United States of America

Please join our mailing list at
www.apocryphilepress.com/free
and we'll keep you up-to-date on all our new releases
—and we'll also send you a FREE BOOK.
Visit us today!

For Christine,
and for H. M. P. – *in memoriam*

Contents

Preface 7
Abbreviations 15
List of Correspondents 17
List of Illustrations 21
Biographical Outline 23
Introduction 29

✍ Letters

    To Voltaire 47
    To Rousseau 57
    To Van den Broucke 61
    To Charles-Antoine de Ligne 73
    To Stanislas-Augustus 93
    To Mme de Coigny 97
    To Ségur 119
    To Potemkin 133
    To Poniatowski 137
    To Princess de Ligne 141
    To Calonne 151
    To Casanova 155
    To Hugh Elliot 167
    To Bonnay 171
    Illustrations 175
    To Müller 177
    To Tallyrand 189
    To Archenholtz 195
    To Gentz 199
    To D'Arenberg 207
    To Paër 213
    To Mme de Staël 217
    To Flore de Ligne 237
    To Metternich 241
    To Saxe-Weimar 245

To Laborde	253
To Caroline Pichler	259
To Mme Panam	263
To My Readers	267
Appendix A, Two Scenes from *Fragments*	272
Appendix B, A letter on the Turks	276
Acknowledgements	279

Preface – Ligne as Man of Letters

When, in 1807-8, preparing her anthology of the writings of the Prince de Ligne, *Letters and Reflections*, little could Mme de Staël have foreseen the fame and fortune that would accrue to her work, the most popular published during her lifetime and the most remunerative. Nor did she have to be concerned by such non-literary considerations. She already had a reputation as what we would call "a public intellectual" of European renown; and she was one of the wealthiest women in the West.[1] Her selection from the Prince's multi-volume *Mélanges*,[2] with supplements from other works, was very clever, and Ligne was a devoted collaborator. On occasion, Ligne attempted to favor her efforts on his behalf with the creation of new letters meant to pacify her, should she notice a few unkind personal remarks about her adored father (Jacques Necker, 1732-1804) in material she already had to hand. She, contrary to his expectations, had the good sense and the taste to pass over such flattery without recognition and to concentrate on her "Preface," in which she stressed the gracefulness of his 18th-century style and the elegance and accuracy of his expression, adding, in a memorable phrase, "He has become a model, and not just an imitator." The pertinence of her remarks has yet to be equaled.[3]

The anthology, which appeared in January/February 1809, was met with considerable enthusiasm, inspiring two imitations and even a sixth printing in 1811, not to mention translations into German (two), Russian (two), Italian, and English (two, including one in America). Although there is an edition in two volumes, marked "Londres:/ B. Dulau et Cie./ 1808(-1809)," until more documentary evidence is available, we do not know whether this work takes precedence over "Paris,/...J.J. Paschoud...,/1809."[4]

With all the foregoing attention, it is not surprising that Ligne's excitement knew no bounds as he congratulated his editor, proclaiming in a letter from 1810 " ma chère Baronne [Mme de Staël] m'a fait homme de lettres"[5] – an expression that was gaining in popularity among the public of the time. She had effectively raised Ligne (and his work) from "the dust of Dresden," where volumes of his *Mélanges* were being printed – and not selling very well. In the time since, more than two hundred anthologies have been published, modeled on this one, both in France and abroad.

To forestall criticism, Mme de Staël had orchestrated a veritable campaign among friends and critics in reviews and newspapers. Her success was far-reaching and greater than even she might have hoped. The publication overshadowed her previous novelistic successes and the high seriousness of her *magnum opus* on Germany, still to come. The material reward was likewise considerable, enabling Ligne to improve somewhat the parlous state of his personal finances.

The Prince's approval of the choice of texts would indicate that there were generally but two aspects of his life around which the anthology was organized: his role as a man about town and his aspiration to a military command. The one topic that is passed over, implicitly, is that of Ligne as a writer or, more specifically, a man of letters. (The sole exception to this lack of critical assessment would seem to be *Literat und Feldmarschall*).[6]

About 1740, the number of *hommes de lettres* (as writers in general were then classified, though women were exluded from this category) had increased. By the time of the French Revolution the original term was inappropriate, and a new one had to be devised. It was *gens de lettres*, and so it continues to this day (including women), with many under the guise of "critic."

Preface – Ligne as Man of Letters

In one version of the *Dictionnaire philosophique*, Voltaire had included an article on *"gens de lettres"* in which he attempted to define the term and to stress its novelty (though not without attacking two of his pet aversions: the Academy and the University) by saying

> Today a man of letters often adds to the study of Greek and Latin, that of Italian, Spanish, and, above all, English. It is not necessary for a man of letters to acquire a profound knowledge [of all branches of learning]: *omnicompetence* is no longer within human reach; but, true men of letters equip themselves so as to move confidently through these difficult terrains, even if they cannot cultivate them all... The men of letters who have rendered the greatest service to the small number of thinking beings scattered across the earth, are isolated scholars, true sages sealed away in their closets, who have neither carried out public disputations in the University, nor said things by halves in the Academy – and they have almost always been persecuted... [Ligne, for flouting some social predjudices, all pertaining either to belief in superstitions, or magic, or fortune telling, or puerile antagonisms – once life-threatening and now contemptible – that served both the state and religion.].... Sometimes we are astounded that what once stupefied us is no longer of the slightest concern.

Voltaire then goes on to refine his ideal and concludes: [Men of letters] get more enjoyment than others from being sociable. But [he warns] a man of letters is *not* what is called a *bel esprit*, or "wit".[7]

There is also the notion of the man of letters as preoccupied with the idea of *belles lettres*. The term perfectly suits the Prince de Ligne, with all his intelligence and enthusiasm. Rare are the critics who have sensed these qualities in him and, having found them, expatiate on them. Aside from Antonio Mor,[8] notable exceptions are Roland Mortier, Jerome

Vercruysse, Manuel Couvreur, Daniel Acke and other members of the "Groupe d'études Lignistes" in Brussels, who bear witness to the appropriateness of "man of letters" applied to the Prince de Ligne. Finally, the term carried with it the idea of a superior intellect to whom the reader could give credence because of the quality of the writer's thought and expression. Sometimes, a word or phrase or even a brief development as in "To My Readers",[9] is enough to convince the public of Ligne's talent. But a thoroughgoing stylistic analysis, such as we have become accustomed to expect in the works of other writers has not been realized.

More recently, Professor Rémy Saisselin has claimed[10] that, even before Voltaire, the man of letters was gaining in prominence because "literature" in the French-speaking world consisted largely of theater, poetry, and history. Such works were not always recognized as "literature" encapsulated in masterpieces from "the classical moment." "Modern literature" proved a late arrival. In fact, the classical age was a false concept, since the genres mentioned were not free from moral, sacred, or religious concomitants. Their absence was said to characterize "modernity." Instead, "humane letters" referred in general to a taste for verse and an acquaintance with writers that would soon become *belles lettres* or the modern notion of "literature." Though not an aspiring professional, like many of his contemporaries, Ligne was committed to literature from his earliest years, thanks to one of several tutors, the abbé Etienne de la Porte (1714-64), who introduced him to "the flower of the humanities... which to this day has been the delight of my life."[11] Thus we may follow Professor Saisselin's explanation, using the tropes of his analysis, since his perspective applies pre-eminently to the Prince de Ligne.

As Professor Saisselin has outlined, there is

Ligne's enthusiasm for, and preoccupation with the world of the theater, dating from his early publication of the *Lettres à Eugénie* (Paris, 1772/4) on amateur theatricals and continuing to the end of his life;[12]

his enormous production of topical verse was likewise a lifelong activity, if we but cast a glance at the twenty-two pages of *incipit* compiled by Professor Vercruysse;[13]

his tentative engagement with the novel in its various forms, emphasized by Professors Couvreur and Mortier in their magisterial edition of Ligne's *Oeuvres romanesques*,[14] as well as in different asides from his correspondence;

his numerous biographies of military leaders (not forgetting his celebrated hoax, *Mémoires du Prince Eugène de Savoie*);[15] or his attempts at historical analysis like "Sur la Révolution française" (*Mémoires et Mélanges 4*);[16] or his attempt at cultural anthropology in *Mélanges 7*, where his expertise fails him and his fantasy prevents him from recognizing that his "boyars" are Muslim and that the yellow of the women's gowns is a symbol of mourning.[17]

From Ligne's viewpoint, texts could, if necessary, allow an overarching appreciation of literature in its several dimensions and demonstrate how completely he had mastered the technical component of the various styles of what were then known simply as "lettres" (not correspondences). In his case, at the root of all these concerns lay his active and stimulating imagination, accompanied by his profound commitment to a life of the mind that far outshines the rhythm of his life. In all, we can easily determine that he knew instinctively how to write, that he daily enjoyed doing so, and that he valued his role as "man of letters."

Despite all these increments to the portrait of Ligne, we must not forget that he himself had chosen texts for Mme de Staël's anthology. The re-orientation I am suggesting is a corrective to the work of succeeding compilers throughout the nineteenth and twentieth centuries. But, modern readers demand more than the replication of his life: whatever our attitude, the Prince remains conscious of his importance as a creative writer.[18] For even considering his life as a social adventurer or discussing the military tactics of a bygone era, these topics remain essentially an excuse for writing: Ligne is wholly and innately a man of letters. Fancy, or the powers of the imagination, are strongly developed in him. His ideas are straightforward and merit due appreciation from us, with his reputation enhanced. How much more probing is this development when read in context!

The same is also true of his epistolary creations. The local color he invokes is sometimes suspect, since he blithely ignores certain facts about native cultures, unless his professed ignorance was but a ploy to alert the reader to his fantasy.[19] Additionally, there are discrete changes that betray considerable reworking by the author.

Further indications of Ligne's preferences are to be found in specific words or threads underpinning his conception of the literary enterprise. When he makes urgent pleas for help of one sort or another (very necessary to his life as an exile in Vienna from 1794 to the end), he cannot keep himself from punning. There are also his critical assessments in *Lettres à M. de La Harpe*[20] or in the (infrequent) reviews of works by contemporary authors, firmly grounded in common-sense attitudes (sometimes masquerading as humor) that go far to confirm his cautious approach to the contemporary novel in line with the views of, say, Jane Austen, William Beckford, or even Goethe.

And so, in the pages that follow, without stressing the third man (of letters) to be found in Ligne's texts, after the man-about-town and the man-at-arms, I hope that this concern may continue the revival of interest in the works of the Prince, revealing his true genius as the authentic creator of literature I have just sketched above.

***

Mme. de Staël added Ligne's journalistic interviews with Voltaire and Rousseau to her collection. I have included, at the end of my presentation, two scenes from Ligne's *Fragments* (Vercruysse ed.) that are perfect examples of his creativity: A – An encounter at a gala, and the Babel of the Court at Vienna. On a more serious note, there is the text: B – of a letter from about 1790 on the Turks, at a time when they were losing ground in Europe, and their threat seemed less imminent.

Notes

1. For information concerning Mme de Staël and Ligne, see Vercruysse, Jeroom. *Bibliographie descriptive.* (Paris, 2008), 255-90. On de Staël's fortune, see Herold, J. Christopher. *Mistress to an Age.* Indianapolis: Bobbs-Merrill, 1968. 259.
2. Prince de Ligne, Charles-Joseph. *Mélanges militaires, littéraires et sentimentaires.* 34 vols. (Vienna/Dresde:, 1795-1811).
3. "Eighteenth-century style," see Jasinski, Béatrice. *Correspondance générale de Mme de Staël.* 16 vols. I:i-lxxvi. Paris: Pauvert, 1961.
4. See Vercruysse, *Bibliographie descriptive*, (Paris, 2008), 255-68.
5. Maria Ullrichová. *Lettres de Mme de Staël ... conservées en Bohême.* Prague: Akademia, 1959. 69.
6. The one exception to this seeming lack of interest is Günther Elbing's *Literat und Feldmarschall.* Stuttgart: Deutsche Verlagsanstalt, 1979.
7. Voltaire. *Œuvres complètes.* Vol. 33:B. Oxford: The Voltaire Foundation, 1987. 121-23.
8. See Antonio Mor, "Le Prince de Ligne, prosateur," *Lettres romanes* ix (1955), 15-37.
9. Prince de Ligne, "Aux lecteurs." *NRL 1*, 3-9.
10. Saisselin, Remy. *The Literary Enterprise.* Detroit: Wayne State University, 1979. 18-19.
11. Prince de Ligne, Charles-Joseph. *Frags. 2,* (Vercruysse, ed.).55.
12. Such as they are, these ideas created a favorable *point d'appui* for writers, actors, producers, and the public itself. See Vercruysse, *Bibliographie descriptive*, (Paris, 2008), 25-37.
13. See Vercruysse, *Bibliographie descriptive*, (Paris, 2008), 255-90, 495-518.
14. Prince de Ligne, *Oeuvres romanesques* (ed. Couvreur-Mortier), 2 vol. Paris: Champion, 2000-5.
15. Prince de Ligne, *Mémoires du Prince Eugène de Savoie.* Weimar: Au Bureau de l'industrie, 1809. See Vercruysse, *Bibliographie descriptive*, (Paris, 2008), 302-12.
16. Prince de Ligne, Charles-Joseph. *Mémoires et Mélanges, 4.* Paris: Dupont 1827. 147-61. Vercruysse, *Bibliographie descriptive*, (Paris, 2008), 349.
17. Prince de Ligne. *Mél.* vii. (1796), 198-210.
18. There is a very subtle analysis and explanation of Ligne's conscious turn from the military to literature by Christoph Dröghe in *Nouvelles Annales Prince de Ligne*, viii. Paris: Champion, 1994. 241.

19. Prince de Ligne. *Frags. 1,* (Vercruysse ed.), 140. "*Je ne me relis jamais*", disproved by any photograph of a page of his writings, either in his hand or that of a secretary.
20. "Lettres à M. de La Harpe," Prince de Ligne. *Mél. x* (1796), 127-34.

Abbreviations

Ligne   *Fragments de l'histoire de ma vie* (Leuridant ed.), 2 vols. Paris:1927-8.
Hereafter, read as: *Frags. 1* (or *2*), (Leuridant ed.), plus page(s).

"   *Fragments de l'histoire de ma vie* (Vercruysse ed.), 2 vols. Paris, 2001.
Hereafter, read as: *Frags. 1* (or *2*), (Vercruysse ed.), plus page(s).

"   *Mélanges militaires, litteraires et sentimentaires*, 34 vols. (Vienna/Dresden: 1795-1811.)
Read hereafter as: *Mél.* plus vol., (plus date), plus page(s).
This is not to be confused with other works combined with *Mélanges* (e.g. *Mémoires et Mélanges*, 5 vols., 1827.)

"   *Nouveau Recueil de Lettres*, 2 vols. (Weimar, 1812).
Read hereafter as: *NRL* 1 (or 2), plus page(s).

Vercruysse   *Bibliographie descriptive des écrits du Prince de Ligne* (Paris: Champion, 2008)
Read as *Bibliographie descriptive*. (Paris: 2008), plus page(s).

Voltaire   *Correspondance*, (Besterman, definitive ed.), 50 vols. (Geneva, 1968-77)
Read hearafter as: Besterman D. letter number

There are, additionally, two important reviews:

Annales Prince de Ligne, 19 vols., (Brussels: 1920-38).
Read: *APL*, plus vol. and (date), and page(s).

Nouvelles Annales Prince de Ligne, 19 vols. (Brussels/ Namur: publication continues).
Read: *NAPL* plus vol. and (date) and page(s).

Letters

Our sole consolation [after the departure of the Prince de Ligne from Ferney] is being able to read him in his letters. Madame Denis, Voltaire's *Correspondence* (BestD.) xxxv, 146.

The Correspondents are numbered as they appear in the following anthology.

1. To VOLTAIRE,
   a- from Brussels, 30 December, 1763
   b- from Brussels, 1777 (includes a note from the *Coup-dœil* (1786).
2. To Jean-Jacues ROUSSEAU, from Paris, 1770.
3. To J-J VANDENBROUCKE,
   a- from Belœil, 12/13 [June, 1774].
   b- from [Versailles?] ii/iii, 1776.
   c- from Vienna, 4 [April 1778]
   d- from Vienna, 15 April, 1786.
   e- from Vienna, 24 August, 1795.
4. To Charles-Antoine de LIGNE,
   a- from Brezno (Czech Republic), 26 June, 1778.
   b- from Versailles, 10 December, 1780.
   c- from HQ, Elizavetgorod (Russia), 12 May, 1788
   d- from HQ, Kameniets-Podolskiy (Ukraine), 8 June, 1788.

e- from My camp in the deserts of Tartary (Ochakov, Russia), 30 July, 1789.
   f- from Vienna, after the attack on Ismaïlia (Romania), [25 November, 1790?]

5. To STAISLAS AUGUSTUS, King of Poland, from Kiev, 10 [April, 1787].

6. To Louise-Marthe, Marquise de COIGNY[?] from Parthenizza [Crimea], [1787, 1801?]. Includes a note on the letters, plus remarks on the addressee/dedicatee.

7. To Louis-Philippe, Count de SÉGUR,
   a- from Elizavetgorod (Russia), 1 December, 1787.
   b- from Ryabaïa-Movila (Moldova). 1 December, 1788.
   c- from Vienna, [undated]

8. To Gregory-Alexis, Prince POTEMKIN, from Cetatea Hora [Suceava, Romania], [24 May, 1788].

9. To Joseph, Prince PONIATOWSKI, from Semun (Serbia), September/October, 1789.

10. To Françoise, PRINCESS DE LIGNE, *Copie* from Vienna, 3 January 1790.

11. To Charles-Alexandre, Marquis de CALONNE, from Belœil, March, 1791.

12. To Giacomo CASANOVA [de Seingalt],
    a- from Toeplitz, 22 September, 1794.
    b- from Vienna, [27 November, 1794?].
    c- from Vienna, 17 December, 1794.
    d- from Vienna, 20th [January 1797].
    e- from Vienna, 21 March, 1798.

13. To Hugh ELLIOT, from Toeplitz, 1799/1800?

14. To Charles-François, Marquis de BONNAY, from Toeplitz, 28 June, 1802.

15. To Jean, Count de MÜLLER [von Sylvelden],
    a- from Toeplitz, 15 July, 1802.
    b- from Vienna, mid-October [1803].

c- from Vienna, 13 January, 1805.
d- from Vienna, 24/25 February, 1805.
e- from Toeplitz, 10 September, 1805.

16. To Charles-Maurice, Prince de TALLEYRAND,
    a- from Vienna, 20 [December],1805
    b- from Vienna, 29 December, 1805.
    c- from Vienna, 12 December, 1806.

17. To Johann-Wilhelm von ARCHENHOLZ, from Toeplitz, 2 Germinal [7 April], 1806.

18. To Friederich [von] GENTZ, from Vienna, 4 June, 1806.

19. To Auguste, Prince d'ARENBERG, from Toeplitz, 20 July, 1807.

20. To Ferdinand PAËR, [no place, no date, but presumably from Toeplitz, 1807].

21. To Germaine, Baronness de STAËL-HOLSTEIN,
    a- from Vienna, 28 December,1807.
    b- from Toeplitz, [23] September, [1808].
    c- from Toeplitz, July, 1809 [?].
    d- from Vienna, [1809/1810].
    e- from Vienna, 24 June, [1810?]
    f- from the Kahlenberg [Vienna], 8 July, 1811.

22. To Flore, Princess de LIGNE, his daughter, from Vienna, 26 March, 1808.

23. To Clemens, Prince von METTERNICH,
    a-from Vienna, [beginning], 1809.
    b-from Vienna, [1810]
    c- [Oct/Nov], 1814

24. To Karl-Augustus, Duke of SACHSEN-WEIMAR,
    a-from Vienna, 12 June, 1810.
    b- from Baden bei Wien, autumn, 1810.

25. To Alexandre, Count de LABORDE, from Vienna/Toeplitz, 1810.

26. To Caroline PICHLER, from Vienna, 1 June, 1812.
27. To Pauline PANAM, (includes *billets*), from Vienna, August/November 1814.
28. To "My Readers", from Vienna [1812].

Appendices

Two scenes from LIGNE's *Fragments:*
    a. Encounter at a Gala.
    b. Babel of the Court (at Vienna).

Letter from Vienna, October, 1790: Who would know the Turks?

Illustrations

No. 1a – Cover. Manuscript page of Ligne's *Fragments de l'histoire de ma vie* (ed. Leuridant), 2 vols, Paris: Plon, 1927; vol. 1, 196.

No. 1b – Cover. Ligne aged about 45 in 1774-5 at the time of Ligne's Crimean adventure. Engraving by Antoine Cardon (1739-1822), after Charles Leclercq (1753-1821). (Courtesy of Fondation Ligne, Beloeil.)

No. 2 - Title Page *Silhouette of the Prince* circa 1780 by François Gonord from the catalog of an exhibition at the Château de Belœil, 1982, *Le Prince de Ligne et son temps*; no. 7:03.

No. 3 – The Ayu Dag (Bear Mountain, 572 m.), about 16 kms to NE of Yalta, and site of Parthenit (Parthenizza to Ligne) – an ancient trading village near the shore, with classical ruins scattered about. Oil painting: *View to the Ayu Dag and Parthenit*, by A. Litzinov, 1894. (Courtesy of Joyce Borkowski, S. Berwick, ME; photo: Geo. Barker, Portsmouth, N.H.)

No. 4 – *Ligne reading in bed around 1794*. Pen and ink by Sauveur Legros (1754-1834). Ligne's Turkish servant Osman, standing at foot of the bed, had been made a prisoner at Ochakov (1791). *Annales Prince de Ligne*, 1934. (Courtesy of Fondation Ligne, Beloeil.)

No. 5 – Portrait engraved after H. Jagemann (1780-1820) by C-A. Schwerdgeburth (1785-1878). *Ligne* as "homme de lettres." (Courtesy Hans Wahl, Anton Kippenberg: *Goethe und seine Welt*, Insel-Verlag, Leipzig 1932, 177)

Biographical Outline

Nota Bene. Dates in this biographical outline are to be read as follows: day in Arabic;month in small Roman; year in Arabic.

23. v. 1735	Baptism in Brussels of Charles-Joseph, 7th Prince de Ligne and the Holy Roman Empire, Grandee of Spain, Lord of Fagnolles and other fiefs. Son of Prince Claude-Lamoral II and Elizabeth, Princess de Salm, he belongs to one of the most ancient families of Hainaut in the Austrian Netherlands (modern Belgium). His father and uncle before him were Field Marshals of the Holy Roman Empire, as would be Charles-Joseph himself.
1737-1751	Educated by tutors at Belœil, the family seat, not far from Mons. Writes *Discours sur la profession des armes* (pub. 1796).
1751	Travels via Strasbourg and Ulm to Vienna, where he is presented to the Empress Maria-Theresa and named Chamberlain to the Emperor Francis I Stephen.
1752	Ensign in the regiment of Ligne-Infanterie, commanded by his father.
vi. 1755	Start of Seven Years' War in America; baptism of fire at Kolin (1757), where he is promoted to Captain; sees action mainly in Bohemia and Silesia; promoted to Lieutenant-Colonel after Hochkirch (1758).

6. viii. 1755	Marries Françoise, Princess de Liechtenstein (1739-1821), honeymoon at her parents' castle in Moravia.
26. v. 1757	Birth of daughter, Princess Christine (died 1830).
23. ix. 1759	Birth of favorite son, Prince Charles-Antoine (died 1792).
xi. 1759	Sent to Paris and Versailles to announce the Austrian victory at Maxen; returns to the war at Berlin and Torgau (both 1759) and Adelsbach (1762).
1763	Following the Peace of Hubertusberg, pays first yearly visit to France (until 1787) with Count d'Artois. Develops *Amabile, conte* (pub. 1996).
3. iv. 1764	Attends coronation of Joseph II at Frankfurt.
vi. 1764	Promoted to Major-General and visits Venice; returning to Brussels, stays with Voltaire at Ferney for a week. Writes *Mes Conversations avec M. de Voltaire* (*Mél. x* (1796), 257-68).
3. xi. 1764	Birth of Prince François-Léopold (died 1771).
7. v. 1766	Birth of Prince Louis (died 1813).
7. vi. 1766	On death of Prince Claude-Lamoral, becomes head of the family and inherits titles and fortune of the Lignes.
20. vii. 1767	Following birth of Prince Adalbert-Xavier (died 1771), visits England.
1769	In Brussels, helps to found the Société Littéraire (precursor of the modern Académie Royale) and befriends Eugénie (1746-1806) and Angélique (1749-1822) d'Hannetaire.
1770	Joins Freemasons at Mons (Lodge of True and Perfect Harmony); visits Jean-Jacques Rousseau in Paris, and in September attends meeting of Frederick II and Joseph II at Neustadt (Moravia). Writes *Mes Conversations avec Jean-Jacques* (*Mél. x* (1796), 268-77).
31. v. 1771	Promoted to Lieutenant General and named Colonel-Propriétaire of his father's regiment.

1772	Awarded the Golden Fleece; visits Amsterdam.
Summer 1773	Visits Spa with the Duc d'Orléans (future Philippe-Egalité of France). Publishes *Mémoires sur ... le comte de Bussy-Rabutin. Mél. v* (1795), xvi-159.
18.vii 1773	Birth of daughter Princess Euphémie (died 1834).
1773-1776	Sponsors literary gatherings at his secondary residence of Baudour near Mons.
1774	Returns to Spa, Paris, and Vienna; publishes *Lettres à Eugénie (Eulalie)* (*Mél. xi* (1796), ii-129.) on amateur theatricals.
iv. 1775	Begins work on the "English" garden at Belœil; fraternizes with Count d'Artois (future Charles X of France), often returning to Versailles to frequent the society of Marie-Antoinette.
18. xi. 1775	Birth of daughter, Princess Flore (died 1849).
1778	Conceives of the Temple d'Amour at Trianon for Marie-Antoinette; participates in the War of the Bavarian Succession at Boesigberg, Bohemia (September).
29. vii. 1779	Marriage of his son Prince Charles to the Polish heiress Hélène Massalska (1763-1815), followed by eight days' celebration at Belœil; for the occasion composes *Colette et Lucas, comédie*.
vi. 1780	Undertakes lengthy trip to Saint-Petersburg to regularize the terms of Hélène Massalska-Ligne's dowry.
17. viii. 1780	Presented to Catherine II at Tsarskoye Sélo; leaves on 5 October, in his pocket a brevet of Colonel in the Russian army and title to lands in the Crimea, near Yalta. Publishes *Préjugés/ Fantaisies militaires (in Mél. i and ii, 1795)*.
ii. 1781	Passing through Warsaw, is created a Polish noble and is elected to the Diet.
26. vi. 1781	Receives Joseph II at Brussels.

6. viii. 1781	Attends entry of the Emperor into Luxemburg and publishes first version of the *Coup-d'Œil sur Belœil*.
1783	Revisits Spa with Count d'Artois. Publishes *Mélanges de littérature* in two volumes.
5. i. 1784	Attends flight of lighter-than-air balloon by Pilâtre de Rozier at Lyons.
x. 1784	Guards the frontier with Holland in the "Seven Days' War" against the Dutch.
1786	Publishes second version of the *Coup-d'Œil*.
End 1786	Returns to Saint Petersburg, arriving home in January 1787.
4. iv. 1787	Publishes *Mémoires sur les campagnes de Louis de Bade*. (*Mél. iii-iv (1795): iii-215, iv-218.*) Joins Catherine II at Kiev for famous descent of the Dniepr in a waterborne caravan to the Crimea.
1787-1789	Participates in Catherine's Second Turkish War in Moldavia and before Ochakov; then, on the Austrian side at Belgrade, where he is named Grand Master of the Artillery and awarded the rank of Commander in the Order of Maria-Theresa (October 1789).
1788	Publishes *L'Amant ridicule, proverbe*.
24. x. 1789	Uprising in Brussels to which his name is (wrongly) attached, entailing temporary exile to Belgrade.
3. i. 1790	*Lettre à la Princesse son épouse* on the Belgian revolt published without his knowledge.
v. 1790	Allowed to regain Vienna, arranges residence ("Little Belœil") on the Kahlenberg.
30. ix. 1790	Attends coronation of Leopold II in Frankfurt, returning to Brussels.
20. v. 1791	Named Grand Bailiff and Captain-General of Hainaut province (Belgium).
14. ix. 1792	Death of son, Prince Charles, fighting against the French Revolution in the Argonne.

Beg. 1793	Presides over Estates of Hainaut in Mons and welcomes French refugees from the Revolution almost daily at Belœil.
26. vi. 1794	Forced into exile in Vienna by defeat of Austrian coalition at Fleurus; French occupation of Austrian Netherlands sequesters Belœil and his revenues.
1794-1814	Acquires a small house on the Moelkerbastei in Vienna ("the Parrot's Perch") and notoriety as a man-about-town.
Summer 1794	Commences almost yearly visits to Princess Christine and her family at Toeplitz (Bohemia); meets Casanova at nearby Dux.
1795	Publishes volumes 8-9 (final version of the *Coup-d'Œil sur Belœil*) of his *Mélanges* at Dresden and sells Crimean properties to Count Valerian Zubov for income.
1797-1814	*Fragments de l'histoire de ma vie* (his immortal memoirs; complete publication, in 2 vols., 2000-2001).
1800	Inspects his regiment at Lemberg (Ukraine).
1802	Publishes *Mémoire sur le comte de Bonneval*.
27. iv. 1803	Marriage of Prince Louis to Countess Louise van der Noot de Duras (1785-1863).
12. v. 1803	Declared a mediatized Prince by Napoleon, receives as compensation the abbey of Edelstetten in Swabia (Bavaria).
29. x. 1803	Sequestration of Belœil rescinded.
28. i. 1804	Birth of Prince Eugene (died 1880), son of Prince Louis and continuator of "the Line."
19. vi. 1804	Sells Edelstetten to Prince Niklaus Esterhazy for income and cedes Belœil and other fiefs to his son, Prince Louis.
1804-1814	Compiles *Ma Napoléonide* (partially published 1921); new edition by J. Vercruysse. *Napoléon, France – Autriche*. Paris: Champion, 2013.

iv.-x. 1805	Flees to Pressburg (Bratislava), then returns to Vienna occupied by Napoleon.
vii. 1806	Inspects his regiment at Lemberg (Ukraine).
v. 1807	Travels to Karlsbad (Bohemia) where he meets Goethe, continuing into Poland where he is reconciled with Hélène Massalska-Ligne.
18. vi. 1807	Named Captain of the Palace Guard (Trabanorum seu Satrapum Turma).
17. vii. 1807	On a visit to Dresden sees Napoleon, but refuses to be presented.
xii. 1807-v. 1808	Frequents Mme de Staël in Vienna.
27. ix. 1808	Attends coronation of Francis II (Francis I) as Emperor of Austria, at Pressburg (Bratislava).
7. x. 1808	Named Field-Marshal.
1809	Publishes at Weimar the very successful hoax, *Mémoires du Prince Eugène de Savoie*.
14. iv. 1809-30. i. 1810	"Annus horribilis." Flees with the Court before Napoleon to Pesth (Hungary).
20. iv. 1809	Accused of treachery because of published correspondence with General-Count de Grünne, is consigned to house arrest for one day.
24. x. 1809	Publication of *Lettres et pensées*, an anthology of his work by Mme de Staël, makes him famous overnight.
1810-1812	Sees Goethe at Toeplitz and visits Weimar, Dresden and Prague.
1812	Publishes at Weimar *Nouveau Recueil de Lettres* ("critical" ed., 1928).
ix. 1814-iv. 1815	Congress of Vienna where he is lionized.
13. xii. 1814	After catching cold at a late-night assignation, dies in bed at his house on the Moelkerbastei, his funeral attended by three monarchs and an enormous throng, followed by interment on the Kahlenberg.

Introduction

The following selection from the letters of the Prince de Ligne (1735-1814) comprises a few, translated by other hands.[1] All – both old and new – have been carefully vetted and, it is hoped, made consistent with current usage in every case so as to provide the interested reader with the means of forming an independent idea of the author. Most of the letters presented here are relatively brief (some are no more than notes); the longest is Ligne's most famous: a meditation from the Crimea (no. 6). Addressed to the Marquise de Coigny (and first published in Ligne's *Mélanges* for 1801);[2] she was not properly a correspondent, rather, an acquaintance who had known Ligne at Versailles in the 1770's. My choice of letters, personally examined by me, is faithful to the originals; others, discovered by Ph. Mansel, are included in his magisterial and, I like to think, definitive biography, *Prince of Europe*.[3]

So far, Ligne's letters have not been the object of a complete, scholarly edition, any more than recent revelations about the existence of other letters from Ligne in, for example, the family archives at Belœil, the archives of the University Library at Ghent, Belgium (Van den Broucke collection), or at the castle of Antoing, Belgium ("Les Livres rouges"), or in the state archives, Děčin, Czech Republic. Additionally there are individual letters scattered far and wide, reflecting Ligne's background in the Frenchified circles of European court society before the French Revolution.[4] Their number will surely increase as more and more are published; it has already reached some 2,000.

Wherever possible, I have tried to identify the place of origin, as well as the date. If there are uncertainties about either, I have included the information available in brackets, followed by a question mark; rarely, the question mark alone. I have not regularized salutations at the beginning or at the end of each letter, indicating, if possible, signatures like "le Prince de Ligne", or "Ligne", or, simply, a straight line, thus "____".

I have normalized (but not necessarily modernized) all proper names following the original, but this has proved to be particularly challenging where localities in SE Europe are concerned – not to mention Ligne's own orthographic fancies.[5]

The examples of Ligne's letters are arranged in groups corresponding in general to the developments in his life and thought, though all the letters in any one group are not necessarily in chronological order.

The notes are as brief as possible to be consistent with clarity. Some go far afield, as "Jane Austen" or "Goethe" (no. 24), on writing novels to direct the interested reader to their possible expansion into comparative topics that reflect Ligne's (perhaps) unconscious awareness of contemporary preoccupations.

While familiar letters do not often seem to treat but one subject only, their primary concern, at least for Ligne, may generally be news about his family or friends old – like King Stanislas, Bonnay, or Calonne – and new – like Casanova, Elliot, or the Duke of Saxe-Weimar – they may include his activities, or his wartime experiences (compare the rather humdrum reflections for Ségur on the Empress Catherine's Second Turkish War (1787-92) with the more visceral reactions of Ligne as an observer of Austria's defeat at the hands of Napoleon in 1805-9). (no. 15) Like many another *ci-devant* [former aristocrat] after the French Revolution, but refusing to acknowledge Napoleon (as in his letter to Auguste d'Arenberg) (no. 19), Ligne's letters to Gentz and Müller reveal all the frustrations of a teen-ager when, resorting to pseudonyms and writing in invisible ink, he assumes that "le monstre" Napoleon, could be undone by the likes of himself and his cohorts utilizing such methods. This attitude was reinforced (in 1790) with the circulation of a letter to his wife the Princess de Ligne (1739-1821) (no. 10), written at the time of the revolt of the Austrian Low Countries, 1787-89, and carefully shifting the terms of his (non) involvement. Politically, he had shown himself to be more astute when in 1786 he had posited that the future of Europe could be assured by a union of Protestant Princes under the aegis of Prussia – *not* Catholic Austria (not included in this collection) but such insidious ideas, going contrary to his liege of the time, are what soured his relations with the House of Habsburg for years to come. A well-known gadfly, he was caught in a treasonable correspondence (not included in this collection) in 1809 that excited all Europe and resulted in Ligne being confined to house arrest for one day.[6]

It is curious how detached are the few letters to his "most cherished son," Charles –Antoine (1756-92), where he speaks in a reserved or distant voice (no. 4). His true warmth and concern are more in evidence in his correspondence with Prince Joseph Poniatowski (1762-1813) (no. 9). And although Ligne's "love letters" easily number one thousand or more, they do not possess the intimacy nor the urgency of Voltaire's to Madame Denis as revealed by Th. Besterman in his edition.[7] The only samples of Ligne's "passion" included here are notes to Madame Panam (his last heart-throb with quasi-comic overtones) assembled by Professor Roland Mortier in an article from 2002 of the *Nouvelles Annales Prince de Ligne* (no. 27).[8]

Then there is also the *exotica*, characterized by his letter to Ségur about life in Moldavia (no. 7), to which was added (as an afterthought?) his quite stirring picture of the Turkish military at a time of decadence and which goes beyond European mythologies regarding "le Turc barbare et cruel," not to mention other minorities from Eastern Europe.[9]

Raised in the military to be a leader in wartime, Ligne was frustrated, after the Seven Years' War ended in an unsatisfactory peace at not receiving any commands – not even later against Napoleon, where he *might* have risen to greatness, as was called to his attention with publication of Archenholz's *Geschichte des Siebenjährigen Krieges* (no. 17).

It is interesting to see how, intellectually, he becomes more engaged with literature, especially as he took more and more to his pen.[10] Thus, the last letter in my selection, addressed to his readership in 1812, broaches several concerns about the profession of letters merely adumbrated in previous correspondence (no. 28). There he had formed his attitude as an astute critic (see no. 26 to Caroline Pichler) and would seem to confirm this re-ordering of his priorities, particularly in regard to publication of his *Mélanges* by friends Alexandre de Laborde, Paër, and Auguste d'Arenberg who were called upon to conspire with him for his charities (nos. 19, 20 and 25).

Scattered among these *varia* are frequent appeals to the likes of Potemkin, Talleyrand, and Metternich (nos 8, 16 and 23) that combine heartfelt pleading and punning – a typical combination. In the end, the letters I have chosen confirm the Prince's idea of self - that of a high-born individual, sure of his status in society, but unable to come to grips with his changed circumstances in post-Revolutionary Europe. Nonetheless, he was able to see (or to sense) clearly the all-too human motivation in History.

Much of the early collection at Ghent (no. 3) concerns his finances, especially as an aristocrat, still very much in the public eye. These letters show him in his most "anti-financier" and spendthrift moments. He did indeed lose a great part of his fortune both before and during the French Revolution and its aftermath, thanks to his fecklessness. Yet, even after 1794, though reduced in fortune, he was never so poor as he pretended. All this changed for the better when, in 1804, his son, Prince Louis, (1766-1813) took charge. And even more so, when in 1809, despite many vagaries, the anthology of his writings by Mme de Staël (no. 21) brought him much favorable attention from the public.

****

Ligne's first letter to be published by him was to Jean-Jacques Rousseau in 1770 (no. 2). Although the intent was kindly and well-meant, the authorial stance was so arch and supercilious (some would say "arrogant") that the public reaction overall was negative.[11] Characterized by Grimm in the *Correspondence littéraire* (13 July, 1770), as the work of a foreigner trying to outdo the French in wit and style -- and Grimm himself, a German of bourgeois origins? -- it was generally felt to have failed miserably. There then followed considerable curiosity, not to say recrimination, as to how this letter had come into Grimm's hands. Who was responsible: Ligne, or Rousseau himself? The question remains open.

Later, at the time of publication, Ligne's *Nouveau Recueil de Lettres* (1812)[12] was capital. But there is no up-to-date critical edition, the originals having probably disappeared. Little or no attention was paid to the fact that the collection contained some imaginary letters (viz. to Christopher Columbus, Napoleon, and the Pope), along with other curious details relating to epistolary exchanges of the day.[13] All such anomalies call for great circumspection in examining the texts, many of which were rewritten and adjusted to the vagaries of the author's intent, even though frequently quoted in biographies and critical studies of the Prince. Many of the lapses in these texts are printed out hereafter, although my intent was not to prepare a critical edition, since my involvement was limited to Englishing the letters and making them intelligible.

*****

Ligne tells us in his *Fragments*[14] that in general, on rising in the morning, he wrote in bed and continued his correspondence until roughly three in the afternoon, after which he dined and began his round of social gatherings.

The Prince does not mention the fact that he probably wrote with a dull quill pen, even though working with an ink-pot on the bedclothes could possibly spell disaster.[15] Such being the case, he then passed the letters on to one of several amanuenses, notably his daughters Christine (1757-1830) and Flore (1775-1849), his step-grand-daughter Titine O'Donnell (1786-1867), or his secretaries Sauveur Legros, father (1754-1834) and Emile, son (1781-1837). Recent inquiries by Professor Vercruysse have proved that from time to time he also had recourse to a friend, Marie-Caroline Murray (1741-1831), "La Muse Belgique."[16]

With such help – and it was considerable – it is incomprehensible (even allowing for the Prince's acute awareness of his reputation) that on various occasions he should have rewritten a number of these and other letters, as was sometimes the case in the eighteenth century: witness his composing a letter for Mme de Staël's anthology where he attempts to rectify any bad impressions his editor may have received from an unfortunate reference to her adored father, Jacques Necker (1732-1804), among copies he had previously forwarded to her (not included in this collection). Thus shamelessly does he attempt to disprove his contention in the *Fragments*[17] that he never re-read his work. In the end, many a page from his pen resembles the (in-)famous proofs of Balzac. On the other hand (according to the originals of Mme de Staël's anthology in the archives at Coppet, Switzerland), close textual readings of the selections made for her anthology prove that she herself was not above "improving" contributions from her colleague.[18]

The topics covered by Ligne in this vast undertaking are those we might expect from such a renowned traveler who was also a military adept with a number of new ideas, feelings, and projects common to any writer of familiar letters from his time, particularly those reflecting his own idea of himself.[19] Despite its highs and lows, perfections and failings, this correspondence with all its problems is as complete a representation of the man – not just the wit, the courtier, the historian or the family-man. – as one could wish.

Careful attention to his texts by Ligne did not make matters easier for his amanuenses (or for us), since in addition to numerous changes or simply fabrications for the benefit of his correspondents (and, ultimately, of himself – as I have pointed out in my Preface above), there were, additionally, instances of coloring the truth of what he was purveying.

It depends in great measure on a singular blind spot in his self-knowledge. One of the most egregious of these examples is a letter purporting to quote from his enthusiastic son, Charles-Antoine, following the surrender of the Turkish fort at Sabatsch on the Save upstream from its junction with the Danube at Belgrade. I quote from the original in Ligne's correspondence with Joseph II.[20] In a letter to Charles-Antoine where I judge the explanation for his outburst to be more than fatherly pride that demanded he come forward as part of an imagined scenario directing attention from the son to him. If so, such actions destroy the charm of some of these correspondences (like the request in verse to his daughter Flore for a concert ticket) (no. 22), while underlining some less agreeable aspects of Ligne's character. On the other hand, angry or threatening letters (such as the one in the archives at Ghent dismissing van den Broucke in 1806 after years of good and faithful service) that do not make for memorable epistolary exchanges – and which I do not quote – are not to be found in my selection. *Cave principem!*

All such details that involve a careful examination of the documents (where available) and measured evaluation of the evidence can sometimes lead the reader far from the accepted character of the writer; they can also add telling increments to his personality as perceived some two hundred years on: such is the perspective in which I have chosen to offer them here. There is always some truth to be gleaned through reading an historical figure like this *intus et in cute* [inwardly and in the flesh], as Rousseau proclaimed about himself, while in Ligne's case a more profound and comprehensible being can be grasped beyond his egomania in his complete humanity, not merely as a wit nor as a social butterfly, for he remains more than either, (or even Professor Blanning's "priapic adventurer"),[21] rather, a fascinating correspondent.

There are many other explanations for the increase in memorable epistolary exchanges during the eighteenth century, most notably improved communications, whether by road, canal, or other means (though postage was still to be paid by the addressee), the spread of literacy, and improved methods of reproduction if the collection were to be printed, assuring greater diffusion, remuneration, and sometimes even fame, whether scandalous or not.

The number of topics concerning relations between private individuals (leaving aside matters of a public—and especially political—nature) are as varied as the personality of the man or woman taking up the pen. While usually no topic need comprise a whole letter, being frequently combined with other concerns or single expressions, the range was considerably extended.

Because of the importance of the letter to the intellectual life of the times, it acquired a double-edged quality. Leaving aside the epistolary novel's capacity for "facts" to become "fictions" that create "character"[22] (and vice versa, as in Richardson's works or Laclos' *Liaisons dangereuses*), whereby the personal becomes universal. When published they traduce Horace Walpole's jibe about "the importance of nobody to everybody" and underline the interest of "one to all", even though in character that "one" may bear witness to a growing concern with alterity. In Clare Brant's categorization there are overlaps from one letter to another (or even within a single letter) just as there are definite modes representing "the writer, the parent, the teacher, the citizen," all contributing to the cultural significance of these exchanges.[23]

Such attitudes helped greatly to define the idea of letter-writing and to attract public interest to private correspondences. One, or several, correspondents (whatever the motives) were aware of a new audience, and this fashion brought about a renewal of the genre. They also recognized that the most intimate thoughts were the materials of a new form for literary expression. At this juncture, recognition could be guaranteed by recourse to the most profound of the modes mentioned above. This feature was characteristic of "feminist" literature and "writing to the moment" with letters of historical play (or re-play). Thus did the mixture of several types make of these creations a work of great and enduring human interest as well as a work of art.

Generally speaking, such letters as these raise questions about the psychology of the self, including ethics and sincerity, while manipulating (and challenging) the audience, both male and female. As Stephen Brown has said in "Letters,"[24] this last factor, while not in itself transparent, underscores the acknowledgement of intellectual equals by engaging one another's ideas and style. Sexual frankness, frequently coupled with intellectual compatibility, also contributed to the over-riding importance of feeling to this revitalized form, buttressed by elements of illusion and performance. All such considerations can be construed as validating and, so, confirming the letter as the period's most distinctive creation.

When a writer published his/her letters—and the new conception of the form involved both men and women—the reader was made privy to gossip, history, adventure, politics. The modern reader recognizes that the writer is playing two roles at once, that a genuine human being (or even a *persona*) wields the pen, according to the ethos of any particular epistolarity. There is a wager in the undertaking: all or nothing? personal expression? or public document? From rules of intimacy to self-respect, from correspondence to narrative, limited only by sense and function, the resources of the imagination enter into full play.[25]

Reading other people's letters was thought to be an "improving" activity and being immersed in other people's thought processes (*in medias res*, so to speak) essential to that improvement. Eighteenth-century letter writers were so convinced of the uniqueness of their material, that they undertook to disseminate it as widely as possible through their correspondences—such were the virtues of multiple correspondents and topics. With the latter, there is also an immediacy, while with the former, there is a distancing, and both are essential to generating interest and involvement, thus explaining the popularity of the form.

Epistolary discourse depends on the interplay of binary criteria, like "form and substance". But in these letters the terms are unstable and wavering, since the limits between the two elements are frequently shifting and never certain. Both restraint and outspokenness characterize this body of writing, where proximity (to the subject-matter) and distance (from the correspondent) play an important, but frangible role. These are the dynamics of a creation almost always in movement, discouraging (or privileging) a single interpretation over others. Without renouncing facts or conventions—least of all those of polite conversation—many writers created a distinct mode for reconstructing the view of their life and times, different from the inspiration or manipulation to be discerned in their other writings.[26]

Amidst similar theoretical discussions of the recent past, there came upon the scene a writer, "famous, but little known." This enthusiast was none other than Charles-Joseph, Prince de Ligne, a faithful servant of the House of Habsburg. Educated for a role in the military, but, so it seems, always to be frustrated in his desire for advancement, until in 1808, he achieved the acme of his career with the award of the rank of Field-Marshal.[27] This was, paradoxically, at a time when he was better known as a man of letters, a second career to which he had ever been drawn, ending his life as an acknowledged writer and stylist. This discontinuity explains and in many ways enhances his letters and has been variously commented upon.

His long and peripatetic life (1735-1814) saw him forced into exile in Vienna with time on his hands, especially after 1794, when the French Revolutionaries' occupation of Belgium sequestered his properties and revenues. Because of his attachment to cosmopolitans in many countries, *genuine* letters written by him are today scattered far and wide.

The word "genuine" above is essential to any collection of Ligne's correspondence, because some letters were dictated by him and hence subject to error, but particularly because of his poor handwriting, leading some previous editors to misread him. But there are also proofs of finagling, sometimes by Ligne himself, at others by well-intentioned, but misguided devotees, unhesitatingly cutting and rearranging original texts to suit their own interpretation of the man and his *Weltanschauung*. This is notably true of his first editor Mme de Staël. In her anthology, *Lettres et pensées du Maréchal Prince de Ligne* (1809), a work which brought Ligne recognition and profit, but traduced some of his ideas and his style. Separating the real from the false in such situations can prove most difficult, which is why I have resorted wherever possible to manuscripts I have seen and copied myself and reliable critical editions of some of the letters that have appeared over time, such as Jeroom Vercruysse on Talleyrand, Maria Ullrichová on Metternich, and Philip Mansel on those to several others in his excellent biography. (Many of the lapses in these texts are printed out hereafter, although my intent was not to prepare a critical edition.)

Some of the errors of fact or interpretation are Ligne's own. He tells us that he never reread his copy. But see our illustration no. 4 His language is the standard cosmopolitan French of the Old Régime[28] and won for Ligne many admirers, not least the Empress Josephine, because of his characteristic fluidity. His obvious facility in writing is nonetheless the fruit of a carefully conceived desire for effect. The patent search for expressions of concision, contrast, or ellipsis, (and many other figures of classical rhetoric) lead him to an abuse of punning that conceals his utter seriousness. Beneath his casual approach there is weighty and often correct observation cloaked in a humorous detachment of apparent simplicity. And while the sophisticated French of his caste was his preferred mode of expression, this did not prevent him from periodically attempting foreign idioms—English, German, or Italian—at which he failed.

The letters I have chosen to include in this anthology in translation have not generally been available in English. Their number could be expanded since, while there may as yet be many undiscovered items, the choice presented here sketches the main outlines and concerns of Ligne's life and times. Not all are of first quality, but the best—of which I trust my work will give some idea—are on a par with those said to characterize the Golden Age referred to by Clare Brant above.[29] Some, especially those to Mme de Staël, were obviously re-worked by Ligne himself when not simply fantasies.

But, whatever the source, the variety of topics and moods should suffice to attract modern readers to the real and sometimes playful, sometimes painful expressions of the author's true feelings. While the subject-matter and style may seem fatuous and irritating in some letters, they are nonetheless genuine in their revelation of Ligne's deep appreciation of his correspondents, the depth of whose friendship might have contributed to Ligne's peace of mind. By the same token, the notes to Talleyrand (no. 16) and Metternich (no 23) serve to confirm him (in his own mind, at least) as the equal of the elite of his time. The selection from the notes to Madame Panam at the end of his life, apart from concluding the adventures of his career, betrays that humanity which, beneath the snobbery and self-centeredness equally on view elsewhere, has contributed so much to his attractiveness (no. 27).

When Ligne does undertake to broach public, political, or military concerns, he frequently repeats himself—but always with an eye to his correspondent whose personal ideas, right or wrong, become truly historic. In a larger sense, the letters to Ségur (no. 7) and Madame de Coigny (no. 6) show considerable originality in undertaking an ethnological presentation of peoples from SE Europe, broadening in the most famous letter here (to Madame de Coigny) into a travelogue-cum-quasi-philosophical meditation that displays how much he had appropriated of Rousseau's confessional writing, made public at about the same time as this letter makes clear (that is, if we are to believe the date of 1787). This letter also gives the lie to his earlier sarcasm involving Rousseau himself. Naturally, such a stance was not seen amiss by Rousseau's nemesis Voltaire, to whom playfulness and assiduity were as one in his own psychic makeup. Finally, the letter to Madame de Coigny is all-encompassing as travel-literature, preceding by but a few years the reporting of Lady Craven in her own *Journey to the Crimea* (Dublin, 1789). The latter text is the only one (so far as I am aware) to contrast with or control Ligne's fantasy. But Ligne is read, while Lady Craven is not.[30]

In the end, literature, the topic that puts all the others into the background, including Ligne's own comments on the military order in which he had been raised and was soon to be outdated, occupies (even incidentally) a distant place in his thought. Just as Voltaire had preoccupied him at the outset of his career (no. 1), so too would Goethe and German letters at the end. His confusion of Schiller's *Kabale und Liebe* with Goethe's *Wahlverwandtschaften*, bears witness to this lively interest, fostered in part by his concerns with writing, as in "To my readers," (no. 28) and style, as in the letter to Caroline Pichler (no. 26). His faulty knowledge of German did not prevent him from approaching these texts through valuable French translations. All of this despite his high-handed (and facetious) tone to Saxe-Weimar (no. 24) regarding publications of his own, confirmed at last by his instructions to Laborde (no. 25) with a cool, calculating eye, not only to profits for his charities, but also to his own mortality and reputation.

Notes

1. Notably Katherine P. Wormeley, *The Prince de Ligne – His Memoirs, Letters, and Miscellaneous Papers*, 2 vol. (Boston: Hardy-Pratt,1899;) and Leigh Ashton, *Letters and Memoirs of the Prince de Ligne*. (London: Routledge, 1927.)
2. Charles-Joseph, Prince de Ligne, *Mél. xxi*, (1801) 3-62. See J. Vercruysse, *Bibliographie descriptive* ,(Paris, 2008), 140-96.
3. Ph. Mansel, *Prince of Europe*. London: Weidenfeld-Nicolson, 2003. See the review by T. Blanning, *TLS*, 13 June, 2003.
4. M. Fumaroli, *Quand l'Europe parlait français* (Paris: Fallois, 2001; 421-37.)
5. See S. Balayé, ed., "Lettres inédites du Prince de Ligne à Madame de Staël." (*Bulletin de l'Académie royale,* Brussels: 1966.) Note, page 288, "Pour éviter..."
6. Ligne, *Napoléon*, etc. (Vercruysse, ed.). (Paris: Champion, 2013; 229-71.)

7. See T. Besterman, *Voltaire: Lettres d'amour à sa nièce, Mme Denis* (Paris:Plon, 1957,) esp. nos 23 ff. Cf. the more conventional view of Ligne's love letters by Ch. Dröghe in *Nouvelles Annales Prince de Ligne, viii* (1994), pages 184-206. Hereafter, *NAPL*, plus volume, date and pages.
8. R. Mortier, *NAPL xv* (2002), 157-77. "Le Prince de Ligne et *La Belle Grecque*".
9. R. Mortier, *NAPL viii* (1994), 207-16. "Ligne et les minorités." For the Turks, see C.D. Rouillard, *The Turk in French Literature*, etc. (Paris: Boivin, 1939,) and B. Guy, "Le Prince de Ligne et les Turcs," *Le Gai Saber* (Cranston, ed.), (Potomac, MD, 1983, 132-45.)
10. See my "Preface" above. The anthology has been reprinted and edited by R. Trousson as *Lettres et pensées du Prince de Ligne* (Paris, Tallandier, 1989; pages 67-379.) Also J. Vercruysse as in note 2 above. This re-orientation is very subtly analyzed and explained in *NAPL viii* (1994), 241.
11. See Leigh's edition of Rousseau's *Correspondance complète*. (Oxford: The Voltaire Fdn., 1989; no. 6740.)
12. Ligne, *Noveau Recueil de lettres*, 2 vols. Weimar: Au Bureau de l'Industrie, with illustrations and 88 letters. See Vercruysse, *Bibliographie Descriptive*, (Paris, 2008), 319-21.
13. Which Pope? Ligne does not say, although we might correctly assume it was Pius VII, Chiaramonti.
14. C.J. de Ligne, *Frags. 1,* (Vercruysse ed.) 170.
15. See Michael Finlay, *Western Writing Implements in the Age of the Quill-pen.* (Carlisle, 1990).
16. See the articles by J. Vercruysse in *NAPL xi* (1996), 51-139, plus many others (though not all exclusively in the *Nouvelles Annales*, by this "Doyen des études Lignistes.")
17. Ligne, *Frags. 1*, (Vercruysse ed.) 140, "Je ne me relis jaimais."
18. J. Vercruysse, "Ligne" in *Charactères et Portraits* (Acke, ed.), (Paris: Champion, 2003), 467.
19. Ligne, *Mémoire sur le Roi de Prusse* (Berlin, 1789), 7: "I greatly dislike speaking of myself" (of course he didn't), and "the eye is hateful to me." (Cf. Pascal, *Pensées*.)
20. Charles-Antoine to Charles-Joseph, from Kleinack (Serbia), 25 April 1788. Vienna: H.H.S.A. – Staats Kanzelei Vortåge : Supplement, 1788. Correspondenz, Josef II, 15.
21. T. Blanning in note 3 above.
22. But see Nicholas Paige, *Before Fiction* (PA: UPA, 2011.)
23. Clare Brant, *Eighteenth- Century Letters* (London: Palgrave – MacMillan, 2000.)

24. Stephen Brown, "Letters" in *Blackwell's Companion to the Enlightenment*, (Cambridge, MA: Harvard UP, 1992; 282-4.)
25. *Archive International de Recherches sur l'Epistolaire*, no. 35 (Paris: PUF, 2009.)
26. C. N. Freidel, *La Conquête de l'Intime* (Paris: 2009).
27. Carlo Bronne, *Belœil et La Maison de Ligne* (Belœil: Fdn Ligne, 1979, 169-203, 229-34.)
28. See the outline by Beatrice Jasinski in her edition of Mme de Staël's general correspondence. (Paris: Pauvert, 1962, vol I: i-lxxi.)
29. See note 23 above.
30. So far as I am aware, Ph. Mansel and S. Sebag-Montefiore are two of the few among our contemporaries to have read this intriguing *reportage*.

The Letters

1

1694 - Voltaire (François-Marie Arouet de) - 1778

In the summer of 1763, at the end of the Seven Years War in which he had fought bravely, the Prince de Ligne stopped by Ferney outside Geneva like many another, to satisfy his curiosity about the greatest man of the age. Voltaire (then aged 67), at first suspicious was soon captivated by his young admirer (28 years old) and asked him to stay over. The visit lasted a week and confirmed Ligne's enthusiasm. Related in a piece of "superior journalism," *Mes Conversations avec M. de Voltaire*. Ligne's witty reportage,[1] revealing a nice appreciation of the master of the house, his feats and foibles, led to a later correspondence that is perhaps the best of those Ligne maintained with a number of personalities, none of whom who was so well known as Voltaire, nor so manipulative. In the mid '70s, Voltaire attempted to draw closer to the Prince, using him as a cat's paw for "the good cause of the philosophes."[2] Ligne resisted, but his enthusiasm did not abate and continued even after Voltaire's death.

I've chosen to group a few of the letters in this exchange – sophisticated, flattering, and perhaps ill-considered, full of ornithological metaphors by both Ligne and his inspiration – to appreciation of the glory of their time.

Letters from Ligne:
    ✉ a - This 30 December, 1763, Brussels
    ✉ b - 13 December, 1776, Ferney
    ✉ c - January, 1777, [Brussels]
    ✉ d - 8 January, 1778, Ferney
    ✉ e - From Ligne's *Coup-d'Œil*

See: R. Pomeau, dir. *Voltaire en son temps*, 5 vol., Oxford: The Voltaire Foundation, 1988-90.

B. Guy, "Voltaire et Ligne," CAIEF 54 (Mai 2002), 103-13

Notes

1. See my article in CAIEF 54 (Mai 2002), 103-13.
2. See J. Vercruysse in Ligne, *Caractères et portraits* (Acke, ed.), Paris:Champion, 2003, 465-8.

Ligne to Voltaire - a
This 30 December, 1763   Brussels

    I find, Sir, that I've had the honor of addressing you before and saying that you have the luck of pretty women. People are proud of your favors when they receive them. They appear so, even though they've not been lucky enough for that. You have little in common with pretty women who've already lost their reputation. Because of the publicity, yours will not have to suffer. Twenty times have I kissed what you deigned write to me. Those who are not so fortunate in knowing you have done as much. My friends have shared in my joy. You've discovered a new way to make people happy. While thus paying homage to humanity in so many different ways, you don't stint trying to enlighten and console us. Accustomed to seeing empresses give you shelter, kings sweet talk you, ministers pay court to you, your name uttered with respect by the most backward nations, with Englishmen, Frenchmen, and Italians at your feet, you should pay attention to what I take it into my head to write you from afar. Therefore, Sir, this letter is merely intended to allow me to unburden myself. Moreover, I'm so used to speaking rapturously about you, it's not surprising that at this very moment I'm giving vent to my enthusiasm.
    Every day, I try to exercise my feeble talent for [writing] comedies that I'll never risk producing at Ferney. Just allow me to have a seat in corner of your charming theater if they're giving one of your plays. I promise to behave like everyone else and be overwhelmed. I've had the pleasure of seeing a play here with all the trappings and magnificence imaginable, undoubtedly better performed in Paris, but surely not better produced. The beauties of *Tancrède*[1] illuminated the darkness of night surrounding us. If I do the honors of my country like this, allow me also to proclaim its good will. Belgian sincerity is what I call to witness my deep feelings for you. Please look kindly on my assurance of

them while I've the honor to remain, with the most tender and respectful attachment,

> Sir,
> Your very humble and obedient servant,
> Charles, Prince de Ligne

Source: Besterman D., no. 11596

Notes

1. *Tancrède*, a play by Voltaire (1760).

Voltaire to Ligne - b
13 December, 1776   Ferney

A very old owl, near death in a hovel between the Jura and the Alps, has been greatly touched at the kindness shown him by an Austrian eagle. The inspiration of this letter from Brussels, dated 25 November [1777], is enough to bring the old bird back to life – if that were possible. He shall remember until his dying moments a trip he once made despite the heaviness of his wings, to the land of this charming bird, a newborn child who since that time has honored him now and again with a letter precious above all.

The handsome bird recently visited the new menagerie at Fontainebleau with the brilliant new specimens who decorate that cage and has judged precisely their different plumage.[1] Now it's up to him to create by example a pretty cage in Brussels.[2] Sometimes it takes but one person to foster good taste in one's native land. Emulation spreads rapidly from one to another. It's as true in intellectual matter as in women's hairdos; it takes but one to start. In the same way, a remarkable man, thanks to the force of his personality and wit, can revive the fine arts and good taste, just as the eagle I've mentioned is doing, the man I'm thanking here, the one whose humble and obedient servant I am, with respect,

                                       The old owl.

                             Source: Besterman D., No. 20397

Notes

1. The court of Louis XVI and Marie-Antoinette.
2. Ligne inherited the title (Prince) and the family fortune in 1766.

Ligne to Voltaire[1] - c
January 1777   [Brussels]

    I know that the owl is the preferred symbol
        Of Wisdom for the Gods.
     If I had not met you, I'd think
         They had placed you
       In that form amongst men
     To correct our frivolous race.

When Minerva[2] comes to your aid, your destiny is assured.
      But, like you, does she know
       How to please and instruct?
    Only while scolding does some good;
     For she's grumpy and atrabilious,
  And her gloomy bird is nothing like you.

  Can we imagine an owl whose melody excels
That Amphion of the forest, the swan of Mantua,[3]
        Who is able to draw
      From the lute of the Muse,
From the trumpets of Mars, or from the flute of Pan
       The self-same harmony?

  If one becomes an eagle by staring at the sun,
      I'm surely such a one:
     I dared countenance that genius
       Who never had his equal
        (Nor ever shall),
  Who dares to criticize foolish ideas,

   And correct the wrongs of Themis,[4]
      Excoriating madness,
      The friend of reason
  And the benefactor of humanity.

> Sublime or charming, you are the one
> Who soars above us all
> In your delirium
> From highest heaven, your own true element.
>
> Rome is no more Rome, there remains but a goose,
> The prey and refuge
> Of the Capitol[5]
> Who saved the city in another age;
> But there are no more eagles.
> Nature is too exhausted
> To form another you,
> And for some time she's been resting.
>
> Now parakeets, with noisy cooing,
> Drown out flocks
> Of jays and crows,
> But here below we'll sooner see
> Two worlds collide,
> And the commingling of two seas,
> Than we shall encounter a second Voltaire.

Source: Besterman D., No. 20522

Notes

1. Voltaire entertained Ligne at Ferney in 1763.
2. In Greek mythology the daughter of Jupiter: as goddess of wisdom and inventiveness; worshipped in Athens, Olympia and Thebes.
3. Amphion, a son of Zeus and Antiope in Greek mythology; a famous musician and ruler of Thebes. "The swan of Mantua" is the poet Virgil (70-19 B.C.), said to have been born there.
4. In Greek mythology the goddess of justice represented holding scales.
5. Geese reportedly saved the capitol in Rome from Gaulish occupation in 300 B.C.. The remaining goose is the pope, Clement XIV (Ganganelli) who dissolved the Jesuit order in 1773 with the brief *Dominus ac Redemptor*.

Voltaire to Ligne –d
8 January, 1778   Ferney

'Neath an old oak an old owl,
Possessed, he thought, of genius,
Was humming in his homely hole
A few notes without melody.
A charming swan with silvery neck
Was heard by the old bird
Singing in harmony,
And the sad old bird
Died on the spot from jealousy.
      No, no, my handsome swan,
That's one lie too many;
He didn't expire so quickly:
He might have swooned with pleasure
If it weren't for his old age.

Source: Besterman D., No 21050.

From Ligne's *Coup-d'Œil,* on a statue of Voltaire in the gardens at Bel Œil -e[1]

Divine Voltaire,
Here will I lay my offerings to you. Although you love your own sheep only in pastorals,[2] mine will come to graze on the flowers I'll plant at the foot of your statue in the gardens of Belœil. My vassals and I devoutly bless the man who has given wit to some and bread to many, as I sacrifice to the author of Epistles from Lake Geneva and On agriculture, the apostle of toleration, humanity and beneficence, to the pioneer of Ferney,[3] and the lord of the manor. If it were merely to the author of the *Henriade*[4] and [literary] masterpieces of every kind, all my wealth would not suffice to raise a temple to him which should be made of gold and azure. I'd outstrip the pagan gods in ostentation; they would then be put in their [proper] place and every 21st of November[5] I'd ruin myself in celebrations worthy of the glory that was Greece.

Source: *Coup d'Œil* (2001), 339, note.

Notes

1. Passage to be found in all eighteenth-century editions, this one from 1786, 14, note.
2. From Voltaire's *Epistle to Mme Denis on Agriculture*, 1761. "Je n'aime les moutons / Que lorsqu'ils sont à moi."
3. See Voltaire's Traité *sur la tolerance* (1762), and *Epître en arrivant dans ses terres près du lac de Genève* [les Délices, NOT Ferney] (1755). Les Délices, Voltaire's home in Geneva from 1755 to 1759. Ferney: village on the outskirts of Geneva – but in France – where Voltaire resided from 1759 to 1778.
4. *La Henriade* (ca 1716-45), epic poem about Henri IV.
5. Voltaire's saint's day (Francis of Assisi). See R. Pomeau, *D'Arouet à Voltaire* (Oxford, 1988), 18.

2

1712 - J-J. Rousseau - 1778

When he returned to Paris from Venice at the end of 1744, Rousseau, a poor Protestant provincial from Geneva, was thirsting to find fame and fortune. Five years later (1749), that thirst was suddenly quenched with publication of his perverse and personal *Discours sur les sciences et les arts*, in which he attacked "the perfections of civilization" – the theater, literature and learning. Surprisingly, the essay was awarded a gold medal by the Academy of Dijon. From then on his ill health and misanthropy sufficed to keep him in the public eye, if not in their heart. After a few misguided efforts to enlist Voltaire on his side, his several quarrels with the Master ended in disaster, and he retreated more and more into his own shell.

In 1770, Ligne visited him in Paris relating the occasion with a certain archness that led Grimm in the *Correspondence literaire* to admonish him for his perhaps unthinking cruelty; but Grimm was also thinking perhaps of himself (both he and Ligne were foreigners in France) saying "The desire to be witty is an incurable malady in this country."

But why should Ligne, by then a famous name among the intelligentsia, have deemed it necessary (unless to rival Rousseau in self promotion) to publish? Or was it Rousseau who chose to reveal this screed to the public?

This is the first published letter in Ligne's extensive correspondence.[1]

See: T. Besterman, *Voltaire*. NY: Harcourt Brace, 1969, 399-400.
        M. Cranston, *Rousseau*, 3 vol, U. Chicago P., 1991-97.

R. Trousson, in *Ligne. Caractères et Portraits* (Acke ed.), Paris:Champion, 2003, 487-92.

R. Mortier, *Clartés et Ombres du Siècle des Lumières*, Genève:Droz, 1969, 145.

Notes

1. Rousseau in *Correspondence complète de Rousseau*, (Leigh ed.), 52 volumes Voltaire Foundation, Oxford, 1965 -90; no. 6740.

Ligne to Rousseau
July 1770   Paris

Sir,

I am the gentleman who called to see you the other day.[1] I'll not return, although I've a great desire to do so, since you, as I, like neither devotion nor devotees.

Consider what I proposed to you.[2] People don't know how to read in my country where you'll be neither admired nor persecuted.

You shall have the key to my books and my gardens. Either you shall find me there or not. You shall have all to yourself alone a very small country house, a quarter league from my own.[3] You may plant, you may sow, you shall do there whatever you wish.

Jean-Baptiste[4] and his wit came to die in Flanders; but he wrote only verse. Let Jean-Jacques and his genius come to live there. Whether at my place or yours, may you continue "to devote your life to Truth".[5] Were you to desire more freedom, I've a very small plot of ground owned by no one else. The sky is fair, the air pure, and it is only eighty leagues from here. I have neither archbishop nor parliament,[6] only the best sheep in the world.

At my other dwelling I have honeybees. I'm offering them to you. If you like honey, I'll leave them there, but if not, I'll move them elsewhere: their little republic will treat you better than the Republic of Geneva,[7] which you have so greatly honored and where you could have done some good.

I like, as you, neither thrones nor dominions.[8] You shall rule over no one, and no one shall rule over you. If you accept my offer, Sir, I shall myself go to call for you and deliver you to [our] Temple of Virtue.

Such will be the name of your dwelling, but we shall not call it so. I hope to spare your modesty the triumphs you deserve.

If all of this does not suit you, Sir, [pretend] I've said nothing. I shall not see you but shall continue to read and admire you without saying so.[9]

                Le Prince de Ligne

Source: Rousseau, *Correspondance complète de Rousseau,* (Leigh ed.), Letter 6740

Notes

1. Ligne had visited Rousseau at his apartment in the rue Platrière in Paris (today rue J-J. Rousseau, 1er arr.) in July.
2. I.e., a country retreat at his property of Fagnolles in Namur Province, Belgium.
3. I.e., from Baudour, near Mons.
4. Jean-Baptiste Rousseau (1671-1741), poet whose name Ligne had invoked in order to gain admission to Rousseau's home, had died in Brussels.
5. Rousseau's motto was "Vitam impendere vero" (Devote one's life to Truth).
6. Two bodies in French society of the time that had condemned Rousseau: the R.C. Church (1764) and the Government (1765).
7. Rousseau had been forced to flee Geneva after publishing his *Lettre à d'Alembert* (1758).
8. "Thrones, etc." two of the nine orders of angels in Thomistic theology.
9. See the text and adverse commentary on this letter in Grimm's *Correspondance littéraire* for 13 July 1770.

1737 - Jean Jacques Vandenbroucke - 1808

Lawyer and faithful administrator for Ligne and his family from 1770 until summarily dismissed in 1806. His papers form an extensive collection of Lineana at the University library, Ghent.

Letters from Ligne to Vandenbroucke,
- ✉ a - from Belœil [?], 12/13/June, 1774
- ✉ b - Versailles [?] vii/viii, 1776
- ✉ c - Belœil/Brussels ? February, 1777
- ✉ d - [Vienna ? 1786 ?]
- ✉ e - Vienna, 24 August, 1795

See: Ph. Mansel, *Prince of Europe*. London: Weidenfeld and Nicolson, (1993), 36-155, and especially page 156.
E. Hubert, "Lettres et documents inédits," *APL i* (1920), 130-43.

Ligne to Vandenbroucke - a
12/13 June, 1774 [Belœil?]

My dear Vandenbroucke,
    I've told you that when I'd see you putting my affairs in order, I'd no longer hold anything back from you. Here's proof.
    Do you remember an annuity for 3,500 florins that I don't remember what lawyer said he wanted to be paid? I didn't wish to render an account to you at the time, but since my confidence [in you] is now complete, I can tell you that after living with Eugénie[1] for seven years, she became pregnant three years ago and went to live in Lyons and have the child there. The child died. But I didn't want to make her more distraught than she was already, since after six months she was aware that I didn't love her.
    Monsieur Desandrouins,[2] to whom I've been paying interest of 300 ducats [per an] now wants to have the whole sum. As it brings interest at 4% and he's enjoyed that for three years, he has agreed to repay me what he's already received in order to cash in the capital – about five thousand florins. In consideration of which, give him 3,000 as quickly as possible. That will be the end of it. As you'll see by these papers, the sum was drawn on my property at Rumpst[3] which inconvenienced me greatly.
    After using the 25,000, for which I've signed as you very cleverly recommended, think about selling 30,000 of the first shares.
    Also, write to Théaulon[4] and have him inquire of the Prince of Nassau[5] about realizing 30,000 livres on instruments that I took out with him on condition of retrieving them at face value, that is, at 10,000 livres. Perhaps they'll bring less. Either the Prince of Nassau or his agent can clarify this or make it easier for Théaulon who knows, moreover, what this gambling with paper money involves, since with less hard cash than usual, we might gain more.
    I've not one sou of debt for gambling: that's my general confession. I'm giving neither parties nor sleigh rides nor costume balls.[6] I need a letter of credit on Paris or Lyons not to exceed two- or three-hundred louis for my Mardi Gras. In addition, I'm

paying off a lot of bills with my two hundred ducats a month. And I'm very careful.[7]

Let Etienne (and I don't know who else)[8] be paid with an IOU or credit before the first of February when I'll be in Paris [and unavailable].

Tell Monsieur de Champ to hurry with the business at Salms. I've finished with Rasse[9] who's demanding to be reimbursed for his expenses. I've told him there's nothing to be done.

Yours wholeheartedly, my dear Vandenbroucke.
                 Le Prince de Ligne,
                 Your servant and friend.

Source: Ghent, Vol. I, f. 125.

Notes

1. Ligne is mistaken here; his ladylove was not Eugénie, but her sister, Angélique d'Hannetaire (1749-1822).
2. Stanislas, Viscount Desandrouins (1738-1821), businessman, an early developer of the mines at Anzin (Nord).
3. Rumpst, a property in Hainaut Province belonging to the Ligne family.
4. Ligne is here referring to his banker, Jean-Etienne Théaulon. (1739-?). Son of a Receveur de la Ferme générale. See, among many others, *Frags. 2,* (Vercruysse ed.), 173, and Mansel, 61-70.
5. Frederick-August, Prince of Nassau-Weilburg (1738-1816), friend and distant relative of Ligne.
6. Ligne here refers to parties, etc. related in the *Fragments* (Vercruysse ed.), see note 4 above.
7. As this note would indicate, "careful" or not, the Prince's financial situation deteriorated steadily until 1794. In that year, French occupation of the Low Countries ruined his already weakened finances.

"In the year 1765, my father left me an income of 150,000 fl. and 7,000,000 in debts. I've repaid a portion of this last with the sale of two estates and increased my revenues by 50,000. Until his death, since I had received nothing from my father for my [expenses] Court [in Vienna], I was supported by Christians – Menou and Lambert , and by Jews – Brandeis and Schimmel.

For all I know, here is what I have since received.." There follows a schematic and simplistic accounting of his financial situation until, roughly, 1795, followed by this telling footnote [ca. 1837] from his grandson Eugène-Lamoral (1804-80): certified inaccurate by us... in debt for more than 3,000,000 of the surplus from the calculations of the antifinancial head of our venerable forefather. (*Frags. 1*, (Leuridant ed.), 169-70, note.)

8. Etienne, a servant in Ligne.'s household; see Mansel, 156-7.
9. De Champ (name? dates?) lawyer in a suit to recover Ligne's inheritance from his mother, presented before the Reichskammergericht in Wetzlar (1774); the suit was never resolved. Since the suit was brought in Germany, the man's name might have been Dechant. (See Mansel, 62)

   The other lawyer, Rasse (name? dates?), was involved in suits to regain possession and monies from estates at Koeurs (Lorraine) and Corbie (Picardy) in 1773. The suits were lost by Ligne in 1775.

Ligne to Vandenbroucke - b
vii/viii 1776. [Versailles?]

Things are going splendidly, my dear Vandenbroucke, yet if I'd not been here, we would have been out of luck. I'm working like a madman. But let me tell you that if I'd not promised a thousand louis to someone,[1] we were in for it, and I'd get off paying interest every year out of pocket. I'll borrow it here, if they finish with what they owe me. Find someone reliable who can arrange to pay it to me here at six percent. We need credit to obtain credit.

Our garrulous friend[2] is working miracles. Herewith, today's letter from him. I'll have recourse to the Queen's bounty,[3] only if the injustice of Justice doesn't come through.[4] While waiting, Count d'Artois and his chancellor, Bastard,[5] have helped me eonsiderably. This damned family of the Cardinal [de Luynes][6] is requesting further delays, thanks to his stroke. I've told H.M.[7] that such a solution would be unberable. Every day he inquires whether he has lost any property. Monsieur de La Galaisière[8] is the only one to have told him that he would not. He'll remember [this], if he makes a contribution.

Adieu, my dear Vandenbroucke. Regards.

Source: Mansel, no.3, 267

Notes

1. Person difficult to identify.
2. Person difficult to identify.
3. Marie-Antoinette de France (1755-93), Queen in 1774.
4. Sarcasm.
5. Artois (1757-1836), King of France in 1830. Bastard, his chancellor (no dates).
6. Paul-Albert de Luynes (1703-85), Cardinal, Archbishop of Sens.
7. Louis XVI de France (1754-93), King in 1774.
8. Henri-François de La Galaisière (dates?), Chancellor of the Queen's household.

Ligne to Vandenbroucke - c
February, 1777 [Belœil/Brussels?]

You've clearly seen – or foreseen – our financial situation, my dear Vandenbroucke, and I'm as sure of beating the French in war as you in business. For most intelligent minds are lacking in common sense. Therefore, stick to your first plan. It's quite likely I'll go to Paris in three weeks: this will be the time our lawsuit on Corbie[1] will be heard. Monsieur Le Clerc seems to be the only honest member of the government;[2] he'll be the presenter of my request. I've still boundless hope in the government. If the memoir I advise you to have printed does not suffice, my family will be our second line of defense; besides, to have them on our side, the decision of the Council of State will have to be nullified.

Be ferocious: use money, Hénin, and through him the Count d' Artois, the Queen, and through her Princess de Ligne along with Madame de Brionne.[3] Speak with business contacts of Count de Lauraguais[4] to ascertain his daughter's share or what we'll lose, which I don't believe will happen. But it's better to have two [illegible].

Believe me, my dear Vandenboucke, your devoted friend.

Source: Mansel, no.4, 267/8.

Notes

1. Among several lawsuits which consumed a great deal of time and money, this one, his most ambitious, dating from 1768, was to demand 50,000 livres per an for twelve years from the King of France in return for giving up his claim to estates sold two hundred years earlier by an ancestor to the Abbey of Corbie near Amiens. Ligne lost his case.
2. A good example of Ligne's navieté in matters like this. M. LeClerc's name was probably not LeClerc, but rather, a noun distinguishing his function in the courtroom.
3. A list of names to show his social prominence: Prince Charles-Antoine d'Hénin-Liétard (1744 -94), a friend; Count d'Artois

(1757-1836), ditto; Marie-Antoinette, Queen of France (1755-93), Princess Françoise-Xavière de Ligne, Ligne's wife, née Liechtenstein (1739 – 1820) and Henriette, Marquise de Brionne (1710-80), Ligne's aunt.

4. Louis –Félicité, Count de Lauraguais (1733-1834), wit and friend of Ligne's, responsible for freeing the French stage of spectators.

Ligne to Vandenbroucke - d
15 April, 1786   [Vienna? 1786
   See infra reference to Helene Massalska-Ligne's pregnancy.]

My dear Vandenbroucke,
   Reforming my household is scarcely possible, yet it is inconceivable that Princess de Ligne[1] should be left without horses or a postillion. I do not at all wish for her to know of any changes, except for the suppers that might be less frequent, less numerous and less well-lit, since we're not obliged to do the honors of the town (Brussels), and there are other houses where she's been invited. She might arrange, as in the past, to entertain once a week. Our finances were very different then; Baptiste's accounts are proof.[2] Two or three small suppers will reduce our expenditures by two-thirds.
   As the cost of too expensive undertakings by the zealots [illegible] has frightened M. de Calonne,[3] I prefer by far to have 50,000 or 60,000 livres in annuities on my life for the three of us[4] and make a better profit from the sale of property we hold in common at Jeumont and Hestrud [illegible].[5] Moreover, the rumor in Europe about the Empress's gift [to me] of property in the Crimea[6] must surely commit her to adding profit to honor. I've already suggested that she allow England to land 1,000 pirates at Cherson,[7] hoping she'll spare a few to help me to colonize and develop the country; it's a very rich corner of the world, lacking only in men. The Greeks were the cleverest in so doing, before the ignorance and cruelty of the Turks came to devastate this fine land.[8]
   I shall visit the Empress next January to cast "the master's eye" over all, and I'm positive something good will come of it. If the extraordinary amount we owe our creditors and the profits from the sale of the least good products that we'll gain from Koeurs with its revenues and improvements will soon see us home free.[9] From now til then, my dear Vandenbroucke, we must be patient, along with the others. Your friendship and the reactions it will inspire will see us through. I'll go over all this with you – from

the first of June to the end of December. We've received and forwarded to Pradel[10] a few documents, including procurations. It seems that Charles' little wife is pregnant.[11] We've suspected as much for the past three weeks. If so, she can return to the Low Countries in September.

Adieu, dear Vandenbroucke, I salute you with all my heart.

Source: Ghent,Vol. 5, f. 15.

Notes

1. Princess Francoise-Xavière de Ligne (1739-1821); born a Princess of Liechtenstein, it is easy to understand her need for a coach and horses.
2. Baptiste, a servant in the Ligne household; cf. Mansel, 156-7.
3. Calonne, Charles-Alexandre de (1734-1802). French statesman, Contrôleur général, 1783-7; his spending policy, designed to restore public credit (Keynesian *avant la lettre*), was mismanaged and ended in disaster; exiled to England by the Revolution; a friend of Ligne's.
4. "The three of us"? Prince Charles-Antoine, Prince Louis and Prince Charles-Joseph?
5. Jeumont, Hestrud—two properties of the Ligne family in Hainaut Province.
6. Did Catherine II make the famous grant to Ligne of Parthenizza and Nikita *before* the famous voyage of 1787 down the Dnieper? According to the date of this letter, it would seem so.
7. "Cherson" the southernmost point of the Crimea, not the "new town" on the Dnieper, about 75 kms ENE of Ochakov and the Liman.
8. The Crimea had been occupied by the Greeks from about 80 B.C. to 250 A.D. (?) then by the Genoese from about 1250 and was conquered by the Turks in 1451.
9. Koeurs (Lorraine), site of lawsuit brought by Ligne as a descendant of his ancestress, Louise de Lorraine, Countess of Chaligny (1595 1667); lasted for more than sixty years; the suit was lost by Ligne in 1775.
10. Pradel (names? dates?) lawyer for Ligne in the Koeurs lawsuit.
11. Helene Massalska-Ligne (1764-1815), wife of Charles-Antoine de Ligne (1757-1792), gave birth to a girl, Sidonie, in Sept. 1786 (died 1828).

From Ligne to Vandenbroucke - e
24 August 1795[1]   Vienna

My dear Vandenbroucke,

Though you've rendered me good service, improved my lands, and put my business in order, the greatest favor of all is having sent to me an intelligent man whom I can send to Basel and Paris, to, first, the Prussian ministers, and, second, to the National Convention.[2] I've written to the King of Prussia,[3] and though my special peace seems like a joke, I've also informed H I M.[4] I've added twice as many reasons, forceful plausible, a bit more historically correct than the memoir for Harmegnies[5] that wasn't very well founded.

I've written to M. Barthélmy[6] and to still others. I've urged Legros[7] to leave immediately for [Brussels]; he already left yesterday. I'm predicting that good will come of it and the Republic will play fair.[8] You'll be useful to him, my good Vandenbroucke, as also to me, for you can tell that She's [The Republic's] already rid of the monsters who would surely have ruined Belœil, had they survived. The present regime is gentle and just, even obliging, so it seems. Please receive the assurance of my gratitude and friendship, my dear Vandenbroucke, without compliment, but as usual.

Source: Ghent, vii, fo. 135

Notes

1. Written after the Terror in France (1793-95).
2. Prussian ministers were in Basel to prepare the Treaty of 5 April 1795, whle the convention in Paris was meeting from 1792-95.
3. Frederick-William II (1744 – 97) reigned from 1786.
4. Francis II (1768-1835) H.R.E. 1790-1806; reigned as Francis I of Austria (1804-35).
5. P.P.J. Harmegnies (fl. 1780-1800), meticulous diarist from Mons.
6. François Marquis de Barthélemy (1747-1830), French ambassador in Switzerland, negotiated the Treaty of Basel (1795), deported to Guyana (1804-15), for his generous terms in the treaty.

7. Sauveur Legros (1754-1834), secretary to Ligne (ca. 1768-1806); see Mansel, 156 and 175.
8. The first French Republic, 1792-99. Ligne, writing after the Terror, is still quite naïve about his relations with his enemies in the government.

4

1759 - Charles-Antoine de Ligne - 1792

Ligne's favorite son. Trained in the military (Corps of Engineers/ Artillery), married Apolline-Hélène, Princess Massalska (1763-1814, div. 1793); Ligne gave an elaborate celebration at Belœil for the wedding in 1779, composing the play *Colette et Lucas*.

Had one daughter, Sidonie (1786-1828) who married unhappily in 1807 a cousin by her mother's second marriage, François Potocki (1778-1853). Had another daughter by Adêlaide Bernardy-Nones (aka Fleury d'Ellignies, 1768-1810?), Fanny-Christine (1786-1867), "La petite Ligne qui n'est pas droite," who married in 1811 Maurice Count O'Donnell de Tyrconnel (1780-1843).

Charles-Antoine accompanied Ligne to Russia in 1787, subsequently fighting with distinction in the Empress Catherine's second Turkish war. Fought against the French Revolution, killed at La Croix aux Bois in the Argonne. See both Byron (*Don Juan*) and Chateaubriand (*Mémoires d'Outre – Tombe*).

Ligne made several attempts to be fatherly, but only to assert himself in his egomania. See Carlo Bronne, *Belœil et la Maison de Ligne*, Belœil: Fondation Ligne, 1979, 205- 16, and contrast with the tone and sincerity of his letter to Prince Poniatowski from 1789, below, characterized by genuine feeling.

Letters from Ligne:
    ✉ a - this 26 June, 1778, from my HQ at Brezno (Czech. Rep.)
    ✉ b - this 10/10/80, Versailles
    ✉ c - 12 May, 1788, from Potemkin's HQ at Elizavetgorod
    ✉ d - 8 June, 1788, from FM Roumiantzov's HQ, in Poland
    ✉ f - 6 - 25 Nov. 1790, Vienna, after the attack on Ismaïlia

Ligne to Charles-Antoine - a
this 26 June, 1778 from my HQ at Brezno (Czech. Rep.)[1]

Well, my genius of an engineer,

So, you are still fortifying, but not fortified, in respect of the genius of our engineers![2] Myself, I've great difficulty in being fortified against boredom.

The Emperor[3] came here to create what might well be called an embarrassment. He claims he wants to make war; but at the same time he does not. "Who wants to bet there'll be war?" he said the other day. "Everyone," replied Marshal Loudon,[4] ever in a bad mood. "It doesn't mean anything to say: Everybody – except for me," said Marshal Lascy.[5] "How much [do you bet]?" said the Emperor, expecting a wager of about twenty ducats. "Two hundred thousand florins," countered Loudon. The Emperor made a devil of a face and realized it was a public criticism.

He seemed kindly disposed toward me, but he fears lest people play games with him. He was satisfied with my troops and said many nice things about you, dear Charles. He had observed you working wonders. Now he's gone, [but] I can still see him from my window.

I laugh at myself and others when I reflect that, not being appreciated, I'm worth more than people think. I'm drilling each squad myself and make myself hoarse

commanding six battalions at a time. Here, there's not even what in Bohemia we call "a <u>kalon</u>", a rotten shed defended only by four soldiers. I go and visit to taste their soup and bread and weigh their meat to see that they are not short-changed. There's not one to whom I don't speak nor for whom I get vegetables or offer something. Not an officer for whom I don't buy food while trying to excite his enthusiasm for this war.

My fellow-officers don't do anything like that, and they're well advised, since no one can hold it against them; none is anxious to fight. Their manner is most pacific in front of the young men they wish at the same time to prepare to be zealous and good generals. It's all the same to me; they'll soon be Field

Marshals, and that too will be all right. I've not spoken French for six weeks. Yet, on the other hand, to repay me for a rather bad dinner, they bow and scrape when about thirty feet in front of me at the end of the meal. You have colleagues. I have only a Capuchin monk whom I send to catch terns among the reeds [in the marsh] every day.

If an infantry officer may salute an officer of engineers and a genius at his job, I give you a big hug, my dear boy. I'm delighted that you're getting ahead for doing worthless work. Goodbye for now, my excellent piece of work and a masterpiece almost as surely as Christine.[6]

P.S. I've just learned that [on 24 June] Marshal Lascy asked the Emperor what he had said in answer to the King of Prussia's letter,[7] received that very day. "He has his back to the wall," he said. "I told him that time was a-wasting, and I wanted some lessons from a past master. When do you expect, my dear Marshal, that I'll have his answer?" Lascy counted on his fingers and opined, "In six or eight days Your Majesty will receive an answer, but the King himself will bring it, since I've learned today that he's now crossed over into Bohemia." "Your count is exact." "So much the better. I've received orders to march with my whole corps."

P.P.S. Since I don't expect you've already returned from Pardubitz[8] to your corps, let me give some more recent news. It has been reported to the Emperor that the King has crossed the frontier with I don't know how many columns. The Emperor galloped madly to Number Seven redoubt and asked twenty times, "Where's the Marshal?"[9] who, at that very moment had already arrived at the trot for the first time in his life. "Well, Marshal, I've looked for you everywhere." "Well, Sire, here, in this telescope is the King." "I believe it's himself on a large English horse, perhaps his Anhalt.[10] See?" – "Perhaps; but they'll not beat us on their own. Look, moreover, at the strength of our columns!" "Ah! There's one with at least ten thousand men, amongst the others." "Are they going to attack?" "Perhaps, but they won't be in formation before two hours." "What time is it?" "They'll be at mess. We will too. They'll not attack Your Majesty today." "Tomorrow?" "Tomorrow? I don't think so. Day after, neither. Nor in this whole campaign."

You'll recognize in this exchange the cold and somewhat bitter attitude of our good Marshal, annoyed that someone else should meddle with his schemes at any time; and the Emperor's attitude on these occasions that it's all too much for him.

Source: *Frags. 1,* (Vercruysse ed.) 232-4.

Notes

1. Brezno, a military encampment in the Czech Republic, on the border with Saxony, some 50 miles Northwest of Prague.
2. That is, fortifying the steep banks of the upper Elbe under Marshal Moritz Lascy (1725-1801), one of the most respected Austrian commanders.
3. Joseph II (1741-90), in 1765 shared power with his mother, Maria-Theresa; emperor in 1780.
4. Marshal Gideon Loudon (variously, Laudhon or Laudon) (1717-90), at the time of this letter, in charge of operations on the frontier with Saxony.
5. This and the following paragraphs shed some light on Ligne's experience on the Imperial side in the War of the Bavarian Succession (or "Potato War" 1778-9).
6. Christine de Ligne, Princess Clary-Aldringen (1757-1830), Ligne's eldest daughter and frequent amanuensis.
7. Frederick "the Great" (1712-86), King of Prussia in 1740.
8. Pardubitz: important center, 65 mi East of Prague.
9. Marshal Loudon.
10. A joke to undercut Frederick's reputation as a military "genius" with his reliance on "old Dessau" (Leopold, Duke of Anhalt-Dessau, 1676-1747), a Prussian commander essential to the king's successes in war.

Ligne to Charles-Antoine - b
this 10/10/80   Versailles

Isn't it droll, my dear Charles, to be married?[1] You'll get along fine, as usual. We're all more or less "fine" according to our situation. Only fools have no knowledge of how to profit by such a state of affairs. In the meantime, you have a very pretty little woman who, without dishonoring you, might be your mistress. Although, you and all of us, from father to son, have borne the name Lamoral,[2] we really don't know whether or not he was a saint. I'm not moral enough, nor moralist, nor moralizing to preach to you while making fun of those who don't appreciate my morality; but this consists only in wanting to make people around me happy. I'm sure that's yours, too. Without a regiment of principles, that's one of four or five I've reserved for your second education.

As with the first principle, I've told you that lying or cowardice can cause great sorrow. I trust, dear boy, that you've already learned this brief lesson.

Well, now we're faced with the others. Take as much money as you need, or that my agents have or will find for you.[3]

The Queen has said she will help in the business of Koeurs;[4] and when I tell her that my affairs of the heart are going nicely without her help, she calls me stupid. If you had heard her, Charles, you'd have become a flatterer for the first time in your life. That's all I'm going to say about Koeurs, and that's the end of two principles. Your uncle [by marriage], the Bishop of Wilna,[5] who thinks that one day you or I might be the next King of Poland, wants us to take Polish nationality. We'll go and collect it. That's another piece of business settled. Our aunt in the Tuileries[6] wants your wife to have court privileges ["le tabouret"] if she's a mind to go to Versailles, and for that I transmit my title of "Grandee" to you.[7] I've already written to the King of Spain,[8] to his minister, and spoken with the Spanish ambassador. [This,] at the risk of catching cold for being obliged to get out of my carriage at the entrance to the Court where only Spanish grandees are allowed [to remain covered], as at the Luxembourg palace and elsewhere.

Here are two sources for saving money: [the sale of] rights and privileges that cost me nothing. What is costly, is listening to witty people talking foolishness, hearing war discussed by those who've only been to the parade-ground and even then have misunderstood what they saw, ladies calling themselves disinterested, who by dint of tormenting the Queen (a thousand times too kind-hearted) and her ministers, who snare pensions, and animus toward those who've had twenty lovers, including schemers, self-important and spiteful. Sometimes these people make my blood boil. Yet a half-hour later, all is forgotten.

Our [Chevalier] de Lisle[9] is tactless, as you know, but unfortunately he's also meddlesome. Yesterday, a Sunday, when all the most illustrious bores in France pay court to the Queen at the Polignacs'[10] after dinner, de Lisle pushes to the front of all the nobles and marshals of France, touches the Queen's dress and says: There, I knew I was right; it's embroidered; what good work they produce today! I nearly died with embarrassment, not knowing where to hide from her and from him. This reminded me of the time when you and I were standing behind the King of Poland[11] looking at prints with de Lisle who turned over one that His Majesty was studying.

Would you like to laugh at another of my mistakes that amused the royal family? You're familiar with my box at the theater underneath theirs. Well, it was terribly cold and the play was *Le Miroir de la fausse magie*.[12] The King[13] complained about the temperature and the stiffness of the actors. That's because, said I, the ending takes place before a mirror. Among several others, the brothers booed loud and long for this bad pun[14]

Life at Versailles suits me very well: a true "vie de château".

Hugs and kisses to your wife and also to your mother[15] who had the sense to produce a Charles like you.

P.S. A propos: I'm already planning in my head a grove of trees for my Charles with a fountain for Hélene amd a bower of roses for your children.¹⁶ I'll do it as soon as as I leave Versailles to go and tell you and "tutti quanti" that I love you with all my heart.

Source: *Frags. 1,* (Vercruysse ed.), 234-6.

Notes

1. Charles-Antoine de Ligne (1759-92), Ligne's eldest son, wed on 14 July, 1779 to Hélène Massalska (1763-1814), a Polish heiress who married after his death on the field of battle a cousin, Vincent Potocki (1751-1825), divorced in 1793.
2. "Saint" Lamoral: there is no such saint, at least not officially recognized by the Church; Lamoral, first Prince de Ligne (1563-1624).
3. Ligne is here referring to his banker, Jean-Etienne Théaulon. (1739-?) Son of a Receveur de la Ferme générale. See, among many others, *Frags. 2,* (Vercruysse ed.), 173, and Mansel, 61-70.
4. Marie-Antoinette(1755-93), Queen of France in 1774, guillotined. Koeurs: locality in Lorraine, subject of a lengthy dispute with the French crown, ultimately lost by Ligne's family.
5. Ignaz Massalski (1724-94), Prince-bishop of Wilna, uncle of Hélène de Ligne, hanged by Revolutionaries.
6. Henriette, Princess de Ligne-Mouhy(1710-87), aunt by marriage of Ligne, *dame d'atours* to the Queen of Spain, residing in the Tuileries.
7. The family of the Prince obtained the title of Grandee, with all the rights and privileges it carried (some mentioned hereafter) in 1621, for services to the Spanish Habsburgs, at that time controlling the Netherlands.
8. King of Spain, Charles III (1711-88).
9. Nicolas, Chevalier de Lisle (1735-83), intimate of Ligne.
10. The Polignacs (fl.1772-1818), clan of courtiers around Marie-Antoinette responsible for many of her follies.
11. King of Poland: Stanislas-Augustus Poniatowski (1732-98), elected king, 1764 to 1791; lover of Catherine the Great of Russia, 1755 to 1758.
12. *Le Miroir...*(1775?): opera in 2 acts by André Grétry (1741-1813), book by J-F. Marmontel (1723-99).
13. Louis XVI (1754-93), King of France in 1774; guillotined.

14. "brothers:" Louis, Count de Provence (1755-1824), King of France as Louis XVIII in 1795; and Charles, Count d'Artois (1757-1836), King as Charles X in 1824; exiled in 1830. Ligne here is making a pun: "glace", mirror or ice; "de glace", stiffness or lifelessness.
15. Francoise-Xaviere, Princess de Ligne, nee Liechtenstein (1739-1821), Ligne's wife.
16. This project for Belœil was never mentioned again, but see Ligne's *Coup-d'œil*. (Guy/Vercruysse, eds.), (Paris: Champion, 2004), 241.

Ligne to Charles-Antoine - c
12 May, 1788   from Potemkin's HQ at Elizavetgorod[1]

My dear Charles,

What have I to say to you that you don't already know about what I felt on receiving a letter from His Majesty[2] full of kindness and grace. It's worth more to you than all the food for rats [like] parchments, titles, diplomas, and patents. It contians such touching expressions for the two of me that, though I'm becoming too important to weep, it was impossible not to every time I wanted to read it. All the generals, Circassians, Zaporogues, Tatars, Kabardiens, Germans, Russians, Cossacks, et al[3] came to me as a group to say charming things I'll never forget.

The best father and friend of my Charles were certainly very much touched by the honor you've earned and which is much more than any I've received in my life; but General de Ligne was greatly pained. Can you imagine, my boy, the fine moment the two of us would have known if I'd been the first man you helped to scale the parapet that you reached before anyone else?

Gods! How stupid I am at this distance from you! I would have wished you were wounded in cold blood in the knee or some other part of your "too, too solid flesh" at Hunerwasser or Niemes.[4] I'm as nervous for you as an old woman. It's not much different in such a state from being a politician, to be sure. Nonetheless, I managed with a few requests for [a troop] of light horse to execute a really serious charge. I've never done so before, except at the head of ten uhlans against five or six drunken Prussian hussars.[5] You'll have to admit it wasn't the most remarkable action of the century. I've never wanted to be enclosed in those squares where you're caught as in a box with only one way in or out. You take charge in a battle as opportunity offers. In that way I'm sure that even lacking troops wherever I may be, matters will only unfold as I wish. I've already learned everything necessary for that, and am beginning to understand a little Russian.[6]

Can you now see, dear Charles, how right I was to insist on wanting you to have a career in the artillery? Engineering[7] has called you, I know. But might you not also have been slightly wounded by chance despite not having written about it to me? Don't ever let a courier from His Majesty to me depart without a letter from you.

A thousand greetings to my comrade Rouvroy[8] whose luck I envy as well as his wound. Poor Poniatowski![9] I'm afraid lest he follow in his father's footsteps. He's already got valor and the military spirit, is personally attached to His Majesty, and generous, etc. Let's just hope that battle doesn't do him in. Give him a hug from me.

Do you know, old friend, that although I'm not spending much, I still appear to be an Oriental satrap with dromedaries, a camel, buffaloes, my herd of cattle, seventy horse, and the devil's share of men and beasts? Write to me often, I beg you again and again. And keep my Charles alive for the best of his friends who's become an admirer. You must let me repeat myself: think about how proud I am of what you've done.

His Majesty will have read, about the same time as this letter,[10] where I tell him how much greater than mine is your worth, foretelling him also that one day you'll be of great use to him.

We've missed by blundering the opportunity to capture Hotin[11] where I was hoping to go. In a fortnight I'll try to find some relaxation and honor at Ochakov.[12]

Nassau[13] is in charge of eighty rowboats with which he hopes to take the fortress from the sea.

Adieu, dear Chevalier of the Order of Marie-Therese for your brilliant work. I hug you and love you as no one else can.

Source: *Frags. 1,* (Vercruysse ed.), 236-7.

Notes

1. Elizavetgorod (mod. Kirovograd, Ukr.): city on the Dnieper, S. of Kiev; Potemkin's HQ in 1788-90.
2. Letter from Joseph II to Ligne about Charles at Sabatsch, from Kleinack, 25 April, 1788; see Ligne's third letter to Ségur in *Lettres*

sur la derniere guerre des Turcs, Mél. vii (1796), 55-9. Sabatsch (mod. Savac, Serbia), a fortified city on the Sava, guarding the approaches to Belgrade; fell to Imperial forces on 24 Feb., 1788. Charles' message, adapted by Ligne runs: "Nous avons Sabatch. J'ai la croix. Vous sentez bien, papa, que j'ai pensé à vous en montant le premier à l'assaut." This must be compared with the original: Vive la guerre, papa, et vive le maréshal (sic). Je suis lieutenant-colonel et Chevalier de l'Ordre de Marie-Thérèse. (Mansel, 242.) The order, founded by the Empress in 1757 as the highest Austrian military distinction: white ribbon, edged with red. Ligne himself was not made a member until 1789.

3. The multi-national army opposing the Turks.

4. Hunerwasser (Sept. 1788) and Niemes (Aug. 1788), two Austrian engagements in Bavaria during Frederick the Great's "potato war" of the Bavarian Succession, 1778-9.

5. Allusions to Ligne's career in the Seven Years' War on the Austrian side. Uhlans and Hussars were two types of light cavalry

6. Ligne needed to know Russian because he was fighting on the Russian side as a colonel in the Russian army.

7. There is a pun here on the word *génie* ("genius and military engineering").

8. Jean-Theodore Rouvroy, Chevalier de (1727-89), Austrian general of artillery at Sabatch; friend of Ligne's; wounded before Ochakov. His "luck" is another example of Ligne's irony.

9. Joseph Poniatowski, Prince (1762-1813), joined Imperial forces at Sabatch in 1788; made a marshal of France under Napoleon; drowned at Leipzig; "le Bayard polonais"; friend of Ligne father and son. His father, Casimir (1721-1800), a political idealist; member of the Confederation of Bar which attempted to annul the Polish constituion of 1791. See no. 9 of this collection.

10. Letter of thanks from Ligne to Joseph II, May 1788, beginning, "Where can I find words to express..."

11. Hotin (mod. Khotyn, Ukr.), Turkish fortress on the Dniester, some 30 mi. North Northeast of Chernivitsi, captured by Frederick Josias, Prince of Saxe-Koburg (1737-1815) for the Imperials in 1789.

12. Ochakov (Ukr.), Turkish fortress on the North side of estuary (*liman*) of the Dnieper and the Bug, opposite Kinburn on the South; taken by Potemkin in 1788. More irony.

13. Charles-Othon, Prince of Nassau-Siegen (1715-1808), famous adventurer from end of the 18th c.; distant relative and friend of Ligne.

Ligne to Charles-Antoine - d
8 June, 1788   from FM Roumiantzov's HQ, in Poland[1]

If you were to ask me, my dear Charles, how I'm doing, I'll always give the same reply. I go from one army and their marshals to the other in order to get them into action. The devil's in it, despite all their Orthodox signs of the cross. Here's the best thing I've done: leaving this joker, this flatterer who claims he admires me[2] for Kaminiec.

If only I had a heart! How love-struck I'd be! The governess, this superb, well-known Greek,[3] admired by all the world, took me in a carriage to within half the range of the cannon at Hotin[4] that were firing a few shots over our heads. I have to admit, I was more anxious to reconnoiter her to discover her weaknesses in order to lay siege to her instead of to the fortress. I'm staying with her. But what a hellish noise of chains all night long! I thought it was ghosts. And so it was, for they kept it up continually with their marching all over the house.. Her husband, commanding at Kaminiec, is served only by people condemned to hard labor. What a contrast between their criminal expressions and the beauty to whom they devote their attention even when being chastised. Even the cook has been condemned to the galleys. It's economic, but horrible.

But there's better, for I have here Ismail.[5] His droll body, so youthful, so childlike, so new (captured in one of our skirmishes), amuses me, and I serve him, rather than the other way round. One day, when laying my sabre on the harpsichord, he began to play on the keyboard. What a funny face he made! Fine! Another day, when he was supposed to offer me a chair, he brings me Mme de Witte's harp that was in the room she had given me; and he played a few chords. He laughs, jumps around touching all the tables, thinking that everything resonates – and that this old castle is enchanted.

I'd like, dear Charles, since I can't do anything with the marshal commanding this place, I'll return to Ochakov[6] and Potemkin[7] to provide me with some glory like yours. You'll be the cause of my attacks, for I want you to have a father worthy of yourself. You thought of me,[8] you're both touching and sublime; you worked on my behalf, I'm going to work for you. Wasn't I right to write a week before Sabatch that you're more worthy than I? I send you tenderest greetings from five- or six-hundred leagues.

Source: Frags. 1, (Vercruysse ed.), 238.

Notes

1. Marshal-Count Pierre Roumiantzov-Zadoumaski (1725-96), "le Turenne russe", renowned for his victories over the Turks in Catherine's First Turkish War, 1768-72. The war was being waged on two fronts: Russians in the East, Austrians in the West.
2. Prince Gregory-Alexandrovitch Potemkin (1739-91), favorite of Catherine the Great; a clever, but disorganized politician, under whom Ligne was to fare no better than with Roumiantzov at Kaminiec (mod. Kaminiets-Podolsky), a fortified town, formerly in Poland, at the junction of mod. Ukraine, Moldova, and Romania.
3. Sophie de Witte (1766-1822), celebrated beauty, known as "la belle Fanariote"; wife of Russian commandant Joseph de Witte (1740-?), then of Stanislas-Felix Potocki (1781-1805) in 1798.
   See (in Polish), J. Lojek, *Works of the beautiful Bithynian.* Warsaw: Institut Widawnifzy, 1972.
4. Hotin (mod. Khotyn, Ukr.), Turkish fortress on the Dniester, some 30 miles North Northeast of Chernovitsi, taken by Prince Frederick-Josias of Saxe-Koburg-Saalfeld (1737-1815) in 1789.
5. Ismaïl (1770-1820?), Turkish prisoner from Ochakov who became a favorite servant of Ligne and outlived him to serve another generation of the family.
6. Roumiantzov, see note 1 above.
7. Ochakov (Ukr.), Turkish fortress on the North shore of estuary formed by the Dniester and the Bug (*liman*); taken by Potemkin in 1789.
8. Note from Charles-Antoine to Ligne; see note 2 to letter no 3 in this correspondence.

Ligne to Charles-Antoine - e
30 July, 1789   before Ochakov[1]

    I'll find a place for your Prussian officer. I'm unable to make Prince Potemkin[2] advance to the estuary,[3] but I can force his officers to do so. I've created generals and majors, erc., but you, you've garnered laurels and make light of what I've done.
    Still no action on this front: 1/3 out of fear, 1/3 out of malice, 1/3 out of ignorance. When this war is over, I'd like to have had 1/4 of your glory in this campaign. Your letters are confident and gay, like yourself. They have a unique physiognomy. I've been obliged to put them aside because a storm is coming.
    [Later] A cloudburst over our camp has flooded the two pretty households I have in the shelter of an immense Turkish tent. I've no place to put my feet. Oh-oh. I've just been informed that one of our majors has been killed by a bolt of lightning in his tent. Every day there are other strikes in our midst. Win some, lose some. The other day they amputated the arm of an officer of light horse for a tarantula bite. As for the lizards, no one can verify better than I that they are friends to man. I'm living with them and trust them more than I do our so-called friends in this country. Sometimes I hear the wind and have someone open my tent but close it very quickly. It's as if the wind were passing over a brazier. Thus, we're enjoying every possible pleasure.
    Let me give you proof of Prince Repnin's[4] good taste. You know how this branch of the service demands courage against the baseness of inferiors and the impertinence of superiors? When Prince Potemkin gives a sign or lets something fall, twenty generals jump to pick it up. The other day, seven or eight wanted to help Prince Repnin off with his coat. "No, gentlemen," he said, "the Prince de Ligne will take care of it." And he called me to him. What a fine lesson! They are more delicate in spirit than in sentiment, and they recognize this; on the other hand, I play the unlucky one. But Sarti[5] is here with an excellent orchestra that you're familiar with: 30 dos, 30 res, 30 etc. Sometimes we lack bread, but not biscuits nor macaroons; neither apples

nor pears, but jars of jam; no butter, but ices; no water, but all sorts of wine; sometimes no wood for the cook-stoves, but logs of sweet aloe to burn and perfume the air.

Mme Michael Potemkina [Praskovia] is here and is extremely beautiful. Mme Skavronskaia, another niece of the vizir or patriarch Potemkin (for he always arranges his religion to suit) is also charming. Mme Samoïlova, another niece, is still prettier.[6] The other day I was acting in a proverb for her here in the desert. She liked it and asked me to make up a riddle for her.

I offered the Prince [Potemkin] an animal some idiot had sent to me. One's name is Marolles, the other's Lafayette[7] who recommends the former to me as a genial leader, destined to take Ochakov. "Good day, general, he says on entering. I'll take the fort in a fortnight. Do you have any books here? Are there any by Vauban or Coehorn[8] in Russia? I want to refresh my memory before I begin." Imagine Potemkin's astonishment! "What a man," he says to me. "I don't know if he's an engineer or not. But I do know he's French. Ask him a few questions." And I did. He admitted he was only a civil engineer. Mr de Stad [L'Estat] who rivals Vigee[9] in difficult confessions makes me happy. He's also French, amazing the Prince [Potemkin], displeasing everyone, writing charming verse, detesting the petulance of Roger[10] with whom he's always quarreling, and assuring me he's dying of fright. He's better when the cannon fire. "You see, he says to me, how Nature suffers." My horse also trembles and cares no more for glory than I.

We have here another character, ridiculous like his name: Gigandet;[11] he's a lieutenant in the Guards from Porrentruy. Yesterday he was burgled. "Furious, said he in his thick Swiss accent, I got up wearing out my feet to go and complain immediately to a cheneral who told me: If it's a soldier, I'll have him repay you; but if it's an officer, it will be difficult."

Another Frenchman whose name is Second[12] came to see me about an affair [of honor], for, said he, "Monsieur, I understand I'll have to fight." I reassured him, saying that with his name, he'd not need another if he spoke that way to everyone. Pretty good – and stupid – isn't it?

Shall I tell you about more of my innocent pleasures? I put my dromedaries on the road to the Golden Door,[13] where, by chance, *Marlbrouck s'en va-t-en guerre*. The other day three or four generals tumbled into a ditch with one-half their escort, while the other half fled.

Oh, Charles! When shall we see one another again? In Stamboul[14] or Belœil? If only His Majesty and my general [Potemkin] did not spend so much time standing on ceremony or crossing the Sava or the Bug, as if going through a door, we should certainly go through the Sublime Porte and find ourselves where I've said before. Well, dear Cineas,[15] while waiting, let us always love one another wherever we may be, no matter what.

Source:*Frags. 1,* (Vercruysse ed.) 239-41.

Notes

1. Turkish fortress on North shore of estuary (*liman*) formed by the Dnieper and the Bug; taken by the Russians in 1789.
2. Gregory Alexandrovitch Potemkin (1739-91), Prince of Tauric Crimea; favorite of Catherine II; a clever politician though profligate; friend of Ligne who left a remarkable literary portrait of him *Mél. 7,* (1795), 168-79.
3. The *liman*, emptying into the Black Sea, defended by two forts: Ochakov to the North, and Kinburn to the South.
4. Nicolas, Prince Repnin (1734-1801), Russian general, served in French army during Seven Years' War, then ambassador to Poland; hated by the Turks; disgraced in 1792; Paul I made him a Field Marshal.
5. Giuseppe Sarti (1730-1802), Italian musician called to Russia by Catherine II.
6. Three of Potemkin's nieces for whom he had an un-natural passion and who followed him to war: Praskovia Potemkina (dates ?), Catharina Skavronskaia (1783-1857), and Elizaveta Samoïlova (1763-1830): see *Mél. 11,* (1796), 295, *Mél. 13,* (1796), 349.
7. Alexandre-Louis, Chevalier de Marolles (dates?), a French captain of engineers, sponsored by Marie-Joseph du Motier, Marquis de Lafayette (1757-1834), a courtier who had fought in the American Revolution; a "liberal royalist" whose politics were suspect to L.

8. Sebastien Le Prestre de Vauban (1633-1707) and Menno van Coehorn (1641-1704), rival French and Dutch engineers in the wars of their time.
9. Baron de l'Estat (1740?-1801?), French officer, served in Russia; dramatic author; and Louis-Etienne Vigée (1768-1830), brother of the painter Elisabeth Vigée-Lebrun (1755-1842), served in Russia (1782-96); also a dramatic author who stole title and plot of l'Estat's *Difficult confessions* (both 1783).
10. Roger, Count Damas d'Antigny (1768-1823), handsome cosmopolitan; fought in American Revolution and before Ochakov; left interesting memoirs; friend of Ligne.
11. Gigandet: character difficult to identify; Ligne here is trying to pun on his name with French *gigantesque*.
12. Jacques Segond de Sederon (1758-1816?); French officer, served in Russia (1788-90).
13. The French text has "troupes", but "portes" is undoubtedly what Ligne meant; see "doors" (infra) leading to the "Sublime Porte", a common metaphor for the Turkish government. Marlbrouck: title of a very popular pantomime from 1784, including the famous march ("For he's a jolly good fellow") that Ligne satirizes here, as had Beaumarchais and Mozart before him. Stamboul (Constantinople).
14. Allusion to the Allies' war on two fronts; one in the West with Joseph II on the Sava; the other in the East with Marshal Roumiantzov on the Bug.
15. Cineas (fl. 250 B.C.), Thessalonian diplomat serving Pyrrhus (319-272 B.C.) who counseled against war, somewhat like Charles-Antoine. Executed by Cyrus the Great.

Ligne to Charles-Antoine - f
6 –25 Nov. 1790   Vienna, after the attack on Ismaïlia[1]

My dear Charles,
So you're making me end this war as I began it, dying with fright for the life of the most daring of mortals, with joy for having given life to you, with tenderness for what you've accomplished, and with chagrin for never having achieved your successes of every sort. In spite of these four dead issues, I'm dong very well and am the happiest of men because I'm going to see you again. Ah! Good God, good Charles, brave Charles, what a scare you gave me![2] I'm the one who's always betting heavily [on you]. If the Turks had cut off your head [saying *néboissé*][3] as they sometimes do during the night, especially when I think of you instead of sleeping, tell me, I ask you, what in the world I'd do? If I were able to survive, would I have what I have without reproaching myself the strength or weakness I displayed in not opposing your departure [for the service]?

Lord, Lord, dear Charles, you're returning, but I can't get over it. I swear to you that with the luck you've had in escaping danger, you shall be immortal, both physically and morally. I don't know what I'll do to hug you – where I'll stand, where you'll put your big nose, where I'll stuff my own, hoping as well to kiss your wounded knee, perhaps myself kneeling before you (or Heaven – though I'm not used to this).

Come quickly, my dear Charles. It will be a fine moment for you. I believe everyone wishes to be your father, for all Vienna is united for the first time in enthusiasm [for you] Dear Charles, how I love you ....[4] [The rest of this letter is addressed to Armand-Emmanuel, duke de Richelieu (1766-1822).]

Source: *Frags. 1,* (Vecruysse, ed.) 241-2.

Notes

1. The date is false, in as much as the fortress of Ismaïlia at the Mouths of the Danube fell on 21 December 1790. Perhaps an honest mistake for 1791.
2. Ismaïlia, a very bloody victory for the allies, 21 Dec. 1790, where Charles Antoine had fought gloriously.
3. This is Ligne's version of a Turkish expression, said to have been uttered before decapitating a prisoner; meaning: Don't be afraid.
4. The ultimate expression of fatherliness in this sequence. Charles-Antoine would later go on to fight on the royalist side in the French Revolution and be killed in the Argonne on 14 Sep. 1792; his father never recovered from this news, received on 22 Sep. 1792 at Belœil; see his letter to Casanova.

5

1732 – King Stanislaus-Augustus – 1798

Stanislaus-Augustus of Poland (1732-98), scion of the powerful Russophile Czartoryski clan, lover of Catherine II of Russia, (1755-58) to whom he owed his elevation as King from 1764 to the third partition, 1795, after which he died an exile in Russia. Knew Ligne during the latter's campaign to the Polish nobility. The tone of this letter bears witness to the quasi-fraternal affection between the two as Ligne tried to cajole the King into joining Catherine's waterborne caravan to the Crimea (1787), to no avail. Ligne airily claims in a letter from Cherson, that the king, waiting at Kaniev on the Dnieper spent "Three months and three millions to have [a last] interview with the Empress that lasted only three hours." *Lettre à la Marquis de Coigny* (H. Lebasteur ed.), Paris: Champion, 1914, page 22 note1.

See: J. Fabre, *Stanislaus-Augustus Poniatowski et l'Europe des lumières*. Paris: PUF, 1952.
I. de Madariaga, *Russia in the Age of Catherine the Great*. London: Yale [1981].

Ligne to the King
King Stanislaus-Augustus[1]

10 April [1787]   Kivovie [Kiev][2]

Sire,

    I beg Your Majesty to forgive me for not arriving at the head of the youthful water-borne caravan.[3] As I never have anything to hide from you, allow me the honor of saying that it's to pay court to you that I'm not going to pay any respects to Your Majesty [in person]. The Empress Catherine II would find in this confirmation that fear reigns here and that we are bored. Pleasurableness leads to Kameniev,[4] in addition to the obligation to pay homage. I'm sure she would say to me you'll have more fun there where never-ending social obligations might be perhaps too much of a burden for you. I prefer to sacrifice myself at this time and prolong the interview at least for myself, or to precede you, if I may. I'd like to remain at Kiev, the most faithful and zealous of your apostles, preaching true religion, and would become a martyr if necessary, knowing with great satisfaction that as a result everyone would return to the faith. In all of this there'd be no other Passion, Sire, than the one you inspire in good and beautiful souls. I'm upset at having to part from this passionate pilgrim who bears on his calm and serene brow the marks of His Passion.[5] He, however, almost scolded me, along with Count Edward Dillon[6] for the manoeuvre I dared make in begging Your Majesty to include him in one or another of your lists of honors. I defended myself by saying that it was not because of what I'd heard. You'd gain thereby a reputation for being humane and glorious through some mark of appreciation, by naming him to membership in one of your orders. I am certain that without revealing my role in this, Your Majesty would deign surprise him at his leave-taking with, say, the Order of Saint Stanislaus.[7] Such a sign of kindness on your part with an award of yours - founded by you - would flatter him more than the Order of the White Eagle (with which you might later honor him as a general or diplomat),[8] as has already been suggested. I beg pardon of you, Sire, for this excess of zeal on my part, but I'm [so] attached to people who are attached to Your Majesty and are not ingrates, for I detest those who are.

I trust that the flotilla will celebrate Saint Stanislaus[9] in the port or at the gates of Kameniev. That is all that's necessary to console me for being afloat. I'll not bother Your Majesty any more with my ideas. I'll say only that your letter, full of grace and goodness, cheered and inspired me. The one useless - but necessary - matter I'll bring up, since we must have more, (rather than less), confidence, is the honor I have more than anyone else in the world of being most deeply and respectfully devoted to you, Sire.

Your Majesty's very humble and obedient servant,
Ligne

Source: Warsaw, Zentralarchiv,
Zbior Popielov 165
Mansel, 270 no.9

Notes

1. Compare the text of this letter with those published by Mme De Staël, all faulty.
2. Kiev: town on the Dnieper where Ligne had arrived on 4 April while waiting for the ice to break up.
3. Catherine's caravan left Kiev on 1 May and ended at Cherson in the Crimea at the end of the month.
4. Kameniev [Kamniv] town about one-third of the way between Kiev and Kremenchug where Stanislaus-Augustus waited, as Ligne says, "three months and spent three millions for an interview with Catherine lasting three hours" (*Lettres a la Marquise de Coigny* – Lebasteur ed., 21).
5. Probably the King himself.
6. Edward Dillon (1750-1839): French aristocrat and diplomat.
7. Order of Saint Stanislaus: Polish order founded by Stanislaus-Augustus in 1765; red ribbon, cotised silver; Maltese cross in

red outlined in silver with gold eaglets wings spread out in the interstices, central medallion in enamel with interlocking "SS" (Saint Stanislaus).

8. Order of the White Eagle: Polish order founded in 1325; red Maltese cross surmounted by a silver eagle with wings outspread, and gold eaglets in the interstices; gold chain of alternating eagles and enameled medallions of the Virgin of Częstochova.

9. Saint Stanislaus of Krakow, murdered by King Boleslas II (shades of Thomas à Beckett!) in 1079; feast day formerly 7 May, now 11 April.

6

1759 – Marquise de Coigny – 1825 (?)

Louise-Marthe de Conflans was probably born at her family's home, le "chateau" de Conflans, rue Geoffroy l'Asnier, in Paris on 4 October 1759. Her grandfather, Louis de Conflans, Marquis d'Armentières (1711-74), was a Field-Marshal in the Army of the King of France, while her grandmother Jeanne-Françoise de Bouteroue (dates?) was from a family of *la robe*.[1]

Louise-Marthe was raised in that forcing-house for French women of the nobility, the prestigious Abbaye aux Bois in Paris and was presented at Court in 1779. In 1780 she was married to François de Franquetot, Marquis de Coigny (1756-1816), son and heir of Marie-François de Franquetot, Duke de Coigny (1737-1821), another Marshal in the military, a tenuous connection between both Marshals and their families with the Prince de Ligne.

The are few facts about her life, but many surmises, along with some telling anecdotes (if true) for a portrait of her in all her spitefulness and abusive language. Such are, for instance, her reputation as viewed by Queen Marie-Antoinette: *Mme de Coigny is the Queen of Paris, while I am merely the Queen of Versailles* (ca 1782); or Napoleon before the Imperial Court: *How is your tongue today?* (1806); or her reply to the poet Rulhière: *R—I've committed only one unkindness in my life. C—When will it end?* (ca 1789); while Tilly pretends that she was the model for Mme de Merteuil in the *Liaisons dangereuses* (1782). And so on and so forth.[2] She may well have inherited her sharp tongue from her grandmother Bouteroue who, like many of her caste, was said to be vehemently anti-royalist.

At the Revolution she "got religion" and became part of the Emigration, passing to England where she frequented the circle surrounding the Prince of Wales (the future George IV) without a noticeable change in her likes and dislikes. She is said to have died in Paris in 1825.

In his life (see his *Fragments*, passim), as in his texts (the *Lettres à la Marquise de Coigny*. (1787/1801); *Réponse aux détracteurs de la reine...* (1814), etc.), Ligne was ever the apologist of Marie-Antoinette. In addressing his *Letters from Crimea* to the Marquise de Coigny, he was not only teasing, but attempting to put her in her place. Thanks to his ambition, vanity and exhibitionism, "See what I might have done for you and your reputation (he implies), if you had not been so outspoken in your vindictiveness toward the late Queen." With such a backhanded compliment, he veered sharply away from the usual playfulness of his epistolary style and was completely serious. They had known one another during Ligne's time at the Court of Versailles in the 1770's. But he had not been in love with her, as intimated by Philip Mansel in his otherwise excellent biography,[3] for surely she was infatuated with the Duke de Lauzun (1747-93) until his death on the guillotine.

Heretofore I've been mystified by "la Marquise de Coigny" in the title of these letters and convinced that the inscription of her name was the choice of someone – anyone – he had known from the same milieu in France before the Revolution, who had survived exile and returned to distribute copies of his work. And Louise-Marthe de Coigny was the one. Or was she?[4]

My most recent interpretation attempts to clarify the matter while remaining true to Ligne's own character and comments in these letters: the posthumous reputation of the beautiful, sweet and innocent Queen (see the *Avertissement*, i-iii), proving that the addressee was not the dedicatee. After all, with the re-establishment of postal service by 1801, could not Ligne have sent copies of the *Letters* himself? And no matter how great his penury, could he not have relied on his correspondents to pay for franking, as was still the custom?

Notes

1. The best succinct account of Louise-Marthe is by Henri Lebasteur in his edition of Ligne's *Lettres à la Marquise de Coigny* (Paris:1914), xvi-xxix.
2. Ligne, *Mémoires 3* (Berlin, 1828), 318-27.
3. See Ph. Mansel in his otherwise excellent biography, *Prince of Europe* (London:2003, 101.)
4. The originator of this idea was Hector de Backer in *Bull. de la Société des Bibliophiles et Iconophiles de Belgique, 1914*, 177.

Ligne to the Marquise de Coigny

[1787?-1801?]　　　　　　　　　　　　　　from Parthenizza[1]

 I'm writing this from a silvery strand of the Black Sea; from the banks of the widest stream formed by torrents from the Tzetterdar[2] in the shade of the two largest walnut-trees there are, as old as the world, at the foot of the cliff where you can still see a ruined column, the last sad remnant of the temple to Diana made famous by the sacrifice of Iphigenia,[3] to the left of the precipice from which [King] Thoas used to cast strangers -- in a word, from the most beautiful and most interesting site in the whole world.

 Sitting on flagstones covered by a Persian carpet I'm surrounded by Tatars[4] who've offered me their hospitality while watching me write and who raise their eyes appreciatively as though I were another Mohammed.

 I can see "the happy shores of ancient Idalia"[5] and the outline of Anatolia [in the distance] while fig, palm, olive, cherry, apricot, and flowering peach trees give off the sweetest fragrance, at the same time as they protect me from the rays of the sun. Ocean waves are rolling diamond-shaped pebbles at my feet. Behind me in a half-circle I see through the branches the houses of my half-savage Tatars who sit smoking on their rooftop which serves as their drawing-room. I catch a glimpse of their cemetery that, because of the site always chosen by the Muslims with care, reminds me of the Champs Elysees;[6] it lies on the bank of the stream I have already mentioned. Where the pebbles dam its course, it becomes a little wider and flows peacefully amid the fruit trees offering the dead a hospitable shade. Their peaceful abode is marked by tombstones capped with turbans, some of which are gilded, and by a sort of funerary urn crudely fashioned from marble. The variety of all these spectacles makes you wonder and causes my pen to fall from my hands. I stretch out on my flagstones and reflect.

No, you cannot conceive of everything going on in my soul. I feel like a new person. Having escaped from magnificence, the hubbub of parties, the fatigues of pleasure, and from their two Imperial Majesties of the North and West, [Catherine II of Russia and Joseph II of Austria] whom I had last seen on the other side of the mountain that extends to the peak made famous by the punishment of Prometheus.[7] I am at last enjoying myself. I ask where I am and by what twist of fate I am here. This is an opportunity for self-examination and, without intending, I recall the follies of my life.

I perceive I'm able to be happy only in tranquility and independence and under conditions I can control. Since I am lazy in mind and body, I always managed to perturb the first in war, in troop inspections, or in travel, and waste the other on people who are not worth the trouble. Cheerful enough in myself, I wear myself out appearing so to those who are not. If, on occasion, I'm preoccupied by a hundred ideas that cross my mind in a flash, they say, "You are sad," it's enough to make me so. Or [they might say] "You are bored," and it makes me boring.[8]

I wonder why, ambitioning neither glory, nor honors, nor money, nor favors, and being true enough to myself not to care, I spend my life at court in every country in Europe.

I remember that a sort of paternal kindness from the Emperor Francis the First[9] who, amused by scatterbrained exploits of the young had attached me to him early on; and that later, loved by one of his loves, it was enough to keep me at court for a long time; but although I had, as was right, the favors of that charming woman, those of our sovereign remained. At his death, although [still] quite young, I imagined myself a lord of the old court; I was on the point of criticizing the new one without being familiar with it, when I became aware that the new Emperor could be just as amiable and possessed the same qualities as the old:[10] I was encouraged to seek his esteem rather than his favor. Certain that he did not like to show his preferences, I could indulge my penchant for his persona, and while I blamed his too-hasty style, I nonetheless appreciated three-quarters of his acts and will forever praise the good intentions of a genius both alert and prolific.

Sent to the court of France[11] at its most brilliant, with news of a victory [for the allies], I never wished to remain and was glad that I had escaped from its formalism even though I recognized it for what it was worth. Chance sent the Count d'Artois[12] to a garrison near where I was inspecting [our] troops. I went to him with about thirty of our officers properly turned out. He looked us over, called me to him, and began as the brother of the king,[13] to finish as if he were my own ruler. We drank, gamed, and laughed. Free for the first time in his life, he was unaware of how to enjoy it. This first expression of gaiety and the charming petulance of youth endeared him to me. The frank allure of his heart which was always and everywhere the same were in evidence and seduced me. He wanted me to go to see him at Versailles; I said I would see him in Paris if he would go there. He insisted, spoke to the Queen about me,[14] and she commanded my attendance [as an Austrian].The attractiveness of her soul and her person, beautiful and pure, and that of her company caused me to spend five months of the year in her entourage. Henceforth I could not leave her for a minute. Moreover, the taste for pleasure, which alone made Versailles an abode of delight, took me there at that time; gratitude drew me back.

Prince Henry[15] was making a tour of the battlefields [of the Seven Years' War]. Our attitudes and military preparation drew us together; I was accompanying him and had the pleasure of pleasing him. Kindness on his part, bustle on mine, with great mutual understanding, and rendezvous for Spa and Rheinsberg [the Prince's country residence]..

At camp in Moravia with the Emperor and the then King of Prussia, as well as today's:[16] the latter notices my adulation of great men and invites me back to Berlin. Good relations with him and tokens of esteem and kindness from this first of heroes, overwhelm me with glory. His nephew, at that time the Crown Prince,[17] goes to Saint Petersburg. A few trysts -- amorous, confidential, financial, and friendly -- concerning a woman in his thrall, had brought us together. In so remote a country, despite the difference of interests, service, and rank, [even] strangers come together. A sort of favor on his part; embarrassment on mine, [especially] when Russia had to be thwarted [politically].[18]

I escaped from the endearing sentiments of two other kings from the North [about 1790].[19] The too-small head of the one, completely deranged soon after, and the stubborn temper of the other, spare me their endless favors that I was promised on a trip to Copenhagen and Stockholm. I was lucky to get out of it by giving parties for the one and being honored by the other.

My son Charles marries a pretty little Polish [heiress].[20] Her family offers us paper money drawn on the Russian court instead of hard cash. I create a Polish personality for myself or am made Polish in passing [through the country]. A crazy bishop, since hanged, the uncle of my daughter-in-law,[21] imagines that I was on the best of terms with the Empress of Russia because he heard that she treated me marvelously[22] and that I might be King of Poland if I became naturalized. What a change in the nature of European affairs! What a blessing for the Ligne and Massalski families! I am skeptical, but I am willing to please the nation, assembled in a Diet; the nobles applaud. I utter a few words in Latin, I hug and caress the moustaches and work behind the scenes for the King of Poland,[23] himself a schemer like all the kings who are too, on condition they follow the wishes of their neighbors or their subjects. He is a good man, likable and attractive; I give him a piece of advice [and] find myself quite intimate with him.

I arrive in Russia. The first thing I do is to forget the reason for my visit, since it seems more delicate for me to take advantage of the limitless kindnesses bestowed on me each day in order to receive other benefactions. The confident and seductive simplicity of Catherine le Grand[24] enchants me, and her enchanting genius is what has brought me to this place of enchantment. I let my eyes wander and let my mind rest.

I find that my recapitulation of events that have always made me do what I did not want to, does not prove that I am mindless, so I let my soul speak.

Today, Thetis[25] does not aspire to lull the sun to sleep. He is calm, he can descend from his chariot whenever he wants, to come into my arms. Nighttime will be delightful. The sea, tired by the slight movement she has had throughout the day, is so calm that she is like a great mirror into which I look and see into the recesses of my heart. I have never known so beautiful an evening, and in my ideas there is the same clarity in the sky as on the water.

Why not? I ask myself in my inmost being; rather than preoccupied with meditating on the beauties of nature, why not relax in the sweet repose that I so idolize? It's because I fancy this sight will inspire me, and the allure of a little aura of authorial glory is attuned to so much extravagance. Shall I cease to exist? So be it. People will read me; it's one way to avoid death. For such reasons, we die, exerting ourselves for posterity who is not in the least grateful.

Perhaps it's here that Ovid wrote.[26] Perhaps he was sitting where I am. His elegies were written from "Pontus" -- here is the Pontus Euxinus [the hospitable deep] of the Romans. The land of Mithridates, the King of Pontus. And since his place of exile, is at best uncertain, I have every right to believe it is here, and not at *Carantschebes*, as the Transylvanians would wish it. Their right to this fiction is [the expression] *cara mea sedes* whose pronunciation according to them has been corrupted to form the name I have just mentioned.[27] Yes, at Parthenizza where the Tatar accent has changed the Greek name "Parthenion" that means "virgin" as in the famous Cape, whence it was transferred to many locales. Here is where mythology inflames the imagination. Everyone in the service of the Gods who did not pass to those of Israel, where temples in such poor taste established their empire. Shall I abandon [if only] for a minute fables for history? I find that Evpatoria (mod. Yevpatoria) was founded by my Mithridates.[28] I can pick up nearby shards of alabaster columns. I came across pieces of aqueducts and walls suggesting parts of a fortification as great as that of London or Paris, and I reflect that these two cities will pass like this one, where the same amorous or political intrigues took place [as in theirs] -- each believing it had left its mark on the world; and the very name of this land transformed it into "Tatary" has fallen into disuse. What a fine lesson for the self-important! Now, turning around, I see and applaud the relaxation of my good Muslims.

Seated on their rooftops with their arms and legs crossed, they have witnessed so much human folly. I have found among them an Albanian who knows a bit of Italian. I ask him to inquire if they are happy or whether I could be of use to them. Do they realize that the Empress has given them to me? They have me informed that they know, in general, that they have been provided for, but they do not really know what that means. They have been happy til now, and if they were no longer so, they would escape on two of the ships they built themselves – I can see them from where I sit -- and would seek refuge with the Turks in Romania. I give them to understand that *I don't dislike lazy bones,*[29] but would like to know how they live. They pointed out a few sheep, like me, lying in a meadow. *I bless these lazy bones*. They show me their fruit trees and tell me that when the harvest comes, the Kaimakan [the vizier's lieutenant] arrives from Bakhchisaray[30] to take a share; that each family sells two hundred francs' worth every year. There are forty-six groups established between Parthenizza and Nikita, another small settlement belonging to me, whose name in Greek means "victory".[31] *I bless the lazy bones* [again] and promise to prevent them from being exploited. They bring me butter, cheese and milk -- not kumiss like the Tartars are said to drink. *I bless these lazy bones* and return to my meditation.

And again, what am I doing here? Am I a prisoner of the Turks? Have I been cast ashore in a shipwreck? Have I been exiled like Ovid because of some [intrigue] at court or my passionate nature? I ask and tell myself: nothing of the sort. There may be a reason or reasons, but...

After my children and two or three ladies I love madly – or believe I do – my gardens are what give me most pleasure in this world.[32] There are few so handsome; I am still working at beautifying them [even though] I am almost never there. I have never been in them following the blooming season, when small forests of precious shrubs perfume the air even to the horizon: I am two thousand leagues from all that. As an owner of seashore estates I find I am now on my own on the strand of the Pontus Euxinus. A letter has arrived from the Empress some eight hundred leagues away recalling our conversations about the great days of antiquity. She proposes that I follow her to this beautiful landscape to which she has given the name of Taurida[33] and, in consideration of my taste, she offers me the place of Iphigenia's sacrifice. Next, I try to forget dominations, thrones, and powers[34] in order to continue my self-examination. All at once, I experience one of those delightful obliterations I am so fond of, where the mind is completely at rest and you scarce know you are alive. What then occurs to the soul? I don't know. But what is certain is that it suspends every movement.

After that, I make plans. Blasé about almost everything, why should I not stay here? I'll convert these Tatars to the vine and, assuming the air of a courtier who will be understood from a distance by any visitor, I construct beyond their dwellings, eight lodges for vine growers with a colonnade linking them together and a balustrade connecting their rooftops. I draw up plans for what would have been done immediately had it not been for the conflict arising from our voyage.[35]

What a shame! I then say to myself that the religious superstitions of the Greeks destroyed these handsome remains of pagan cults so favored of the imagination.[36] My Albanian cut mine short as soon as he showed me the spot where a bishop was assassinated, and the ruins of a monastery that thankfully is no longer to be seen. The commercial enterprise of the Genoese was sufficient to spoil this lovely site, today alive with white minarets, like needles, long and slim and a sort of oriental architecture that confers a pretty style on even the most humble cabin.[37]

My reflections, leading me to consider the ravages of time, bring me to consult the state of my heart. I think that nothing here below remains in a state of stagnation and that as soon as an empire or power no longer increases, it declines, just as the day we love no more, we love less. My heart! What is this word I have uttered? Is it the spectacle of my heart, or nature which takes me outside myself? I burst into tears without knowing why; but how sweet they are: a general affectation, an overflow of sensibility without being able to discern an object. At this moment at the conjuncture of so many ideas, I weep without being sad. Alas! I say to myself while addressing a few people who are frequently my inspiration, perhaps I am sad. You, too, separated from me by oceans, deserts, remorse, relatives, bores and prejudices? Or else is it for yourselves? Those of you who love me without saying so and whom I abandoned for want of understanding you? Is it for you, superstitious slaves of so many obligations? Love of verse and the countryside, our readings together, our walks, while still other bonds brought us unwittingly together. [Ladies!] Is it because you feel guilty for not wishing for a little more confidence, warmth, and daring? Is it for you that chance or inexperience cast you into my arms? The answer will ever be clear to me with the first fruits of a sensitive and naive heart. Is it for you who, under the pretext of blunders, treated me the same? Is it for you, whom a writer of parties, plays, woodland, gardens, travel, worked on your feelings, even in our innocent encounters leading to the loss of innocence? Let me be precise: being separated has deprived us of satisfaction since we were undoubtedly virtuous.

My tears will not be staunched. Is it the presentment of some heart-rending loss that I will one day suffer? I put that fearful thought from my mind. I pray to God and say "This vague melancholy, like the one we feel in early youth out of a need for love, does it perhaps announce some celestial object completely worthy of my love that will forever end my career in the empire of Love?" It seems to me as though the future wishes to be revealed. There is but a tiny step from the exaltation in which I just found myself to enthusiasm and from there to divination and the art of interpreting oracles.[38]

Then I remember all that has preceded and followed, less in significant periods, both happy and unhappy enough when unhappiness itself had many charms. I recall that, worn out by spending the night in snow to catch the moment of deceiving a mother or husband at the risk of receiving a hundred lashes of the whip or being mistaken for a thief (which did happen once), I was sorry to renounce easy conquests that were simple to maintain. I was loved at the Comédie française because, I told myself, this theater is the School of Taste and demands the greatest skill. But nonetheless I added soon afterward a faery from the Comédie italienne! The pretty sound of a voice goes to the heart; the applause that an air draws from the public is shared. And scarcely was I happy there than a dancer from the Opera seemed to me to personify voluptuousness to perfection. Each movement, said I, leads to that; the arms they raise, the toes they lower *en pointe* are signs of pleasure. Soon out of sorts for not noticing further contrasts, I reappeared in society seeking the charming misfortunes I'd complained about shortly before.

Thus one thing followed another in my recollection and came to preoccupy me; for such in my memory was the picture of my past, present, and future love affairs.

Alas! Why can I not at least recall in the same way my friendships?[39] Yet "*O mes amis*, there are no longer any such," as the Ancients used to say. This precious diversity can be found only in statuettes on buffets or on mantelpieces. Porcelain or alabaster are used, while more often still canvases portray sacrifices to friendship. But when does this happen in reality? I've more friends than many another without pretention to anything in any sense. I've achieved no outstanding success, nor are my qualities alarming. Everywhere I meet sociable friends with whom I dine and trifle all day long. Yet, have I found one who has been kind enough to me so that I'm under any obligation? I'd like to be obliged to others. [On the other hand] several were obliged to me, although they didn't seem to be aware of it. From time to time I like to play the ingrate, but lest I am truly so, I frequently prefer to be generous to excess. Deceptions of this sort seem excusable in my eyes.

Without weeping over humanity, without loving or hating too much (hating is wasteful and tiring), I'm not more satisfied with mankind than I am with myself. In examining myself I find but one good quality – I'm always happy about the good that comes to others.

I judge the world. I watch it like a slide-show while waiting for the moment when Time, raising his well-honed scythe, orders me to disappear. Nine or ten campaigns, a dozen battles or skirmishes in which I took part next come to me as in a dream.[40] I think of the nothingness of glory – glory ignored, forgotten, envied, attacked, revoked, or questioned, yet -- I say to myself – a part of my life has been spent in seeking to love (life) whilst chasing "glory".[41] I say nothing about my valor, no doubt brilliant enough; but I do not find it "pure", for there is only a false appearance to it: I tend to play too much to the gallery. I prefer the valor of my good, dear Charles who never checks to see if people are watching him.[42]

When I look more deeply into myself I find a score of faults. Then I think of the nothingness of ambition. Death has deprived me, or soon will, of the favor of a few good warriors and a few great sovereigns. Capriciousness, inconstancy, spitefulness will make me lose hope of replacing the former and of serving the successors of the latter. Intrigue, separating me from one and all, may cause my soldiers to forget "the voice of their vizir".[43] I let my present flow with the current of my destiny without regrets for the past nor fears for the future

After laughing at my paltry merit and my adventures at Court or in the military, I'm glad I am no worse than I am. I congratulate myself on my talent for making the best of everything to my own satisfaction. Child of nature, and perhaps even a spoiled child, I see myself at last as I've been taught, reflected in this vast sea (as I've already said about my soul) as in a mirror.

Already the veil of night is beginning to obscure the sea. The father of light [the sun] is expected to appear on nearby horizons. The sheep near my Persian carpet are calling to the Tatars who, gravely descending from their rooftops, are going to enclose them with their women whom they've kept hidden all day long. The muezzins are calling to the mosque from the top of their minarets. With my left hand I feel for the beard I don't have; I place my right hand on my breast and *bless these lazy bones.* I bid farewell [to all], allowing them to see in me their master, as I would wish them to be always their own.

I collect my wits, heretofore so scattered on the magic lantern of my life. I look around me with emotion at these lovely scenes that I may never see again and that have allowed me to enjoy the most delicious day of my existence. A fresh breeze suddenly coming up decides me against [using] the boat that was to take me to Feodosiya. I mount a Tatar horse, and, led by my guide, I plunge into the horrors of the night – the roads, the torrents – to recross the famous mountains and find at the end of two days' journey their Imperial Majesties at Karasubazaar.[44]

O Parthenizza! splendid spot that recalled me to myself! O Parthenizza! Never will you leave my memory.

Source: *Lettres à... Coigny*, Lebasteur edition, 45-68.

Notes

1. Parthenizza: "virgin land" (mod. Frunzenskoye in the Crimea) so-called to commemorate Iphigenia, the virgin priestess of Diana in mythology, the name dating from the Genoese occupation in 1290-1475, site of a considerable grant of land to Ligne in 1787, evocative for him of his past life, thought, and feelings translated in this letter. Nearby is Cape Parthenion with the Ayu Dag (Turkish for Bear Mountain, 1695 feet) in back.
2. "The Tzetterdar" is Ligne's adaptation of the Italian for Chatyr-Dag (Tatar) the highest massif in south Crimea (1527 m, 5010 ft), where he may not have traveled; the most likely spot for his visit to an ancient temple is the Ayu-Dag (572 m, 1877 ft) a coastal hill.

Its Eastern slopes lead to the ancient settlement of Partenit, called Partenope for the virgin goddess Diana.

3. Iphigenia, in Greek mythology, the daughter of Agamemnon, delivered from Calchas' sacrifice in Aulis , she became an exile and priestess of Diana (the virgin goddess) in the Crimea, from which she planned to escape with Orestes, her brother, and Pylades to her homeland; heroine of a play by Euripides (ca 410 B.C.) and an opera by Glück (1781). Thoas, in Greek mythology, a King in the Crimea who sacrificed to the gods by casting from the Tzetterdar all foreigners who came to his kingdom. Cf. the recent excellent edition of Goethe's *Iphigenia auf Tauris* by M. Swales (London: Angel, 2014).

4. Modern archeology prefers the spelling "Tatar" to contrast with the Tartar hordes of Genghis Khan who invaded Eastern Europe as far as Liegnitz, Germany, until 1241; so-called from confusion with the Ancients' Tartary, or Hell.

5. Quote from Voltaire, *La Henriade* (1723), 9:1-2. It is unlikely that Ligne could have seen so far from the Crimea.

6. The Champs Elysées, a famous avenue in Paris, whose name derives from the abode of the blessed in classical antiquity, formerly an elegant promenade, now highly commercialized.

7. Prometheus (classical mythology) was chained to Mt Elbruz (5642m, 18510 ft) the highest point in the Caucasus (hence in Europe) for having taken the part of mankind against the gods, especially Zeus. Ligne's geography is, at best, a fancy.

8. For further reflections on his life and thought, see Ligne's *Caractères et portraits* (Acke ed.), Paris, 2003.

9. Francis, I (1708-65), Emperor of Austria and King-Consort of Marie-Thérèse (1717-80).

10. Joseph II (1741-90), Emperor of Austria, reigned (1765-90).

11. In 1759, as courier for the allies after the battle of Maxen (21 Nov. 1759), Ligne was sent to the court of France at Versailles.

12. Charles-Philippe, Count d'Artois (1757-1836), younger brother of Louis XVI and Louis XVIII, later King of France as Charles X (1824-30). There was a twenty-year difference in age between him and Ligne.

13. Louis XVI (1754-93), King of France, guillotined.

14. Marie-Antoinette of Austria (1755-93), Queen of France, guillotined.

15. Prince Henry of Prussia (1726-1802), younger brother of Frederick II the Great (1712-86); honored as soldier and gardenist at Rheinsberg (near Neuruppin, N. Germany); a friend of Ligne's.

16. Frederick the Great of Prussia and Joseph II of Austria met at Neustadt (Moravia) in September 1770, with Frederick-William II of Prussia (1744-97), nephew and successor of Frederick the Great, and Ligne in attendance.
17. Crown Prince, later Frederick-William II of Prussia.
18. Because of Russia's desire for territorial expansion in Poland, resulting in the Confederation of Bar (1768), leading ultimately to the First Partition (1772).
19. Kings of Denmark (Christian VII, 1749-1808, died insane), and Sweden (Gustave III, 1745-92, assassinated). Both knew Ligne about 1780.
20. In 1779, Charles-Antoine de Ligne (1759-92), eldest son of the Prince, married Hélène Massalska (1764-1815), a Polish heiress, amid great festivities planned by Ligne at Belœil.
21. Ignace Massalski, Bishop of Vilna (1728-94), uncle of Ligne's daughter-in-law, hanged by revolutionaries in Warsaw.
22. Allusion to Ligne's "special relationship" with Catherine II of Russia; see their letters, edited by Marie, Princess de Ligne in 1924 (new edition by J. Vercruysse, to appear).
23. Stanislas-Augustus Poniatowski (1732-98), last King of Poland (1764-95).
24. Epithet coined by Ligne; normally "la Grande". Catherine II of Russia (1729-96), about whom there is much to be said, reigned from 1763 and was intimate with Ligne, fully merits this epithet.

If, according to my contention, this marks the end of one letter and the beginning of another – very difficult to prove because of the absence of manuscripts – though a not uncommon practice among artists (see the conflation of two themes in some of Schubert's late piano sonatas, to mention but one example from a sister-art). This development is not a recapitulation: the tone, treatment of several topics broached earlier, and the mood are quite different.

25. Thetis: in classical mythology a sea-goddess, the mother of Achilles.
26. Ovid (43 B.C.-16/17 A.D.), poet, exiled from Rome in 8/9 A.D.; died at Tomis (mod. Kustendji, Mouths of the Danube, Romania), where he wrote the *Tristia* and *Epistolae ex Ponto* (A.D. 912).
27. *Cara mia sedes* (mod. Karansebes, near Timisoara, Romania), where formerly it was believed Ovid had been exiled and died (A.D. 17).
28. Mod. Yevpatoria (Crimea), named for Mithradates IV Eupator (the Great), who reigned in Pontus from 120 to 63 B.C.

29. This phrase, repeated several times, almost as a refrain in imitation of Danton's speech of 12 September, 1792 ("De l'audace") before the Revolutionary tribunal in France.
30. Modern Bakhchisaray, capital of the Crimean Khans until 1783, with a neo-classical palace by Catherine's favorite architect, Charles Cameron (1743-1812); see Pushkin's *Fountain of Bakhchisaray (1822)*.
31. Nikita, site of another grant of land to Ligne in 1787, SW of Parthenizza, near mod. Yalta.
32. Allusion to Ligne's interest in gardens and to an early edition (1786) of his *Coup-d'Œil at Belœil*. See Guy/Vercruysse eds. (Paris: 2003).
33. "Tauride", literary name for the important Black Sea peninsula (now in Ukraine), formerly the Chersonesus (peninsula) Taurica, when the Crimea was supposedly a land of hellish darkness, the pasture of a giant, sterile cow, Taura.
34. A souvenir of Ligne's religious training? In Thomistic philosophy, three heavenly choirs: in descending order, a) seraphim, cherubim, and thrones; b) dominions, virtues, and powers; c) principalities, archangels, and angels.
35. Catherine's second Turkish War (1787-92), begun with the siege of Ochakov (1788), ended by the Treaty of Jassy (1791), to facilitate the Empress's desire to reduce the Ottoman Turks and see her second grandson, Constantine (1779-1831) on the throne in Constantinople (Istanbul). The war was preceded by a famous flotilla descending the Borysthenes (modern Dnieper), 1787.
36. See *Les Ruines*, by Volney (1792) and R. Mortier, *La Poétique des Ruines* (Paris: 1974).
37. The romanticism of these paragraphs is witness to the influence of J-J. Rousseau (1712-78) whom Ligne had read and pretended to know personally. See A. Monglond, *Le Préromantisme* (1930), II, 167-9.
38. The cultural importance of "friendship" at this time has yet to be studied in philosophy, literature and the arts.
39. See A. Béguin, *L'Ame romantique et le rêve* (Paris: 1939).
40. On "glory", see B. Guy in *Mélanges Niklaus* (Exeter: 1975).
41. Prince Charles-Antoine de Ligne, Ligne's eldest and best-loved son, was brave to the point of foolhardiness and was killed fighting the forces of the French Revolution in the Argonne in 1792.
42. From Racine's *Bajazet* (1672), I:i.

43. Karasubazaar: an important trading center near the middle of the Crimea, on a river flowing NE and emptying into the Zivach, or Putrid Sea. "Their Imperial Majesties" were Joseph II of Austria and Catherine II of Russia who had met at Cherson to visit the newly-conquered Crimea.

There are several proofs of the re-working of this letter for publication in 1801; e.g. mention of the *Coup-d'Œil* and the death of Prince Charles-Antoine, as well as that of bishop Massalski, etc.

Professor J. Vercruysse of the Free University of Brussels has discovered an "ante-text" for another letter in the collection, justifying the date "1787." See his *Bibliographie descriptive*, 264.

Commentary on Letter number six in my collection.

This letter – number five "from Parthenizza" – was placed by Ligne at the very center of his collection of nine *Lettres à la Marquise de Coigny* in his *Mélanges militaires, littéraires et sentimentaires, xxi* (1801), 28-45, and is the longest and most important of all. Divided in two unequal parts, it is, first, a summary of the Prince's life, and, second, (as Lanson called it in 1909) "a lyrical meditation" on that life and some of Ligne's ideas. There are also reflections on his situation at the moment of composition. The break occurs, according to my division, at note 24, between the paragraph ending "I... let my mind rest," and the one beginning, "I find that my recapitulation...."

Supposedly written from "Parthenizza" in the Crimea, so named in honor of Iphigenia, the daughter of Agammenon in Greek mythology; she was to be offered as a sacrifice here so that the Greeks might proceed to Troy in the *Iliad*. Instead, she was allowed to choose exile and became a priestess of Diana under the guise of the virgin goddess, Parthenope.

This collection, "from the Crimea," but especially this letter, seems to have been seriously re-worked, though we cannot say for sure, since there is no trace of an original manuscript. The first complete version appeared in Ligne's *Mél. 21* for 1801, since when this letter has inspired both fans and critics.

Frequently, there have been readers wanting to identify Ligne in this letter with an early generation of rousseauistes, but they are mistaken, for there is no rousseauism here, even though the lyrical Rousseau had appeared in the *Rêveries* at about the same time as Ligne's meditation. There may be a seeming transfer of sensibility from one to another; nonetheless, there is no direct mention of either Jean-Jacques or his writing in Ligne's text. The Prince knew Rousseau personally and seems to have kept abreast of his work. Yet the critics are knocking down an open door, while at the same time ignoring an eighteenth-century type of melancholy in the midst of Nature to be found in Delille and other poetasters like Pezay, Dorat, Colardeau, and Lebrun. Even so, some of Ligne's fans are willing to accept his anachronisms in matters both factual and stylistic.

For the former, there is mention of several characters whose dates are ignored (like those of his son Charles-Antoine who died fighting the forces of the French Revolution in the Argonne in 1792, or that of Archbishop Massalski of Poland (a distant relative) who died in 1794). As for style: Ligne's repetition of "lazy bones" in discussing the Islamic occupants of his land-grant of some thousand acres from the Empress Catherine II is perhaps an echo of Danton's "de l'audace" in a speech before the Convention in 1792, or Volney's melancholy in *Les Ruines* from 1791, or Chateaubriand's in the *Itinéraire de Paris à Jérusalem* (1811). There are several more examples (historic and/or stylistic) in both parts of this letter, while the Prince's abuse of "poetic license" (no matter how annoying to the modern reader) merely adds to the attraction of his style.

Despite such details, the charm of his lyricism remains. Thanks to his expression, he succeeds in combining melancholy with sincerity, while he evokes images of a distant past amidst beauties of natural splendor. And his sustained treatment of passing moods has captured and defined for us the meaning of romanticism at its most profound. Included under such a heading are seemingly incidental remarks about Ligne's commitment to friendship, the picturesque (already partially addressed elsewhere), and dreaming. The high seriousness of this meditation does not exclude some quirkiness that gently amuses, while offering his proverbial coquetry, impervious to his theme, leaving traces of his mischievousness in emotion without ignoring that emotion completely.

Since the greater number of these comments apply more specifically to the meditative quality of the second part of this letter, we may wonder if there were not in the Prince's mind around 1801 reason enough to utilize them in a separate letter which, on second thought, he might couple with the original of the first part to create a single expression for the two?

Quite simply, this very sociable man kept, in spite of all, a proper distance from worldly concerns. His contemplative attitude offered the Prince the opportunity to recapitulate certain facets of his life, subsumed by an "examen de conscience" so to speak. Nonetheless, he is content with a rapid review instead of undertaking a genuine analysis. Ligne seeks in vain a number of personal faults, but we shall never know which ones. In the end, this very stylish missive, copiously re-edited is not a sustained romantic diffusion nor a detailed autoportrait.

Such, in brief, are the considerations suggesting that letter number five "from Parthenizza" is really two, cobbled together to form one of the more curious anomalies from the pen of the Prince de Ligne in his collection "from the Crimea", dedicated NOT to Mme de Coigny, but to the memory of Queen Marie-Antoinette (see the "Avertissement").

Starting with note 24, the shift in tone indicates a second text (if not a complete letter) that Ligne has added to his first in order to complete his self-analysis. For want of manuscript proof for this assertion, the content and footnotes are plausible justification for this interpretation which I have not found in any other edition.

Select Bibliography

Lanson, G. "Le Prince de Ligne", *Choix de lettres du xviiie siècle*. (Paris: Hachette, 1909; 557-63.)

H. Lebasteur (ed.). *Lettres... Coigny.* (Paris: Champion, 1914; 45-68.)
Monglond, A. "Le Prince de Ligne à Parthenizza", *Le Préromantisme*, 2 vols. (Paris: 1937, rpt Paris, Corti, 1965; I:167-9.)
Gross, L. "L'exotisme oriental dans l'oeuvre du Prince de Ligne", *Revue de l'Université libre de Bruxelles, xiii* (1960-1) 150-6.
Lecomte, F. "Le Prince de Ligne à Parthenizza", *Lettres romanes, xxxviii* (1984). 283-6.
Lope, H-J. "Sur les traces d'Ovide," *NAPL ii* (1987). 175-92.
Trousson, R. "Lettres et pensées du Prince de Ligne", *D'après l'édition de Mme de* Staël (Paris: Tallandier, 1989; 53-4, plus notes.)
Lope, H-J. "Ligne et la Mer Noire," *NAPL viii* (1994). 143-67.
Guy, B. "Parallel Voyages: Ligne and Custine in Russia," *L'Invitation au Voyage.* (Oxford, Voltaire Foundation, 2000; 250-62.)
Mouriau de Meulenacker, P. *Lettre à la Marquise de Coigny, De Parthenizza.*
Extrait des *Mélanges 16,* (1801). 59 pages, format minuscule (25x47 mm.). Bruxelles: privately printed, 2003.

7

1753 – Louis-Philippe Count de Ségur – 1830

Diplomat; fought in the American Revolution and awarded the Order of the Cincinnati; knew Ligne in Saint Petersburg (1785) and accompanied him on Catherine II's waterborne caravan to the Crimea (1787). Rallied to Napoleon; Grand Master of the Court (1804). Left interesting memoirs in which Ligne figures prominently.

Letters from Ligne:
　　✉ a - 1 December, 1788, [Ryabaya Mogila]
　　✉ b - This 6 October, 1790 plus (1793?) as per note 24, Vienna

See:　　Ségur, *Souvenirs et anecdotes*, 3 vols. Paris, 1840

Ligne to Ségur -a
1 December, 1788[1]   [Ryabaya Mogila]

On returning from camp at Czezora to the one before Ryabaya Mogila, or rather, Jassy, where I have my headquarters. "Relaxing from the din of battle, / our friend will tell of boyars at table."[2]

I might have made a fine tale of our easy victory over Sultan Gerai, *Prince in partibus* of the Crimea, over Ibrahim Nazir, relentlessly harassed by the Austrians from the Yedisan, [and] over the seraskier of the fort at Ismael, Ghazi Hassan Pasha, where the [few] survivors are now consoling one another.[3] Having seized this site because of its impregnability, the Turks, like game-birds, always utilize the same runs and lines of withdrawal, assemble [here] at the beginning of each campaign; this time they were clever enough to set up the site in another way and would have easily been overcome if we had so desired.

The attack by Nassau[-Siegen] and Masson, was made by our other corps; the second name, as you know, is that of our celebrated Frenchman, André-Pierre Masson.[4] I had counted on the Feast of St Gregory, patron of Prince Potemkin [to get him moving]; but [because of his dilatoriness] I left his corps and am still *vox clamans in deserto*.[5]

I could send you a literary portrait as piquant as others, but I'll keep it for myself.[6]

The 15 or 20,000 men [the Turks] pretended were 50,000 have left. After New Serbia [and] the country of the Nogais and Budjiak, Tartary and the steppe of Bessarabia where I've just been,[7] I find myself in a land of enchantment.

Last winter was terrible. [I was living] in a hovel amid snow and a dung heap of a redoubt, six months' campaigning without other views than the sky and the sea for 300 leagues, and weeds covering a plain that is unrelieved and green as a billiard-table – it's enough to make me find everything superb. Since my departure from Elizavet[gorod] I've seen nary a horse nor a tree, except in the Pasha's garden. Near the entrenched camp of Ochakov I hugged a few trees under the hottest gunfire, I was so happy to see them. I even picked and ate some delicious apricots. The only drink available for five months of the year was some brackish water polluted by the corpses of 5,000 Turks killed, burnt, or drowned by Nassau-Siegen, [and] driven by the wind to the shore of the estuary. Otherwise, it was water from the Black Sea – not so saline as that from other seas.

Imagine then my happiness at finding a charming fountain on a rise overlooking Jassy. I kissed the wet before drinking and devoured it with my eyes before moistening my lips that, until then, had been tasted with nothing so agreeable.

I'm housed in one of those superb palaces the boyars have had constructed in Oriental style. More than 150 of them rise above the other buildings in this capital of Moldavia. Read the description of them in my book on gardens.[8]

Charming ladies, almost all from Constantinople, and from ancient Greek families whose [traditional] costume they wear. They sit about on divans and relax with their heads thrown back or resting on an arm like alabaster. The men who visit them lie almost at their side and did not appear to me to cross their arms on their chest nor their legs as freely as those of the ladies? A light, short and clinging skirt doesn't suffice to hide the lovely silhouettes of these last, while gauze shaped like a pocket marvelously outlines two charming swellings that are like the entrance to "the garden of love" [the pudenda]. The black or red scarf covering their head sparkles with gems, and forms a sort of bonnet creating the sweetest effect in the world. Pearls of the first water are worn around their neck and shoulders, unless they're interwoven with net and covered in sequins or demi-ducats to mark the seams of their costume, on some of which I must have counted up to 3,000 coins. The rest of this costume of oriental luxury is worked or woven with gold or silver thread hemmed with precious fur, like the boyars'. Their headdress is like the Turks': atop their red skullcap [winds a length of material resembling] a turban.

Like the sultanas, the boyars busy their fingers with a sort of rosary [worry beads] made of diamonds, pearls, coral, lapis, agate, or a rare kind of wood which seems to reassure them, like the fans of our ladies. I've been told that the suppleness of their fingers has been strengthened using these beads and that telling them over and over has given birth to the creation of a language of love. I even surprised some husbands glaring at the women out of curiosity [or jealousy?], [for] I had already learned a little of this pretty alphabet of gallantry. The time for trysts can easily be mastered in this way, but how to arrange for the rendezvous itself?

Seven or eight servants of the boyars and an equal number of girls who serve their wives, young and with suggestive shapes are always in the apartments, circulating among almost every level of society; they differ only in the richness of their costume from the heads of household. Each one has his or her specialty. As soon as you go in to pay your respects one of these youths will bring a pipe, maybe even more; one of the girls will bring a dish with rose petals [rahat loukoum?] and a spoon; still another will burn or pour out some attar for perfuming the rooms; another will bring a cup of coffee, another, a glass of water. The same acts of hospitality and kindness will be repeated at the homes of twenty boyars if you were to visit them all on the same day. It is considered the greatest insult to refuse even one [invitation].

We're comfortably lodged here, [though] it's warm. I'm dressed like the boyars; I go often among them to observe, for I know but few words of Vlach and none at all of the Greek spoken by the ladies who despise the language of their husbands. What's more they're not very loquacious. Dislike of the Turks, the fear of receiving bad news from Constantinople or from the hospodar [governor], all have accustomed them to an unspeakable sadness [because of the uncertainty of life]. Fifty people assembled every day in one house or another appear to be awaiting the fateful cord [of strangulation].[9] You hear over and over again: my father was killed here by orders from the Porte [Constantinople], and here my sister by order of the governor.

When I say I go among the boyars to observe, [I] should say, rather, in order not to have to think. At my fourth pipe I've already said this about the Turks [and] am fit for nothing. I've not a single idea and not thinking is the best I can do, far from you and all I love.

I greatly appreciate the religious air with which the youth of both sexes who leave their slippers at the foot of a stair in order not to spoil the fine carpets nor sully the sanctuaries of their masters; after finishing with the duties of their office they go back to pick up and sit down in a corner on their knees. I'm happy I don't have to ring for valets or shout. If by chance they are on duty, you call for them as in the seraglio [harem] with handclapping or by applause, as it were.

Constantinople sets the tone for Jassy, as Paris does for the provinces, and new styles are sooner available. Yellow is the favorite color of the sultanas; it's now the preferred one for women in Jassy.[10]

In Constantinople pipes of jasmine-wood have been replaced by long ones of cherry. That's all we other boyars now own. Servants carry them behind the carriage of these gentlemen; they're the only ones allowed to do so, are never on foot [and] are all as lazy as the Turks.

The ladies might easily forego having distended stomachs; such is one of the standards of beauty in this land. One mother sought my forgiveness because her daughter did not show any development. "It will come soon," said she, "for though it's now shameful, she's [nonetheless] as straight and thin as a reed." Such costumes and customs make the pretty women prettier, while the ugly ones become more so; besides, to tell the truth, the ugly ones are rare in this society. Because of their manner of sitting or lying down in a circle, I happened to mistake some of them in a badly lit apartment for [a pile of] furs that had been forgotten on the divan. Daughters of the boyars are put away, as are Turkish women in harems behind grilles that are frequently gilded. Thus they can look out on the real world of men and select their husband-to-be; but the latter look on them only as an object for having sex after a brief ceremony of the Greek [Orthodox] church.

I've just given a charming party that turned out to be successful: a hundred boyars and their wives to table, a ball where we danced the *pyrrhique*,[11] as well as other Grecian, Moldavian, Turkish, Wallachian and gipsy dances. There you can see the origins of such entertainment that is stupid if there is no purpose: there can be only two purposes in society, celebrating a victory over one's enemies or voluptuousness in more tranquil times. If we are now happily arrived at this last, which always dominates, wherever Mohammed's standard is unfurled before the eyes of the Turks.

You hold hands to stay together, you do a few turns – but always face to face. You look intently at each other, you almost let go [of your partner], but you hold on, get closer (I don't remember how), you continue to stare, you understand one another, you appear to love one another.... Such dancing seems most reasonable to me.

As for me, I enjoyed myself immensely by saying nothing to a few of the women. After several helpings of jam and a few drinks laced with rose water, and about six pipes, I realized I was alone.

Nothing can compare with the [political] situation of these people. Suspect to the Russians for preferring the Austrians, likewise to the latter for being secretly attached to the Turks, they long as much to see the first go away as they fear the return of the others.

You who are the arbiters of the fate of mortals so frequently armed by your treaties, repair the evil you've done, more than we who are but the executors of your high and mighty schemes. Favor these human beings as well as the policies of several empires incapable of leaving the poor Moldavians alone and in peace. Their land is so beautiful that the rest of Europe might object. Grant them independence from Oriental despots, let them govern themselves, instead of being under an [appointed] governor who has to be a tyrant of necessity, paying court to the Ottomans. Give them, for their betterment, two boyars as governors, to be changed every three years. Since, after a while, they must rejoin the rest of humanity, they'd not dare to abuse their authority and be made to pay dearly for it at the end of their triennium.

Let mediating courts be amused by this, and frame for them a sample code of laws not conceived by "philosophers,"[12] but by a few reliable thinkers or priests who are not "intellectuals", but are familiar with the climate, the character, the religion, and the customs of the country, and who would accord a truly sovereign authority to the two great and mighty lordships [Walachia and Moldavia] in charge of the administration.

What a blessing for the soul and spirit! But [let there be] no flight of fancy. Become Montesquieu and Louvois, if you can, without ceasing to be Racine, Horace and La Fontaine.[13] You can make great strides if you follow in their footsteps. Labor on behalf of my dear Moldavians in the best way you know how. They treat me so well.

Like everything about them, especially their language, which reminds me that they are descended from the Romans, it's a harmonious blend of Latin and Italian. They say *szluga* for "salut", or *formos coconitza* "a pretty woman", *sara bona* for "good evening" and *draga mi* for "I love you". I can think of no better way to end than with this truth: I can speak to you in at least twelve languages and you'll reply, I'm sure, in good French.

Source: *Mél. 7*, (1796), 198-210.

Notes

1. Ryabaya Mogila ("Hill of the serfs"), now a suburb of Jassy (Iasi) in Moldova.
2. A couplet by Ligne himself.
3. Sahim (Selim) Gherai (? -1787), hated governor of Moldavia, deposed and strangled.

    Ibrahim Nazir (? -1789), governor of the Yedisan (area between the lower reaches of the Southern Bug and the Dnester, conquered by Austria). Ghazi Hassan Pasha (1714-90), formidable military commander of Ismaïlia (Mouths of the Danube, Rom.), site of a massacre by the Austrians 23 December, 1789.

4. Charles-Nicolas-Othon, Prince of Nassau-Siegen (1743-1808), adventurer and friend of Ligne, André-Pierre Masson (1759-1820), French surgeon serving Russia.
5. St. Gregory of Nyssa, feast 9 March, observed by Christian churches, both East and West. Gregory, Prince Potemkin (1739-91), consort of Tsarina Catherine II of Russia, general in charge of her Second Turkish War (1787-92), died at Jassy.

   "Vox clamans..." (A voice crying in the wilderness. Matthew iii:3)
6. There is such a portrait from this period; see the letter to Ségur, from Ochakov, dated 10 August 1788, *Mél.* 7, (1796),171-4. Is Ligne being absent-minded, or is this another sign of tampering with the originals?
7. Territories occupying lands between the Dnester and the Pruth, Southern Russia.
8. Either the first or the second version of the *Coup-d'œil sur Belœil* (1781 or 1786).
9. Strangulation was the typical mode of execution under the Ottoman Turks.
10. Yellow was the color of mourning among these people. See E. Trelawny, *Adventures of a Younger Son*, ch. iii.
11. The *phyrrique* was a stately dance in 2/4 time.
12. "Philosophes" was a pejorative term for Ligne, as is "intellectuals" later in this text.
13. Montesquieu (1689-1755) and Louvois (1639-91), two authoritative writers on politics; Racine (1639-99), Horace (65-8 B.C.), and La Fontaine (1621-98), were all classical writers.

Ligne to Ségur -b
This 6 October, 1790¹   Vienna

To him whom I thought the best of friends, the most amiable of men, the philosopher, the least "philosophical," a most distinguished man of letters, a brilliant officer of dragoons, with time and opportunity the most honorable of courtiers and the most enlightened of ambassadors, who since... but then he was all that.

Source: *Mél. 7,* (1796),149.

Louis Ségur, your signature is not anonymous and yet is not yours, for it bears the stamp of error. Your coat-of-arms suited you to a T. At one time it was the sign of genius.² Your attitude alarmed me. The vile and stupid daring that caused the honor of your respectable father to be attacked by people without honor,³ and their lack of concern for severed arms will prevent (said I to myself) my friend from throwing himself into theirs. Alas! Unfortunately I was deceiving myself. When people know how warm-hearted you are, they must expect some exaggeration [of enthusiasm]. Let not your love for an imaginary good make you forget whatever is possible. Greece had her Sages, but they were only seven.⁴ You have 12,000 at eighteen francs a day who are, unwittingly, the amazement of Europe. With no other mission but themselves, without experience in business, without knowledge of foreign countries, without an overall plan, with no interest in the public good (although this word may include particular benefits), with no respect for the nobility who have ever been useful, brilliant and clear, without an ocean capable of protecting the phraseologists and the laws of a country it surrounds, how can you maintain such an attitude? Let's suppose that by some misfortune for France there remained only gaunt "philosophes"⁵ approving neither of celebrations nor hunting and [who] will acknowledge that their children will be deaf to the call of pleasure and love, alone capable of undoing "equality"....

Wits, however respectable, have precious little talent for creating their own kind. So young, so alive, so exalted a nation which at this moment prepares to sow thorns among roses that are to die, will that nation keep its facile promises? I can imagine an unforeseeable and dreadful event – nonetheless profitable to tiger-monkeys as Frenchmen were called by M. de Voltaire,[6] overthrowing a King but never the throne, while a sovereign, an imagined "philosophe" or a businessman – no matter who – will be seated thereon, even if it were called a curile chair, as you will.

If a Bourbon won't be named immediately, perhaps it will be the handsomest, bravest, most amiable, most beloved of the French who'll mount a throne that was once surrounded by myrtles and laurels[7] The commonalty of names and principles will take flight before a young Prince or dictator who will have read of the battle of Coutras and the amulets of youthful courtiers with lovers' monograms rather than the Social Contract.[8] He'll condemn the unfortunate moment when France drew around herself a cordon of mere ciphers for her first neighbor to break whenever he will. A scepter of iron will prevent a return of horrors and will prove most necessary. Such is the result of liberty: you've become slaves, and you'll deserve to be so. The very names of today's wise men will be erased because they believed they were the cynosure of the universe. One hundred boring pages of declamation will be rejected by History. And from Klostercamp, after bypassing a few pretty celebrations at the Petit Trianon and the costume ball for the Count du Nord, people will seek new challenges and new pleasures under another reign.[9] My friend Plato is not worth following, either in love or in a republic.[10] I prefer the barrels to tuns.[11] In France, Diogenes would have destroyed his lantern.[12] People were mistaken about him: he was not looking for honest men – there were as many in Athens as in Paris. Rather, it was little boys, for he was afraid of being misunderstood, the dress of streetwalkers favoring such errors. Are you men, my lads, the prettiest in the world? If kings, to avenge themselves on the majesty of the monarchy want to crush you, I challenge you to find the [opportune] moment to oppose them.

You'll need to give yourself a lot of time to organize your corps, your hearts and your wits on the Plain.[13] I know your nation can be cured and that it is capable of the grandest accomplishments, thanks to the superiority of your talents of every sort; but I trust you'll not be so awkward as to let yourself be had. Without taking the trouble to make war on you, let a cordon be drawn around France, a large one, as against the plague, and every power, armed to the teeth along your borders, depriving you of all commerce, all communication, will force you to kill one another in a civil war, or to do what they want.

The witness to Catherine's greatness and Joseph's misery[14] will get the better of the man of letters and the philosopher, who, in the quiet reflection of his study, will forget what goes on in the salon of a minister or the cabinet of a king, even when sometimes under the eye of the master. How many additional abuses will there be, good Lord, [once] these are corrected? The ambassador of an erstwhile great monarch at the thought of an important and tricky treaty he had engineered would disdain the insignificant results incurred by a vague and mistaken imagining. Louis Ségur would never go so far as Count de Ségur.[15] Then adieu pretty verses and songs. Adieu poetry, divine and delicate, along with cutting epigrams and genuine madrigals. Adieu passing fancies and gallantry. Vergil, Horace, and Ovid[16] would never have supped with two such brutal brutes [who] would have been only severe and mediocre [as] individuals, without suppleness, sensual delight, flattery and abuse. You'll all become quite boring, and already you yourself have not begun too badly.

Leave a country where people are always either better or worse than themselves, where the destruction of armies proves they will become sorry entities, especially when needed, where coats-of-arms are broken and mottoes effaced, while chivalry is consigned to the madhouse. Leave a country where the tempest, whether external or internal, beats on your remains and will soon be recognized by its thunder and lightning. Those signs of reason[ableness] are but will-o'the-wisps leading weary travelers toward cliffs [of destruction]. Leave a country where the more intelligent you are, the more you are envied, contradicted thwarted, and the less you'll be believed. Wait before returning til the French become more amiable, and do not return alone!

Say, like the Russian in Paris: I'll return when they've changed.[17] Use the miserable friends you ought not to have [anyway] to get you out of all difficulties, and when you've enlightened them as much as possible, get yourself named ambassador to a post where you'll put everything in order, or at least in a more moderate condition. I already sense that there'll be crimes considered necessary to maintain one's self as well as horrible expressions like "the need for crime," "great misfortune for individuals in order to create general well-being," "to the lantern [string 'em up]", etc.[18] Alas, I feel I can no more return to your Paris since it has been sullied with the blood of unfortunate people: imagine the revulsion of every upright person in Europe if blood still flows in the streets there. Oh! Louis Ségur, let your Christian name which you've so ingeniously taken up remind you of the glorious days of Louis le Grand,[19] where you'd have played a nobler role than you do now. The very prim and proper moralists of austerity aren't worthy of those whose celebrations honored the victors from the Rhineland.[20] Offer your hand to Louis XVI and help him regain his throne instead of forcing him to lose it. Let everyone be more royalist than he. Alas! Might not people say to him, instead of keeping him in prison: One fall leads to another?[21] What would you gentlemen become if this fall was complete and you were reduced to governing yourselves? Under what flag have you marched til now? Fishwives have replaced the Longuevilles, the Chevreuses, the Montbazons.[22]

I doubt if you ever get dirty in the sewers of Paris, but you're already up to your knees in filth. Come away, old friend, I beg of you, and proclaim before leaving: Gentlemen your "national debt" and your "deficit" are mere laundry chits.[23] Maintain your priests, and they'll take care of payments. Your King has been too good, your Queen too indulgent toward the enemies she acquired without ever knowing how. Your nation's burdens will be relieved. The supposedly wealthy will no longer be hanged while those in need will be helped. And France and Europe will be peaceful and happy.

Think on these things, Louis Ségur: there's still time, and if your actions bring success, even if you have to work hard at these challenges, let us both be good friends as before.

Source: *Mél. 13*, (1801), 125-31.

Notes

1. The date is important as indicating Ligne's attitude, in accordance with the chronology of the French Revolution up to this time. References to subsequent events are evidence of an obvious reworking.
2. Coat of arms: Quarterly, 1 chequy, or and azure; 2, 3 gules, a lion rampant or; 4 argent. Under Napoleon, the arms were changed to: azure, between a chevron, three roses, or. The motto quoted is false; it should read: *quantum mutatus ab illo* ("How changed you are", Ligne is here paraphrasing Æ. ii:272, where the hero encounters the ghost of Hector.)
3. Philippe-Henri, Marquis de Ségur (1724-1801), Minister of War 1781-7; lost an arm in the Seven Years' War.
4. The Seven Sages of Greece were: Thales of Miletus, Pittacos, Prias, Cleobulus, Periander, Chilon, and Solon.
5. "Philosophical" a pejorative term in Ligne's vocabulary, equivalent to "intellectual" today.
6. Tiger-Monkeys: term used by Voltaire in *Candide* (1759-61), ch. 22, to characterize the French.
7. Perhaps an allusion to Ligne's friend Count Louis de Narbonne (1755-1813).
8. Coutras (Gironde), site of a victory of Henry IV over the Ligue, 1587. *The Social Contract* (1762) is a chef-d'œuvre of political theory by J-J. Rousseau.
9. Klostercamp (Westphalia), site of a victory of the French over the Hanoverians in 1760.

    Petit Trianon, neo-classical chateau by Ange-Jacques Gabriel (1755), now part of Versailles.

    Count du Nord, the alias of Emperor Paul of Russia (1754-1801), while traveling in France in 1782-4.
10. Plato (429-347 B.C.), in the *Republic*.

11. Du Barry (pronounced like "*barils*/barrels" in French), referring to Jeanne Bécu, Countess du Barry (1743-93), acknowledged mistress of Louis XV.
12. Diogenes (413-323 B.C.) lived in a tub and carried a lantern looking for an honest man.
13. "Plain" and "Mountain" two hostile factions in the French Revolution, politically equivalent to today's "Right" and "Left".
14. Catherine II of Russia, Empress in 1762 (1729-96) and Joseph II of Germany, Emperor in 1765 (1741-90).
15. Louis-Philippe, Count de Ségur (1753-1830), as this letter indicates, had at this time renounced his title.
16. Vergil (71-19 B.C.), Horace (65-8 B.C.), and Ovid (43 B.C.- 17 A.D.) Latin classical writers greatly admired by Ligne.
17. *The Russian in Paris* (1760), a tale by Voltaire.
18. These expressions were current in the French Revolution.
19. Louis le Grand or XIV, (1638-1715), reigned alone from 1661; at the peak of glory, 1679.
20. Victories of Louis XIV against the Dutch and their allies in 1668-78-97.
21. Louis XVI was in prison after the return from Versailles, 6 October 1791.
22. "Fishwives" refers to the women from Paris who forced the King and Queen to leave Versailles in October 1791.

    Anne, Countess de Longueville (1619-79) and Marie, Duchess de Chevreuse (1600-79) were two conspirators against Mazarin in the Fronde (1648-53). Louis, Prince de Rohan-Montbazon (1635-74) conspired against the King and was beheaded; a distant relative of Ligne.
23. "National debt" and "Deficit" refer to economic causes of the French Revolution, but like much else in this letter reflect a certain historical carelessness on the part of Ligne, if not tampering. Briefly, the events alluded to herein were as follows: Affair of the Queen's Necklace (Mme Deficit), 1785; the National Assembly (1788-91), where civil equality was guaranteed and feudalism abolished, 4 August 1789; The royal family imprisoned in Paris and the King reluctantly agreed to a limited constitution, 5 September 1792; 17 July 1790, when the use of coats-of-arms was prohibited and priests were made to become civil servants; 1 October 1791 the terms "Plain" (Right) and "Mountain" (Left) came into use; 10 August 1792, the King was deposed and 21 January 1793, and executed; 6 April 1793, there were riots in Paris because of paper money (*assignats*); 16 October 1793, the Queen was executed.

8

1736 – Gregory Alexandrovitch Potemkin, Prince of Tauris – 1791

One of many paramours of Catherine II of Russia and after 1771 (perhaps) her husband. Knew Ligne in St. Petersburg and the Crimea. Ligne left a perceptive portrait of him in *Mél. 7,* (1796), 168-79.

See   I. de Madariaga, *Russia in the Age of Catherine the Great.* New Haven: Yale [1981]

S. Seebag – Montefiori, *Potemkin: Catherine the Great's Imperial Partner.* New York: Penguin, 2005.
-----*Prince of Princes: A Life of G.A. Potemkin.* London: Phoenix, 2000

Ligne to Potemkin
This 24 May, at midnight [1788][1]   from Ceitra Hora [Rom.][2]

Prince,

Please find herewith a letter from my comrade Coburg[3] whom I'll go to consult after an hour spent with the Marshal.[4] Thanks to you, he will be in a position to refuse me nothing. I'll send a courier to you post-haste after our discussion, followed by another from our camp before Hotin,[5] where I hope to arrive Tuesday. There, I'll be able to judge for myself the possibilities and hopes remaining to us.

Prince, dear to my heart, please do not give any more public interviews with newspapers. The immense services you've rendered to us by your letters to the Marshal regarding the Emperor[6] will make me happy at small cost and will prove that the journalists are right.

You can also do me a great favor, again concerning His Majesty, (and Marshal Lascy),[7] by naming my nephew Browne,[8] to be aide-de-camp to the Empress.[9] This is the last wish of his elderly father.[10] I found a letter here, in which he begs this grace of you for which he wrote to Her Imperial Majesty in February.

This will be the 100th obligation I'll have to a Prince I love dearly and respect wholeheartedly and who shall ever be my great, handsome [hero], my worthy Agamemnon, soon to be the victor at Troy,[11] taking only as many days as his forebear took years. Dear Prince, please forgive this prophecy.

[unsigned]
Source: private collection

Notes

1. Entire date in another hand.
2. A fortress in old Moldavia near Jassy. Suceava (mod. Rom.)
3. Frederick-Josias, Prince of Saxe-Coburg (1737-1815), general in the wars against the Revolution and Napoleon.

4. Peter, Count Roumiantzov-Zadoumaskii (1725-96), Russian FM.
5. Hotin: Fortress at an important river junction in Bukovina (modern Khotyn, Ukr.).
6. Joseph II (1741-90), Holy Roman Emperor from 1765.
7. Moritz, Count Lascy (1725-1801), Austrian FM and patron of Ligne.
8. Jean-Georges Count de Browne (1767-1827), Austrian F.M.
9. Catherine II (1712-96), Empress of Russia.
10. Jean-Georges Count de Browne Sr. (1698-1790), Austrian F.M.
11. Ligne's fantasy has Potemkin overcoming Ochakov (Ukr.), in ten days, as the Greeks had overcome Troy in ten years.

9

1762 – Joseph, Prince Poniatowski – 1813

Polish soldier, friend of both Ligne and his son, Charles-Antoine; French F.M.; drowned at Leipzig (1813); "the Polish Bayard."
In the case of this correspondent, Ligne's handwriting and his son's, are difficult to distinguish, but a key is to be found in the salutations: "Mon Prince," for Ligne; "Pépé," for Charles-Antoine; as well as in the tenor of their respective letters.

Ligne to Poniatowski
24 September [1789]   Semlin [mod. Zemun,
suburb of Belgrade]

My dear Prince,

I've received your letter, read it, and the first thing I want to do is to write a reply.

There's nothing in your letter that's uncomplimentary, except for the army of H.I.M.,[1] who adores you and gave expression to his feelings some time ago. What you accomplished last year, what you've attempted, and what you've so impetuously avenged, proves he's right. How you alone who are not aware of yourself can be unaware of how well-liked you are and esteemed, how you can think that what we know is the effect of the first of your duties, might do you an injustice.

The reason for tears, as I read you, is that I thought of the trouble you are currently experiencing[2] and that, with the talent you have for not lacking one, you'll create a thousand and one others. I'm not talking about myself. If our damnable situation of uncertainty were past, I was preparing to be greatly in your debt. My head and my heart were all in your favor. And while imitating me, Charles[3] could continue for hours at a time. What pleasure I'd take in adding to your glory. And what a pleasure for your sensitive and eager soul to be useful to your best friend, and the father of your best friend.

Here I am lost in my [illegible], of all my advanced posts that were impatiently expecting you. I already planned a dinner like one of your Polish feasts for the day of your arrival on the fifth.

Apparently, dear Prince, I love you more than I thought, for my feelings in this are very strong. At the same time I'd be chagrined if you made up your mind to go away. You owe yourself to your fine and illustrious nation whom your example can regenerate. Your sureness [of touch], your countenance, your faithfulness, and your desire will thwart those who in your country are lacking [these qualities], while those who are superficial intriguers of no consequence will perhaps come to their senses.

You'll be the only consolation for the king,[4] upholding his glory and the happiness of his old age.

Stanislas (who is not august, though possessed of great merit) is not much loved. You, on the other hand, are loved by all parties. You'll get the better of them by making eyes at their handsome eyes and staring at the rest. In any case, I predict the most brilliant of destinies for you.

Be clever enough to enjoy life now, and take good care of your health. I've inquired of your men if you need cash. And though they were in tears at my sensitivity and at the idea of your leaving a situation where you're adored, they all laughed when I added with regret that I don't have any [cash] myself. Heavens! I'd steal if I had to.

Adieu, dear good and handsome Prince. This farewell has taken its toll because it is the farewell of a soldier. But don't frighten me otherwise, for we love one another too much not to seek each other out and meet together without end.

[signed] le Prince de Ligne.

Source: Craków,
Polska Akademia Nauk,
Poniatowski Archive,
fo. 41. Mansel no. 14

Notes

1. H.I.M. is His Imperial Majesty, Francis II (I), 1752-1835, Emperor from 1792.
2. Poniatowski had been trying desperately to receive a command in the Imperial army to no avail and was considering offering his service elsewhere, finally achieving his ends in Napoleon's army, becoming FM at the battle of Leipzig (1813), where he drowned.
3. Ligne's eldest son, Charles-Antoine (1759-92), a very close friend of Poniatowski, through whom Ligne got to know the Prince and began to take an avuncular (?) interest in him.
4. Stanislas-Augustus Poniatowski (1732-98), King of Poland (1764-95), a relative of Prince Joseph.

10

1739 – Françoise, Princess de Ligne – 1821

Princess Françoise-Marie v/z Liechtenstein, wed Prince Charles-Joseph de Ligne at the Liechtenstein castle of Feldsberg, Austria, on 6 August 1755. He was 20 years old; the Princess, 14. She gave birth to seven children, two of whom died in infancy.

"My wife is an excellent person, full of delicacy, sensitivity and nobility. She's never intrusive. Her ill-temper is quickly passed, distilled in her moist eyes with tears over nothing at all. She is not cumbersome, for she has a very kind heart. From time to time she is somewhat contradictory and, after seeming to take a bit of pleasure from it for a split-second, she grants her children everything they ask and is even obliging to me."

In the context of the *Copie*, she was "pro-patriots" until it became apparent that both she and her husband had more to gain by remaining faithful to their sovereign than by patronizing the rebels

So far as we know, there is no study devoted to her. The best thumb-nail sketch is in Carlo Bronne, *Belœil et la maison de Ligne*. Belœil: Fdn Ligne, 1979, 172. But even here the author begins: *La Princesse... demeure une énigme*. Despite this lukewarm attitude, most historians agree that the couple became more intimate in their time of sorrow and retirement [post 1780]. See Louis Dumont-Wilden, *La Vie de Charles-Joseph de Ligne*. Paris: Plon, 1927, 39, et seq. Compare as well the more skeptical remarks by Ph. Mansel in *Prince of Europe*. London: Weidenfeld and Nicolson, 2003, 133-212, passim.

Source: Ligne, *Frags, 2* (Vercruysse ed.), 214.

Ligne to the Princess, his wife
3 January 1790[1]   [Vienna]

I cannot believe it. There has never been in history—and I say more: there never will be—such a revolution.[2]

Since this time[3] it's obvious, the article of the Joyeuse Entrée is clear and definitive.[4] I'll admit that for the movement in favor of a few readily adjustable changes that could have been made quickly three years ago. Belgiojoso,[5] through stupidity and obstinacy insisted on having his way. I felt that either too much or too little had been done. People were saying: we are going to revolt. This time they've not said it, they did it—and in a way that speaks as highly of its inspiration as of its realization. It's a fine thing for our Nation to have cast out the Austrians with as much humanity as consideration and covered half a dozen generals with shame. The calm that existed after the Estates were quashed[6] must have been terrifying for the cruel and stupid General Government. I remember how the Duke d'Ursel[7] and I, when reading the sorry news, treated this nascent army with ridicule: What do these émigrés want? We imagined they were but a few workers or deserters thinking only of pillage. I was even thinking that the country would stand up to those they were calling "bandits and brigands".

It's like the second part of *Long Live the Gueux* (beggars).[8] Yet, when I observed the fine tactics of Van der Meersch[9] at Tournhout, the successful crossing of the Scheldt and the courageous attack on Ghent,[10] I was admiring the spirit of Van Der Noot.[11] The primary motive, it seemed to me, of all that, was combined with the spirit and talent of Van der Meersch. They should raise two statues in Brussels to d'Alton and Trautmannsdorf[12] and two others to the two gentlemen who militarily, politically, and humanely conducted themselves so appallingly yet did more for this revolution than the Princes of Orange for the other one.[13] Ferdinand Trautmannsdorf with his foolish letters became merely disobedient and an embarrassment to his master.[14] He wanted to re-establish the Estates the day following their suspension with but few changes, and pointing out to him that it was by a similar act of weakness that the King of France[15] was the cause of his own downfall.

But old d'Alton is a monster against whom I wrote a formal complaint to the War Council, this year. Despite all the other disagreements I had, and which might have sufficed to have him cashiered; [but he has been confirmed in his position.]

Being almost at the head of the armies and always in the last two years commanding a considerable number of troops,[16] you will understand that my career is too far advanced for me to quit the service. I will be neither a traitor, nor ungrateful; and even then I would not expect to please my Nation. I will neither serve against her nor with her against the Emperor.[17] But I will serve her with the last drop of my blood against all the other Powers of Europe.

Source: *NAPL 5* (1990), 37-8.

Notes

1. Date supplied by Ligne; not printed until 23 January 1790 in the *Journal de Bruxelles*, apparently supplied by Van den Broucke on authorization from the Princess de Ligne.
2. "La Révolution Belgique" began about 1787 (before the fall of the Bastille in Paris, 14 July 1789), and ended in 1794 with the fall of the Low Countries at the Battle of Fleurus (25 June).
3. In the course of the Révolution belgique (1787-94).
4. The "Joyeuse Entrée," the charter of civil liberties in the Low Countries, dating from 1356, and preciously guarded.
5. Louis-Charles, Count de Belgiojoso (1728-1802), Austrian plenipotentiary in the Low Countries in 1787; see J. Vercruysse, *NAPL v* (1990), 100.
6. The Duke of Alba, master of the Low Countries (1567-73), abrogated the terms of the "Joyeuse Entrée" in 1567 and caused a great uprising.
7. Wolfgang, Duke d'Ursel (1750-1804), relative and friend of Ligne.
8. "Long Live the Gueux," War of Beggars against the authorities in 1566-76. The phrase became a national refrain.

9. Jean-André Van der Meersch (1734092), one of the leaders in the national revolt.
10. The attack on Ghent (17 November 1789), a victory for the insurgents; see J. Vercruysse in *NAPL v* (1990), 77.
11. Henri Van der Noot (1731-1827), lawyer and leader of the insurgents.
12. Richard d'Alton (1732-90), a Scot commanding in the Imperial Army, committed suicide (as a result of the Révolution belgique?). Ferdinand, Count Trautsmannsdorf (1749-1827, Prince in 1807), diplomat, Austrian minister in Brussels (1787-90), then Grand Master of the Court in Vienna.
13. Prince of Orange, especially William the Silent (1533-84), helped the Gueux in 1566-84.
14. Joseph II (1741-90), Emperor in 1760-90.
15. The King of France was Louis XVI (1754-93).
16. Ligne is referring to his experience in Catherine's Second Turkish War, 1787-92.
17. This is the same as 14 above.

JV Commentary

In his lifetime (1735-1814) Ligne was known as a scatterbrain who would have liked to become an "intellectual" or a "politico". Did he ever achieve his ambition to be taken seriously? The jury is still out.

At the time of the Belgian revolt (1787-90) he added fuel to the debate by publishing a letter to his wife, attempting to establish his reputation in both camps – that of the Rebels (or Pirates) and that of their opponents, the monarchists, with the Emperor Joseph II (a great personal friend) at their head.

For twenty years or more, starting in 1787, the Austrian Low Countries (or, modern Belgium) were the scene of violent contestations within their hereditary limits as a province of the Holy Roman Empire. Beginning with arguments, pro and con, the political, religious, economic, and social interests of the time unraveled and soon rose to great heat, erupting in "la Révolution belgique". This was, as is obvious from the dates, before the outbreak of the French Revolution, and in some respects served as a model for the latter. The disturbances (including military encounters) lasted until roughly 1814 and the Congress of Vienna which had thought to put an end to the problems of the Austrian Low Countries. The Powers did not succeed until 1830 and the creation of modern Belgium.

Though initially absent on assignment in the Crimea, the Prince de Ligne was soon apprised of the situation in his homeland, and desired the military to take action. First, however, he was gazetted to the siege of Belgrade against the Turks (1787-9) as Major-General in charge of the Artillery where he won plaudits for his strategies and the award of Commander in the military Order of Maria-Theresia. Because of rumors relating to confusion within the Révolution belgique and suspicions about his role, he was not allowed to return to Vienna until early 1790, when he had a memorable interview with the Emperor, Joseph II (or so he claimed). Nevertheless, his concern for the situation in the Low Countries encountered success for first, one side, then the other, in the struggles merely intimated above. In later life, while composing his memoirs, *Fragments de l'histoire de ma vie*, he at last understood that in his political naiveté he had had some success in trying to bring together conservatives and patriots in the struggle between good and less good. But in the situation then existing between the two sides was a letter he had composed for his wife, dated 3 January 1790, that was partly sympathetic to the rebels and was made public that year in the *Journal de Bruxelles* on authorization from the Princess de Ligne.

From the beginning, the Copie elicited criticisms pro and con, but especially one question: was it authentic? Why were the two cardinal points so antithetic? What was the role of the Princess de Ligne in all this? How was it possible for a man of Ligne's reputation to be both pro-rebels and pro monarchy at the same time? Etc. Recently, the Doyen of Lignistes, Professor Jeroom Vercruysse, attempted to shed some light on the problem in an analysis of the *Copie d'une lettre* (1790) *du Prince de Ligne à la Princesse, son épouse*. The following remarks are adapted from his presentation in the *Nouvelles Annales Prince de Ligne* v (1990), 36-45.

The words and ideas are proof alone of its authenticity, claims Professor Vercruysse, while the context confers a meaning that is the opposite of what a literal interpretation might allow. The reader will also note that the text of the *Copie* seems to be truncated, with neither formal salutation nor complimentary close; both merit closer scrutiny. The generally short sentences create tensions to be exploited for the readership. At the same time, we cannot exclude the possibility of a re-writing (whether partial or complete) so long as the original has not been found.

From the outset, Ligne's astonishment, faced with the reality of the Révolution belgique, seems to bear witness to his disbelief (real or pretended), unless it is a literary tactic meant to show his disappointment in what followed. Antitheses govern the writing of this text. Ligne appears to be happy to add praises for the conduct of the patriots and their leaders Van der Noot and General Van der Meersch. He frequently uses admiring words or phrases, like: it's a fine thing, humanity, valor, heart and great talent, grand manoeuvre, a fine passage (of the Scheldt), admirable, etc. On the contrary, there are harsh terms condemning the local people responsible for the conflict, like: shame, stupid and cruel, silly letters, narrow-minded and disobedient, monster, appalling, etc. There is no dearth of irony either; the Prince suggests raising statues to the heads both civil and military, judging them very severely and contrasting them with the leaders of the patriots.

Ligne then defines his personal attitude: faithful to his commitments, respect for the unstable neutrality between "the Powers that be" and the "patriots". If we compare the *Copie* with one he wrote on the same day [3 January, 1790] to his secretary Legros, we are struck by their parallelism. In the *Copie* the terms are more incisive, but the themes are identical and had been known since 1787. The acuity of the printed version is the result of the special circumstances in which it was composed and which must be taken into consideration.

Publication of this letter contributed greatly to feeding rumors of Ligne's attachment to the Révolution belgique, a false report that had been some time in circulation. The *Gazette de Hervé* and the *General Journal of Europe* are perhaps the first newspapers to have cast doubt on the matter, for, on 17 November 1789, they had declared that the patriots were wrong to vaunt the idea that the Prince de Ligne had embraced their party and that he, with all his family, had left the province of Brabant. The chargé d'affaires of Liége in Brussels, Dotrenge, writing on 18 November 1789 to the revolutionaries in Liége, nevertheless sees some ambiguity in this and claims that it is, rather, a question of Prince Louis de Ligne [and not Prince Charles-Joseph]. Following publication of the *Copie* in the *Journal de Bruxelles* for 2 February, 1790, after the *Journal des Pays Bas* had announced the return of the Prince de Ligne and his son Charles to Brussels, it was claimed through the Duchesss d'Arenberg and d'Ursel that they would join those relatives who had already embraced the revolutionary cause. (See J. Polansky, *Revolution in Brussels*, 1987, 125-6.) Moreover (but privately) the Princess de Ligne had approved the "pathetic" options of her husband and their elder son. On 29 December, 1789 she had written to Van den Broucke, the family agent, that the Princes were in an impossible situation that prevented them from following their inclinations, "which, I guarantee, are all for their nation." Five months later the Princess would limit herself to stressing their prudence and declaring that they would never bear arms against their country. Meanwhile, the Princess would underline those qualities in her family like the unshakeable faithfulness of Prince Charles-Joseph toward their legitimate sovereign that had long since given the lie to continuing rumors of an eventual rally in favor of the Révolution belgique. This false report, encouraged by publication of the *Copie* - perhaps the result of a singular request by the moribund Joseph II [d. 20 February, 1790] to Prince Charles-Joseph---can cast some light on the "patriotic content" of this letter to be found mixed with protestations of loyalty.

We must recall that in the aftermath of the fall of Belgrade in 1789, Ligne could not return to Vienna because of his earlier comments vis-à-vis the insurgents. The Prince confirmed in a letter to Marshal Lascy that the Emperor, on learning the truth of the matter, rescinded his decision to exile Ligne, who then returned to the Austrian capital around New Year's 1790 and was granted an interview with Joseph II at a time when the latter's health was seriously in question. Thus, the beginning of Ligne's work *Espèce de campagne de 1790* (APL 3 (1922), 50-9), has the dying emperor say to Ligne, "Your nation will be the death of me. I have here", he added, pointing to his heart, "the weight of the stroke resulting from all of this is suffocating.... What are you going to do? Your whole future is compromised. Don't hold back because of your great devotion to my person: you'll be recalled [to duty], or your fortune will be seized. Think about it." The 24th of February 1790, shortly after the demise of the Emperor, Ligne reports using approximately the same terms and the same ideas in a moving letter to the Empress Catherine II [of Russia].

The words of the Emperor, very high-minded, did not fall upon deaf ears; quite the contrary, for the Prince replied, according to the *Espèce de campagne*, I've thought it out. My honor is more precious that my lands." The august moribund had then suggested a solution to Ligne's problem: "Pretend to take care of your business [at Brussels], speak to [the insurgents] without appearing to be concerned about me, and say to them that the revolution is just and that it would never have occurred if, as I had ordered, they had re-established the Estates the day after they had been dismissed." The Emperor foresaw exactly that the Low Countries would never have been supported from outside [one of the favorite themes of Van der Noot] and that they would go from misfortune to misfortune." In the opinion of Joseph II, the Prince would remain two weeks on his estates, [long enough in passing] to advise the insurgents to submit, having surrendered their ancient constitution [the *Joyeuse Entrée* of 1356." Ligne would return thereafter to Vienna. Despite the Emperor's health, continues the narration, he made Ligne promise to carry out this plan, even though the Prince understood its futility and foresaw its dangers. "One week after my interview with H.M., every folly that took place in the Low Countries furnished me with an opportunity to go back on my word, and he acceded to my reasoning.

Thus, Ligne believed himself engaged to act and committed the error of writing a letter "that people were stupid enough to circulate and malicious enough to print." [We are reminded of Talleyrand's remark after the judicial murder of the Duke d'Enghien: Ce n'est pas un crime; c'est une erreur.] Ligne was counting on a limited readership; he was compromised and bitterly disappointed. Happily for him, (as he recalls the essentials) the letter quickly fell into oblivion. A long passage in the *Fragments 1,* (Vercruysse ed.), 313-14 confirms this interpretation. In such a way can it be shown beyond a doubt that the *Copie* is authentic, without repeating Professor Vercruysse's last caveat: We are as far from an apocryphal text as we are from a pretended union with the troops of "the patriots".

11

1734 – Charles-Alexandre, count de Calonne – 1802

French Foreign Minister, Contrôleur des Finances in 1783. As a Keynesian "avant la lettre" convoked the Assembly of Notables (forerunner of the National Assembly) in 1787, but was disgraced; fled to England until recalled by Napoleon in 1802, at which time he died; friend of Ligne.

Ligne to Calonne
March 1791 [Beloeil?]

You cannot imagine what I've been through. What I returned home,[1] I was overcome with pleasure [and] hopefulness, horror and despair. Everything passed through my mind, except fear. You've preached to a convert, my charming apostle. The result for me is ever (or [so to say] all the replies I've received to what I've said) that, as we stated this evening, we must put up with

1 –the certainty of danger through inaction,

2 –the uncertainty of danger through action

3 –the hope of no danger because of the sermon I've been preaching these last three months

4 –the hope of an obligation [to be] forced on us by the over-rated services of the [Holy Roman] Empire, especially if, in a similar circumstance, we should desire it, should we allow the Princes who have suffered in their rights to be attacked?[2]

5 –the certainty of success if the Queen escapes danger (as I believe she will), to put her back on the throne[3]

6 –renouncing the idea of ambition and special need on the part of a young Prince,[4] whose honor and gracefulness I've observed increasing day to day with admiration, as well as the agreeableness of his virtue, wit, and talents developing without losing any of the charm and candor he was given at birth.

Oh that I might win some glory from all of this, to the glory and enhancement of a nation that I used to adore![5] If I'm allowed, I'll be seen carrying the standards of Austria and the Empire to the banks of the Rhine and the Scheldt to go and slit the throats of the monsters on the charming banks of the Seine.[6]

May the most illustrious, the finest of ministers, and the most loyal and admirable of men put paid to his great [project] and may he speak as I do to the young gentleman I like. In the same way as a former Parisian and bourgeois spoke about his own ancestor called Henri IV telling [four illegible words] the one and the other about my faithfulness, my discretion, and my tenderness.[7]

Although I don't like to tell lies, tonight I'll tell the Emperor[8] that I've promised to tell him everything. I'll say that I've promised nothing and will appear to let him abandon all these ideas as a result of the attachment I truly feel for him. His interest, it seems to me, as I've already told him, is linked to his dignity, his glory, and his humanity.

Adieu to you whom I love, just as everyone loves you- and that is all.

Source: PRO (UK),
PC/ 129/ 152. Mansel, 15.

Notes

1. From Russia, the Ukraine, and Belgrade
2. Ligne is unwilling to admit that the nobles' rights had been abrogated by one of their own, the Viscount Louis de Noailles (1756-1804), before the Assembly, the night of 4 August 1789.
3. Restoring Marie-Antoinette (1755-93, reigned 1774-93) to the French throne was one of Ligne's fondest hopes. See J. Vercruysse, *Bibliographie descriptive*, (Paris, 2008), 190-1
4. Count d' Artois (1757-1836, reigned as Charles X, 1824-30), brother of Louis XVI and XVIII. Judged by modern standards, Ligne's choice was "lamentable," but after all he was a friend.
5. The French.
6. Sarcastic allusion to Voltaire's *Henriade i* (1728), 69-70.
7. Probably Voltaire's letter to Ligne, BestD. 13437.
8. Léopold II (1747-92, Emperor 1790-92), brother of Marie-Antoinette

12

1725 – Giacomo-Girolamo Casanova [de Seingalt] – 1798

Famous Italian adventurer, known for his presumed sexual exploits, author of a celebrated autobiography, written in French, supposedly on the recommendation of Ligne whom he knew in his last years in Bohemia, where he was librarian toCountWaldstein, a nephew of Ligne's who became a friend.

Letters from Ligne
- ✉ a - 22 September 1794, from Toeplitz (?)
- ✉ b - [November 1794?], from Vienna
- ✉ c - 17 December 1794, from Vienna
- ✉ d - "This 20th [January 1797, from Vienna]
- ✉ e - 21 March 1798, from Vienna

Bibliography

M.F. Luna, *Casanova mémorialiste* (Paris: 1998).
John Masters, *Casanova* (NY: Viking, 1961).
Sylvia Ostrovska, "Les lettres du Prince à Casanova" *NAPL xiii* (1999), 155-80.
M.L. Prevost et al., *Casanova: la Passion de la Liberté* (Paris: Seuil, 2012).
François Roustaing, *Le Bal masqué de Giacomo Casanova* (Paris: Eds de Minuit: 1985).
Octave Uzanne in *Annales Prince de Ligne,* i (1920), 221-42, 320-41, ii (1921), 114-9.
Helmut Watzlawick, in Ligne, *Caractères ét Portraits* (Acke, ed.), Paris: Champion, 2003, 501- 40

Ligne to Casanova - a
[September 22, 1794] [Toeplitz?]

One third of your charming second volume,[1] dear friend, made me laugh, one third gave me an erection, one third made me reflect. The first two will make people love you madly; the third will make them admire you. You've got the better of Montaigne.[2] That's the greatest compliment, according to me.

You convince me like a skillful doctor; you overwhelm me like a profound metaphysician; but you offend me as a timid pervert, unworthy of your country.[3] Why have you neglected Ishmael (the Bible) and Petronius; are you sure that Bélisse was indeed a girl?[4]

Send the third volume to me right away. Count Salmour,[5] who pays you a thousand compliments, has just devoured this last volume and wants to do the same with every one. Your conversation with Jossouf is sublime,[6] just like your reflections on happiness.

I used to believe, like you, in the superiority of the mass of good over the mass of evil. But two years ago today, the most unhappy day of my life, I learned that my poor Charles had lost his.[7] I feel that all my pleasures together (and I have had a prodigious number of them) have never caused me, either in mass or in detail, the thousandth degree of pleasure that this dreadful loss has caused me pain.

Take away from me this sort of destruction of part of my being. I agree with you. The loss of my finest possessions and of my entire fortune has not caused me so much pain as the kiss a seventeen-year old Jewess gave me pleasure yesterday in the garden at Toeplitz.[8] All the pleasures of the body, the soul and the mind are a force for good, and there are only two real ills: sickness and poverty to the point of not having enough to eat. Too bad for the fools who [think they] know others' [misfortunes].

Can I place the life of my poor Charles beside his death? I adored him for his courage, his character, his naive, funny and expressive gaiety; but he has never given me as much pleasure by living as he has given me pain by living no more. Forgive me, my dear friend, I'm sorry. I did not expect to finish so sadly after beginning [this letter] so differently. I'm shaking myself now; see, the bad moment is passing. Come quickly to get beaten at checkers, and gaze on those [ladies] who, like me, are always glad to see you.[9]

Source: *APL 1* (1920), 335-7, and Mansel, 180-1.

Notes

1. *Histoire de ma vie jusqu'en l'an 1797.* Long before Jean Laforgue massacred Casanova's text (1826), the author himself had prepared a number of bound volumes containing an autograph version of his text, referred to here.
2. Michel de Montaigne (1533-92), eminent French philosopher and essayist.
3. Allusion to Casanova's presumed bisexuality; the French is "antiphysicien timide" (timorous un-natural man – here: timid pervert). See the Pléiade edition of Casanova, vol i, 128n.; and John Masters, *Casanova* (N.Y.: Viking, 1961).
4. For Ishmael, see Genesis and I Chronicles in the Bible, and Petronius (1st c. A.D.), author of the *Satyricon*. In the *Histoire de ma vie* ("Florence", ch. vii), Thérèse Bellino is a castrato.
5. Count Joseph Salmour (1750? - 99), a friend of Ligne's in Vienna; see Ligne's *Frags. 2* (Vercruysse ed.), 324.
6. For Jossouf Ali, see the *Histoire de ma vie* ("Constantinople", ch. xiv); perhaps a fictitious personage.
7. Charles-Antoine de Ligne (1759-92), Ligne's favorite son, killed in action in the Argonne, 14 September 1792, fighting the forces of the French Revolution. Ligne received the news at Belœil on 25 September but claims (*Frags. 1* (Vercruysse ed.) 94) he received word only on September 22.
8. Person difficult to identify; possibly Johanna-Karolina Meyer (1777-1825), sister of Ligne's friend, Baroness Eybenberg, and the compiler of a *Diary for Love and Friendship* (1802); and perhaps also Evangéline Knydat (1777-1832), and with whom according to Ligne's grandson, Charles-Clary, Ligne was "madly in love"

in 1794; later, under her married name of Spazier, responsible for a German translation of Mme. de Staël's anthology (Leipzig – Amsterdam, 1812).
9. There is a pun here on the word "*dames*" (ladies and checkers).

Ligne to Casanova - b
[November 1794?]   Vienna

    My dear friend, I do not have the same pleasure in writing to you as from Toeplitz, because you give me an immediate reply yourself with alacrity, whilst the post usually discourages me. I prefer to take the risk of not informing you that our promise to share our news once a month gives me the greatest pleasure.

    Your erstwhile companion in adventure, literature, conversation, and wit recently passed away in Rome.[1] I'm terribly sorry. You taught me to appreciate him more, while he loved you steadfastly.

    A few weeks ago I was hunting at Feldsperg,[2] and there was, as natural, the Chief Huntsman, count Hardegg.[3] I went to seek him one morning in his room. He had gone out. But in an armchair I found a huge nose. In front of a mirror, there was a pair of eyes, made perhaps to be lively and even almost religious, but seemingly inoculated by someone who has eagle eyes and genius. I spoke to the huge nose: Good day, Mr Costa,[4] and you cannot imagine his surprise. How the devil do you know my name? – I know more, I know about your scrapes, your misfortunes, your travels, your fisticuffs with the Duke, your courage against robbers when leaving Coburg, etc.. He thought I was a witch. After I had observed how embarrassed he was, I ended up telling him that you had said much good about him to me: his faithfulness, his worth, his budding wit, his discretion and devotion. It was one way to get him to speak good of you, and, as I like to hear this, he served my purpose very well and did not hesitate to expatiate in praise of you – that's what I do without being Mr. Costa. I tell everyone about the pleasure I have in seeing you, listening to you, reading you.

    General Souvarov[5] has just, my dear friend, created the matter for your fourth volume. As we can scarcely read characters writ in blood (for there was some spilled in the suburbs of Warsaw), I'll collect all possible materials to pass on to you next summer so you may write about all that with your spirited characters.

Nonetheless Europe is going to the devil. Holland is long gone.[6] Our friend Horace would say we'll have to accept that fact; he always adopts the principle that we must be content with life as it is and profit by each minute: *dum res, et aetas, et sororum/ fila trium patiuntur atra.*[7]

These days you'd be rather hard put to build the pyramid for Mme d'Urfé and Mr d'O.[8] There are other cabals like courts and the army that take away all guesswork. My prediction is that you can [do it], and I shall be tenderly devoted to you with all my heart.

Source: *NAPL XIII* (1999), 159-60.

Notes

1. Cardinal François Joachim de Pierre de Bernis (1715 - 94).
2. Feldsperg (Valtice), Moravia; fabulous country house of the Liechtesteins. Ligne had been visiting with Prince Dietrichstein (Karl-Jean-Baptiste, 1728-1808) and Ligne's relatives, the Clarys.
3. (Johann) Anton-Leonhard Count Hardegg auf Glatz (1740-1813). Soldier, created Feldmarshalleutenant in 1813; friend of Ligne.
4. Gaetano Costa (1734-1801), valet of Count Hardegg, and sometime secretary to Casanova.
5. General Alexander Souvarov (1722-1800), powerful military figure at the Russian court; organized the Polish repression of March 1794, in the course of which the town of Praga (across the Vistula from Warsaw) was destroyed.
6. The Kingdom of Holland was abolished by Napoleon in 1794 and the territory absorbed into the Empire of the French.
7. Horace, *Odes II*, iii: 116.
8. Allusion to a project of Casanova's to benefit the Marquise d'Urfé (1705-75) and Mr d'O (perhaps *not* the famous British banker, Thomas Hope (1704-79), famous banker in London, who did not have a daughter "Esther", mentioned by Ostrovska, letter 1, page 156, but may be a family of Dutch Jewish bankers named Symons with whom Casanova had dealings in 1758-59).

Ligne to Casanova - c
17 December, 1794   Vienna

    Although I'm in the blissful position of not receiving nor giving orders to anyone, I've decided, my dear Casanova, to give you one, not "de par le roi," but "de par mon coeur."[1] And you disobeyed me. The order was that you not speak to me of your end which, happily, is merely deferred for a very long while.

    You were so lucky not to be punished,[2] why do you insist that it's the fault of your writings? Leave the story of your life as it is. From now until you have it printed, few people alive today will still be here then, or they'll have forgotten anecdotes that will be more and more indistinct.

    We should not have a *History of the love life of the Gauls*, if Bussy had, like you, wished merely to develop his memoirs.[3] Do as I do, and sell your [work] whilst you're alive. Take your manuscripts to the Walther brothers at Dresden; let them offer you a life annuity of one hundred ducats (or less, if it's an absolute necessity) and when, twenty years from now, you leave us, your charming memoirs will be worth four or five thousand to them.[4]

    Spread it around that you've burned them [and] go to bed. Call in a Capuchin monk[5] and have him throw several batches of paper on the fire while pretending that you've sacrificed your works to the Virgin Mary.

    My dear nephew[6] will be very sorry if he had speculated on them. But your confession… your conscience…your Capuchin… the Walthers will surely let you in on the secret: then [receive] two hundred copies of what they print. As for what they'll print after my demise which will apparently occur just about the same time as yours and perhaps, wherever we may be, we'll laugh at the [funny] faces of those who'll be reading us.

    I'll never tell you enough, my dear friend, how deeply attached I am to you.

Source: *NAPL XIII* (1999), 157-8.

Notes

1. Style of formal announcement of royal edicts under the Ancien Régime in France.
2. Casanova was frequently embroiled in arguments (some violent) with servants at Dux.
3. Roger de Bussy-Rabutin (1618-93), author of the "History" in question (1665).
4. Walther Brothers, three generations of publishers in Dresden, working with Voltaire and Ligne, among others.
5. Monk of the Order of Saint Francis (1525), renowned for its austerity.
6. Charles-Joseph-Emmanuel, count Waldstein (1755-1814), nephew of Ligne's by his mother, a sister of Ligne's wife; owner of the castle at Dux.

Ligne to Casanova - d
This 20th (January, 1797)   Vienna

    My dear Casanova, your letters give me so much pleasure that I beg you to entertain me often in this way: I always find in them new settings and lifelike portraits.

    My whole family has recognized you in the last one by your charming, lively style and your friendship for us all. We thank you and love you.

    I'm under the spell of your neighborhood and urge you to explore it often; it's also lucky for you to have Dux [as the occasion] for an excursion. I would wish that our general and pretty little friend[1] would wait for us at Toeplitz.

    I'm not so unkind as you about the lovemaking of "Black Bottom." I've got one too, but lively and noisy [according to] what she says. She has beautiful eyes and is "black, but comely."[2] I often look [out of the corner of my eye] at my *Melanpyge* who knows her name and is solid and firm.

    My dear nephew is magnificent in his uniform of the hussars,[3] and since he has a severe head cold, he appears to be returning from some advanced positions.

    Today or tomorrow we're expecting news that the siege of Mantua has been raised.[4] Italy's fate is now clear. I just wish that Venice [Vienna?] would take care of mine.[5] We now have a charming ambassadress: quite young, blonde and sweet – Mme Grimani,[6] whose family name can be found in your delightful notebooks. People asked her yesterday where she'd spent the evening, and she replied "*chez moi*; we went to bed at nine, for we've been married only three months."

    Think often of me who am very fond of you and miss you wholeheartedly. I am annoyed at having to spend so much time without seeing you. I'll have a feast when I read you soon again.

    My thanks to the Walthers who can breathe at last.[7]

Source: *NAPL XIII* (1999), 165/6.

Notes

1. A dog. The black cocker bitch of Casanova's.
2. Cf. *The Song of Songs*, I:5 – hence the name in Greek in the next sentence.
3. Charles-Joseph Emmanuel, Count Waldstein (1755-1814), nephew of Ligne's by his mother, a sister of Ligne's wife, owner of the castle at Dux.
4. Mantua: fortification in North-Central Italy, the lynch-pin of Austria's quadrilateral. Besieged by the French for at least a year; the siege was not raised until 2 February 1797 – hence Ligne's "news" was premature.
5. Ligne was hoping for an improvement in his situation as an exile.
6. Marina Donà Grimani (1775-1830), in 1796 the wife of the last Venetian ambassador in Vienna.
7. Ligne was pleased that the Walthers in Dresden had begun publishing his *Mélanges* (34 volumes) in 1795.

Ligne to Casanova - e
21 March, 1798   Vienna

    Quick! Quick! My dear friend. Give me news of your health. Mine demands that yours be good, for I'm flabbergasted by your suffering. Reassure me by adopting another routine, perhaps the waters at Bilina[1] to make you sweat, a nice [light] diet, with small portions.
    I am anxious to see you without aches and pains, for without them I can say hello to all my pleasures at Toeplitz.
    Our dear general has now left for Russia.[2]
    Reassure Fanny and her family[3] [to whom] I've written a letter that will do some good, I hope.
    I think of you often. We all love you with all our heart.

Source: *NAPL XIII* (1999), 167.

Notes

1. Bilina: Spa not far from Toeplitz.
2. Probably Charles-Othon, Prince of Nassau-Siegen (1744-1806).
3. *Not* Fanny Arnstein, as in *NAPL* 13 (1999), 179; more likely mistress to the dancer Campion from the time when he was in Toeplitz. See Casanova, HMV (Pleiade), III:480. Possibly also Josephine and (Fanny) de Canale-Malabaila, Countess Pachta (1770-1833) madly in love with Ligne in 1794, but of a quite different disposition in 1810; cf. *Frags. 1,* (Vercruysse ed.), 321-455 passim.

13

1752 – Hugh Elliot – 1830

British diplomat "as dangerous to know as he is amusing in society" (Lady Liverpool). Ambassador to Denmark, playing an important role as peacemaker between Sweden and Denmark in 1788; friend of Mirabeau "l'ami des hommes"; in Dresden 1792 - 1802, where he knew and was admired by Ligne; buried in Westminster Abbey.

Letters from Ligne
    ✉ a - [?]   from[Toeplitz]
    ✉ b - [1801?] from Toeplitz

See: *Dictionary of National Biography* sub Elliot.

I. de Madariaga, *Russia in the age of Catherine II*. London: Yale, 1981, 402-09.

Ligne to Elliot - a
[?]   [Toeplitz]

Mon cher ami,
   If you're wanting a valet, and if you should want me, I'll enter your service immediately. But, if you take [someone] like our friend [illegible] under whom I don't serve very well, I beg you, please accept the one I'm sending. He'll serve you better than Pitt and Coburg and our four Austrian marshals from Italy.[1] He'll not betray you and he'll put order in your house. If you've no need of him, you'd give me great pleasure in placing him in some good English house, for I'm very much interested in him. He's the brother of my valet Angelo Molinari. And if you do take him, I'll be, I think, very envious, I who envy no one. But since I'd know the happiness of being constantly in your presence, I'm allowed to be jealous of him.
   Don't be so likeable or so infrequent [a visitor], come and see us again. Quite by chance I'm making this confession to you: never has a man inspired me so much with the desire to spend the rest of my life with him. No one has *ever* combined so many distinguished, piquant, good, new, attractive and essential things like the wonderful minister England is so stupid as to leave in Dresden.
   We're going to welcome a double cloud of émigrés[2] who are so simple as to believe that their half-baked projects and their indiscretions could not possibly cause them to be refused a domicile here. I'm really afraid lest they become martyrs of another Saint Bartholomews or of Barthélemy himself,[3] that's what vigilance and the insidious moderation of the French demons will get you: Europe gone to the dogs, with the Rhine about to be republicanized like the Po.[4] Lucky for me that I'm no longer concerned about the four corners of the world, any more than they're concerned about me. Pleasure is my only business, from time to time collecting the wreckage of my heart and spirit, conversing only with the small number of people I like, of whom you are the first, my dear naughty neighbor.

PS   You've never refused to give pleasure to women. My pleasure and what I'd like most is to see you come with us by boat to Meissen.⁵ We need the minister of a powerful maritime nation for such a cruise. Good day, dear old friend, the most likeable man in the three kingdoms, such as I've rarely seen in three empires or in half a dozen republics.⁶

Source: Mansel, 283, nos. 19-20

Notes

1. William Pitt the Younger (1759 - 1806), English Prime Minister; Frederic-Josias, Prince of Saxe - Coburg (1737-1815), German military leader; these two names were understood in the popular mind as representative of reactionary Europe. General Baron Beaulieu (1725-1819), defeated at Lodi in 1796; General Count Bellegarde (1760-1845), defeated at Arcole in 1796; and General Baron Alvinzi (1735-1810), defeated at Rivoli in 1797; Field Marshall Wurmser (1724-1797), defeated at Castiglione, 1796. Ligne is mistaken, since, as here, only one of the four generals was a field marshal.
2. As a result of the abolition of the Holy Roman Empire in 1802 - 03, there were two groups of émigrés: religious and civilian (largely nobles).
3. St. Bartholomew's (24 August 1572), massacre of Protestants by Catholics in France. François, Marquis Barthélemey (1747-1830), member of the directory, negotiated the treaty of Basel (1795), for which he was exiled to Guyana, liberated in 1815 to serve in Napoleon's court.
4. The republics of northern Italy to which Ligne refers are: the Lombard Republic (1796), the Ligurian Republic (1797), the Republic of Lucca (1799), and the Italian Republic (1800).
5. Meissen, a city in Saxony, not far from Dresden, where porcelain was first manufactured in Europe (1710).
6. The three kingdoms: England, Scotland, and Wales. The three empires: the Holy Roman Empire, Russia, and Turkey. The half dozen republics were: Holland, Belgium, Venice, Geneva, Switzerland and Naples.

Ligne to Elliot - b
[1801?]   [Toeplitz]

You've never refused to give pleasure to the ladies. The one I have[1] and the ones I'd wish to have would like you to come with us by boat to Meissen. We need the Minister of a Maritime Power for a [fluvial] navigation. *Bonjour*, dear old friend, the most amiable man in the three kingdoms,[2] such as I've never seen in three empires[3] or six republics.[4]

> Source: Edinburgh,
> The National Library of Scotland,
> MSS 12988,
> "Elliot" and Mansel, no 20.

Notes

1. Princess Marie-Xavière de Ligne.
2. England, Scotland, Ireland.
3. The Holy Roman Empire, the Napoleonic Empire, and the Russian Empire.
4. The Genevan, the Italian, the Venetian, the Ligurian, the Helvetic, or the Batavian Republics.

14

1750 – Marquis de Bonnay – 1820

Charles-François, Marquis de Bonnay, witty soldier at court of Louis XVIII and intimate of Ligne. His epitaph for the Prince runs: *Cigît le Prince de Ligne, / Il est tout de son long couché; / Jadis il a beacoup péché* [fished/sinned]/ *Mais ce n'etait pas à la Ligne.* [Here lies the Prince de Ligne / Stretched out to his full length. / In days of yore, / He fished galore / but not with rod and line.] Private secretary to Louis XVIII for six months at a time.

See: Mansell. *Louis XVIII.* Cambridge: UP, 1981

Ligne to Bonnay
28 June 1802   Toeplitz

    With little enough talent for lying, I used [what little I have] to sum up the business of the unfortunate Chevalier [de Saxe][1] by telling you it is settled. That was one way [to proceed], and by announcing the site of the dueling-ground on the borders of Saxony, I succeeded in making it inevitable.

    When you saw me on the street [in Toeplitz] on the evening of my departure, I was taking a second letter from Zubov to him.[2] I again lectured him at the door of Mme Lancronska's,[3] repeating the nasty things about nasty deeds that the newspapers were repeating, starting with the beginning of the affair.

    If I'd succeeded in making him determined to give up, Scherbatov[4] would not have come, and we'd not have to weep for him who, by I know not what intimation, what invisible and inexpressible connection, has made me more unhappy at this moment than I would ever have believed possible.

    The stupid acceptance of the challenge from Gielgud,[5] and Zubov's lies to me about all that, made the Chevalier's situation understandable. Unfortunately, the wrong was not on his side, while Scherbatov, by appearing to repent him of the start of this unfortunate quarrel, his innocent air, and his regret in saying that it paid for the errors of his youth. The person who had the idea of telling him to come has much to be sorry for. Although two governments were informed of both duels, I don't like to name the Chevalier's second, about whom the police in Vienna[6] will want to investigate.

    But I defy anyone to question his conduct in all he said, did, and arranged with more exactitude and justice, character, reason, and honor in protesting against dueling at four paces, saying that it might befit the person who had formerly refused to fight, but not the Chevalier whose constancy was well known.

    Each one with but one pistol, later fighting with the saber, and fighting at will, it's inconceivable that a shot fired from sixteen or seventeen paces might be the misfortune of our time.

Other details are still so painful to me, that I have not the strength to relate them to you. Alas! The Chevalier shook my hand before going to his doom[7] [in a way] that left me trembling—me! Superstitious! Christine[8] burst into tears. As you know, the Chevalier was not one to seek compliments, for I've never had the pleasure of telling him how much I liked him. He was so voluble, so happy all day long, you'd have said he never believed in forebodings.

His second, with an unbelievable strength [of will] that he paid for dearly on the dueling-ground, found himself sick afterward. Then, spitting blood, and unsettled and sad, he tried to hide all the fears he was unused to. [But] that's enough. Now, what will Gielgud do? Where did Scherbatov go? Did he stop in Vienna? When does Zubov go to Prague? Or wherever? The Chevalier, at a word or a glance from his second, [saw that he] had not killed his opponent; obeying me, he struck him with his saber exactly where I'd pointed out to him, was covered with glory, thus ending without suffering a life he so little esteemed since his family was of two minds about him,[9] and he didn't care.

I guess you can understand our emotion. That's what prompted me to write this to you. There's perhaps a glimmer of consolation [in all of this] for me since I can tell you that I write with much love,

Ligne

Source: Mansel,
281, no. 128

Notes

1. The Chevalier Joseph de Saxe (1767-1802).
2. Valerian Zubov had fought a duel with the Chevalier at Toeplitz on 18 June 1802.
3. Pélagie, Countess Lancronska, née Potocka (1775?-1846?).

4. Nicolas Scherbatov had pursued the Chevalier de Saxe for more than seven years and fought with him at Toeplitz on 23 June 1802.
5. Gielgud: no information available; probably one of the seconds.
6. This statement refers to the two duels mentioned in notes 2 and 4 above. Duelling was a punishable offense in Austria at this time.
7. See *Frags. 2*, (Vercruysse ed.), 124.
8. Marie - Christine de Ligne (1757-1830), wife of Prince Clary - Aldringen.
9. The Chevalier had been snubbed by his family because of the morganatic marriage of his parents.

The Ayu Dag

Ligne Reading in Bed

Ligne as "homme de lettres"

15

1752 – Jean de Müller [von Sylfelden] – 1809

Swiss historian and diplomat; first served in the Electorate of Mainz; next, in Vienna where he became a friend of Ligne; then in Prussia; finally in Westphalia. Used the pseudonym "Tacitus" when spying for the allies against Napoleon.

Letters from Ligne:
- ✉ a - 18 July 1802, from Toeplitz (?)
- ✉ b - [Mid October 1803?, from Vienna?]
- ✉ c - 13 January 1805, from Vienna
- ✉ d - 24 / 25 February 1805, from [Vienna?]
- ✉ e - 10 September [1805], from Toeplitz

See: L. Wittmer. *Le Prince de Ligne, Jean de Müller, Genz et l'Autriche*. Paris: Champion, 1925. (First published in *APL*) F. Jost. *Essais de littérature comparée, i.* Freiburg: Eds Universitaires, 1964; 32-59. "Un pèlerin de la Suisse romande: Jean de Müller."

Ligne to Müller - a
18 July 1802   Toeplitz

Dear Baron,

I'd like to see one man of worth go and see another immediately. The second has often been heard to speak of the amiable, enlightened, and illustrious Germanic Tacitus[1] who's been cast into the depths of a dreary library in order to render him harmless.

Gentz[2] has the greatest desire to make your acquaintance and is quite likeable and without pretense.

What did the police intend by having me scolded at the War Council for twenty-one or so volumes in my works?[3]

1—was it for having them printed abroad—which I didn't know was forbidden,[4] or

2—was it for having revealed some political secrets in number 24?[5]

Dear Baron, please try to find out about some of this tempest in a teapot and make it subside, so I may be permitted to go on writing—my only pleasure that compensates for want of glory, or a job.

In all my works I speak favorably of the Austrian government, of the sovereignty of its rulers, and of the authority that ought to be the purview of the Catholic faith. These are matters to be treated if you want to be read and make an impression. What I say in volume 24 about my campaigns against the Turks [in 1787-9] relates only to historical circumstances fit for gazettes as much as for politics.[6] People in Vienna no longer know how to read and have forgotten their French.

Please accept, dear Baron, the assurances of eternal attachment from your faithful and enthusiastic admirer,

Ligne.

Source: *APL v* (1924), 250-51.

Notes

1. Tacitus (55-177 A.D.). Roman historian with a high moral tone; a severe critic of Rome. The "Germanic Tacitus" is Müller himself.
2. Gentz, Friederich "von" (1764-1832), famous anti-Napoleonic publicist; secretary to the Congress of Vienna. Gentz and Müller already knew one another through their writings.
3. Censorship: Ligne had already been chastised for his "*Copie d'une letter à la Princesse son épouse*" (Brussels? 1790).
4. His works were being printed in Dresden, in 1802 a part of Napoleon's empire.
5. It is possible to detect some political matters in Ligne's *Lettres à S.M. l'Empereur* [Joseph II], volume 24 of his *Mémoires et Mélanges*, 3-70. See J. Vercruysse, *Bibliographie descriptive*. (Paris: 2008), 179-81.
6. On the Turks and politics, see Ligne's *Mél.* 7, (1796), 147-226, *Lettres sur la dernière guerre des Turcs*; also J. Vercruysse as above 153-54.

Ligne to Müller - b
[mid-October, 1803?]   [Vienna?]

A word, dear friend, to give you my authorization to write immediately to your friend, whom you'll soon be seeing in Dresden. Write with invisible ink, since letters for Dresden are customarily opened, and the Saxons must be unaware of your trip.

Unsigned

Source: *APL 6*, (1925), 235.

Ligne to Müller - c
this 13 January, 1805[1]   Vienna

This letter is not from me, but, rather, from the Court. They are pleased with the way in which you have begun this business and approve the secret promises you've made to everyone, especially Stadion and Razumowsky.[2] There's not a shred of truth in the gossip that claims we reveal everything to Champagny.[3] On the contrary, we have said nothing to him about the major problems: Imperial affairs arranged since peace was concluded between Austria and France—to wit, the idemnification and damages awarded to the Elector of Saxony,[4] done at Paris. The only Court in which we have confidence is Russia, where they read dispatches from our ambassador in France. Here, Champagny deals only with special cases, like captured ships taken from our ports, etc. Even his own government doesn't inform him of major concerns. For the rest, he is well-treated because in effect he's very conciliatory and the mutual interest of the two Imperial Courts [Austria and Russia] is that France should not think we want to attack her and that the extra publicity from people who've no experience in diplomacy have spread in Russia about the consequences that Emperor Alexander's resentment might have, forced us to re-double our efforts to avoid suspicion—all of which has been done in the meantime without giving France any adverse knowledge about our "enmity" with Russia since we have never hidden from "Bony" how deeply attached to this relationship is Francis II.

As for the other obstacle, how little people know our master[5] if they think they might influence his choices by the means of a certain party of which he is cognizant. Markov[6] has been welcomed here like any of the Emperor Alexander's ministers. He's flaunted his personal dislike for "Bony" wherever and whenever he has the chance. According to him, a fully armed and well - prepared Russia must now force Prussia to make an open declaration [of war] and, to that end, either advance against her or have her advance against France. That [last option] would set the continent ablaze at a time when other nations are unprepared and when, as a result, "Bony" would have the advantage and would eagerly seize the opportunity to use this way out of difficulties where he now finds himself because of his incursion [into Baden].[7] By assuring Markov of the undying attachment of Francis II to our alliance with Russia, we've merely repeated the explanations he's already heard and that we're still expecting from Saint Petersburg. The former don't seem to me to extend to such chancy solutions as Markov proposes.

We've learned that Razumowsky has announced he's returning [here] well in advance of his [scheduled date of] arrival. He's probably afraid lest Markov trick him out of his post—a change that would undoubtedly alarm France greatly. Razumowsky's relations with a certain [political] party known to us and the unreliability of his reports have left us completely indifferent to whether he returns or not, so long as he's replaced by someone wise and favorably disposed [to Austria]. We still know nothing certain in this matter. You might go to Berlin to see what details you can pick up that would be useful to us, but always with the greatest secrecy. You'll be reimbursed for your extra expenses.

Unsigned

Source: *APL 6*, (1925), 235-7.

Notes

1. Given certain remarks in the text, the date is unreliable: either 1804 or 1805?
2. André Prince Razumowsky (1752-1856), Russian ambassador in Vienna, 1801-09; Johann - Philip, Count Stadion (1763-1824), Austrian statesman.
3. J-B. Nompar, Count de Champagny (1756-1834), French ambassador in Vienna.
4. Frederick – August, Elector of Saxony (1750-1827) until 1806, when he was made King by Napoleon, then Grand Duke of Warsaw [1807].
5. "Our Master" was Francis II of Austria (1768-1835) Emperor in 1804.
6. Arkady-Ivanovitch Markov (1747-1829), Russian diplomat in Vienna.
7. Allusion to Napoleon's capture and summary execution of the last Prince de Condé, end of the Bourbon – Condé line, Duke d'Enghien (1772 – 1804), seized in Baden, an independent principality, which scandalized Europe, as well as to rumors of monarchist plots in France, signs of growing dissatisfaction within the Empire. See Talleyrand's outraged reaction: *Ce n'est pas un crime, c'est une erreur*/blunder.

Ligne to Müller - d

24/25 February, 1805 [Vienna?]

Dear Baron,
I'm s[p]ending my carnival with you since I've never known how to place a bet nor dance, I prefer to reflect and chat with a superior being whose superiority is hidden behind his modesty and his indulgence by his amiability.

Our admirable Archduke John[1] who would win battles like the illegitimate Don John of Austria[2] if he were given a free hand, has the same opinion of you and likes and esteems you more than anyone.

Although, since your departure, your "late" library has no other attraction for me.[3] I go there [sometimes] to seek consolation with those who work there and who are sincerely devoted to you. I've been touched by all they've said about you, even though they don't write; they still miss you every day just as I do.

As for everything [else] I mention in a brief memoir, [the official "line" is that] we've neither money, nor enough mounts, nor matériel. Frederick the Great[4] was lacking this last article from Rossbach (5 November 1757) to Leuthen (5 December 1757). We've re-established part of the cavalry that needs it, while for the artillery and baggage-trains we'll improvise as we go along. We'll live off the country we cross and have only to sell 800 acres from among the possessions of the monarchy.

Moreover, let England, who is ruining herself in this war without fighting, give us all the silver and gold she'll take from Spain.[5]

I've lately learned that you're going to write the history of my hero.[6] Although frequently correct, I [may have] made several errors in my histories of the Seven Years' War and that of 1778 in my *Mélanges*.[7] I beg you to glance at my texts and see if I did. Tempelhof [one source] was a sergeant at Hochkirch (14 October 1758) and Arkenholz [another source] a captain at Torgau (3 November 1760). Also Retzow.[8]

The brave and respectable captains von Mollendorf, von Kleist, von der Goltz, and von Schmettau[9] will prove useful for such details, while anecdotes about Frederick's private life will fare very well in your hands. Frederick, finally, deserves your wise and heartfelt eloquence.

Continue your friendship towards me, my dear German Tacitus.[10] I am - and will always be—your tenderly devoted

[11]

[P.S.] Kotzebue[12] will also tell you how much he liked our dear Archduke. I'd like for him to meet Prince Louis[13] sometime this year: they're made to like each other.[14] Sundays I visit Mmes W. and K.[15] Everybody who, like me, has had the pleasure of knowing you is as faithfully devoted as I. Stay well in your quiet solitude, and give our tender respects to Countess Ferdinand.[16]

Unsigned

Source: *APL 6* (1925), 39-41.

Notes

1. Archduke John (1782 - 1859), military commander taxed with the loss of the campaign of 1805, but L. always had faith in his abilities.
2. Don John of Austria (1547 - 78), victor at the naval battle against the Turks at Lepanto (1570), off the coast of Greece.
3. Müller's role as "librarian" at the Prussian court.
4. Frederick the Great (1712 - 86), King of Prussia in 1740. See Ligne's *Mémoire sur le roi de Prusse* (1789).
5. On 5 October 1804, England had seized 2 Spanish galleons from Cartagena filled with silver.
6. "my Hero" - Frederick the Great.
7. Ligne wrote of the Seven Years' War in vols. 14-16 of his *Mélanges*.
8. George-Frederick v. Tempelhof (1737 - 1807), Prussian general, had written on the Seven Years' War (1783 - 1801), as had John-William, Baron Arkenholz (1743 - 1812) in 1793, and Frederick-

August v. Retzow (1729 - 1812) in 1802. Ligne wrote about the Seven Years' War in his *Mélanges* (see Note 7 above), and the war of 1778 in *Mél. 12,* (1796).

9. Richard von Mollendorf (1724 - 1816), Frederick von Kleist (1762 - 1823), Charles von der Goltz (1772 - 1822), and Frederick von Schmettau (1742 - 1806) were all Prussian officers with whom Ligne had had talks about strategy. 10.   A key to the secret connection in this correspondence: Mueller was "Tacitus".

11. Ligne's playful way of signing himself.

12. August von Kotzebue (1761 - 1819), playwright; victim of a political assassination.

13. Prince Louis - Ferdinand of Prussia (1772 - 1806), musician and cultural hero of the young Romantics; pursued Madame Récamier in Paris; killed at the battle of Saalfeld.

14. Discreet allusion to the men's homosexuality.

15. Wentzlowska, Mme (dates?), pursued by L. in Toeplitz in 1803; see *Frags. 2,* (Vercruysse ed.), 130, and Countess Catharina Kolowrat (1748 - 1812).

16. "Countess Ferdinand", probably Louise von Brandenburg - Schwedt (1738 - 1820), wife of Ferdinand of Prussia (1730-1815), moved in Müller's circle in Berlin.

Ligne to Baron de Müller, Counsellor to H. M. the King of Prussia in Berlin - e

10 September [1805]   Toeplitz

Dear Baron,
What news? Things are becoming interesting right now. Try to find out and keep me informed. Here's the crucial point: is it true that Prussia has made an agreement with France to go against the aggressor?[1] It couldn't be us [Austrians], even if we were to attack, since so many things have been charged against us that we'd be justified. What a misfortune for Europe would be a war between four players![2] For Prussia, protected only in the direction of Silesia, is open to Cossacks who'd come and ravage her.[3] Russia, who has nothing to fear, stands to gain everything, for she could perhaps protect the Prussians. The court in Berlin has nothing to fear from France who cannot spare a sufficient number of troops to attack. It was a good idea to have sent Merveldt to you as ambassador;[4] he's a general officer of outstanding merit and intelligence, born to succeed.

By addressing your reply [to this letter] to François Baudelet,[5] Chamberlain to the Prince de Ligne, and falsifying your hand, you can write to me without alerting the censor.[6] Be a good friend, my dear Baron, and be assured of my devotion and affection for life.

"If you go about this correctly and quickly, success will surely be ours."[7]

Unsigned
Source: *APL vi* , (1925), 163-5.

Notes

1. Allusion to the presence of Gérard Duroc, Duke of Friuli (1772-1813), in Berlin and flattery of Prussia in French papers. Ligne may have heard about this shift of alliances (as in 1763) through friends.
2. Ligne was thinking of a possible war as follows: France/Prussia against Russia/Austria.

3. As ever, Ligne is alert to geographical/military details.
4. Maximilian, Count Merveldt (1766-1815), Austrian general and ambassador.
5. François Baudelet (dates?), from Belœil. A devoted servant of Ligne who sometimes called him "Léonard"; see *Frags. 2*, (Vercruysse ed.), 490.
6. If things were as secret as Ligne claims, it goes without saying that Müller would not have replied openly, but perhaps by entrusting a letter to a friend going to Toeplitz.
7. Quotation difficult to identify.

16

1754 – Charles-Maurice de Talleyrand-Perigord – 1838

Bishop of Autun before the Revolution, then ambassador and Foreign Minister under Napoleon; Prince of Benevento by the grace of Napoleon. Ambitious, corrupt, cynical, witty and dissolute, but a good European.

Letters from Ligne:
  ✉ a - This morning, 20 [December] 1805, from Vienna
  ✉ b - This 29 December 1805, from Vienna
  ✉ c - This 12 December 1806, from Vienna

See the complementary views of this controversial character:
  Crane Brinton, *The Lives of Talleyrand* (NY: Norton, 1963).
  A. Duff Cooper, *Talleyrand* (London: Cape 1932, rpt. 2009).
  E. de Waresquiel, *Talleyrand* (Paris: CNRS, 2011).

Ligne to Talleyrand - a
This morning, 20 [December] 1805[1]

I wanted to go to Paris to speak to Your Excellency about some concerns of mine, and here you are in Vienna! Really, you are too generous. I could just as easily have forgotten the object of my concerns. For the one on which my heart is set is paying my respects to you.

I was wanting to sign [this note] "one of your admirers," or "a friend of your friends (or lady-friends)," but as you have many of both kinds, I'll sign completely anonymously, requesting Your Excellency to accept the assurance of my respectful devotion.

Ligne

PS – I beg Your Excellency to tell me where and when I might have the honor of seeing you here. Without that, no peace with me.

Source: *NAPL* ix (1995), 154

Notes

1. This note was written after Austerlitz, when Talleyrand was busy preparing treaties with one or the other of Napoleon's victims, and perhaps even his betrayal of the Emperor, hence the final sarcasm about "peace."

Ligne to Talleyrand - b
This 29 December, 1805[1]   Vienna

The Prince de Ligne begs Your Excellency to please help him in an affair where, without thinking of doing harm, there might be a misunderstanding.

Forced to surrender the ruinous remains of his fortune to Louis de Ligne,[2] his son, he kept only his private mansion in Aix-la-Chapelle.[3]

The Prefect of the Roer[4] has declared it now to be [French] government property, and has prevented me from selling it and, I believe, has established an office there. He based his decision on the indemnity the Prince de Ligne received in the [French] Empire, yet this has nothing to do with a property that has not been mediatized.[5] Out of consideration, [the Prince de Ligne] at first requested very little, and out of tactfulness gave his canonesses more than their sovereignty is worth.[6]

If Your Excellency can, by your authority, credit – direct or indirect – influence or force the Prefect to return the property to me so that I may sell it, or have him pay [me] its full value, I shall be extremely obliged to you and to the Prefect if necessary or agreeable to him.

The full value is a small matter and can interest only a ruined man in need of a small sum to pay his debts. These are owing to a rather indifferent government that wanted to offer the Prince de Ligne 18,000 or 19,000 good German florins. That amounts, I believe, to 24,000 florins of this nation in bank notes.[7] I might, perhaps, be able to cash them immediately if Your Excellency has the honor to acquiesce to this request and deems that this business with the Prince de Ligne should be concluded in this way.

Such would be combining Grace with Justice and therefore deserving of being granted by Your Excellency.

Ligne.

Source: *NAPL* ix (1995), 156.

Notes

1. Obviously written after Austerlitz, when Talleyrand was busy preparing treaties with one or the other of Napoleon's victims and perhaps even his betrayal of the Emperor.
2. Prince Louis de Ligne (1766-1813), second son of Prince Charles-Joseph, served France, then Austria, then France and retrieved Belœil from sequestration by France in 1804; guaranteed the continuation of "la lignée."
3. Aix (modern Aachen, Germany). As part of Ligne's mediatization, he had been allowed to keep his mansion here, the seat of an Imperial council.
4. Jean-Charles Laumond (1753-1825), Prefect of the Département of the Roer, one of 26 new Départements added to the French Empire in territories occupied by Napoleon between 1795 and 1807.
5. Mediatization was the indemnification of original title-holders with new properties by re-distributing territories seized through conquest by French arms.
6. Canonesses at Edelstetten: mediatization of Ligne for Fagnolles in Belgium, was a chapter of abbesses in SW Germany, between Bavaria and Wurttemberg, said to be worth 15,000 florins per an; young noblewomen admitted became honorary canonesses; Ligne visited in 1804 and left after a week; sold in 1804 to Prince Nicolas II Esterhazy (1765-1833) for 11,000 florins, but only intermittently repaid.
7. Because of the war with France and the occupation, Austrian currency was worth only a fraction of its value at this time.

Ligne to Talleyrand -c
This 12 December, 1806   Vienna

Prince,

It would be a waste of time [for me] to write to another minister, but since we've seen orders signed and dated from Headquarters in the Levant, the Midi, the West, and now the North, [and] His Imperial Highness going into the most minor details, as if he had nothing else on his mind, I'd like an order "from I don't know where" to send me 6 or 7,000 ducats for my mansion at Aix [mod. Aachen] that is certainly worth 30,000 or more, suitable for a Prince [of the Imperial family] or for some other authority.

I realize that Your Highness has been good enough to intercede for me.[1] I beg 1 000 pardons for having to speak about this one more time, for I know that His Imperial Majesty spoke of it to Maret, Secretary of State,[2] which act of kindness, coming from so high [in the hierarchy] will at the same time bring both honor and pleasure.

Prince, people are right to say "God preserve us from those with but a single idea." I'm annoyed for you and for myself that I have none other. The Revolutions and subsequent changes have relieved me of one of my last [possessions]: the King of Bavaria has deprived me of my one remaining consolation of sovereignty:[3] like Cicero[4] I'm obliged to plead in my own behalf.

I expect my recompense "from the shores of the Hellespont."[5] My faithful and respectful attachment will follow you there [while] I assure you of the gratitude with which I've the honor to be, Prince,

                              Your Highness's most humble and obedient servant,
                                                                        Ligne.
                              Source: *NAPL* ix (1995), 160-1.

Notes

1. See the foregoing letter from 29 December, 1805.
2. Hugues Maret, Duke of Bassano (1763-1839), Secretary of State under Napoleon, future minister and peer under Louis XVIII.
3. Maximilian Joseph (1756-1825) Duke of Bavaria (King in 1806), by adhering in July of 1806 to the Confederation of the Rhine, revoked the sovereignty of Edelstetten. Nonetheless, Ligne had already sold this territory; was this simply a lapse of memory, or one way to strengthen his appeal?
4. Cicreo: *De Domo sua*, an oration from 57 B.C.
5. "The Hellespont" or the Dardanelles, a strait where Talleyrand as Foreign Minister was supposed to travel to convince the Sultan to join with the French in thwarting the British Navy in the area.

17

1743 – Johann-Wilhelm von Archenholtz – 1812

Swedish author writing in German a famous history of the Seven Year's War in two volumes (Berlin 1793) which evoked Ligne's enthusiasm.

Ligne to Archenholtz
2 Germinal [9 April], 1806[1]   Vienna

Dear Sir,
    Here I am, repaid with a little of the glory I've tried to acquire [in my life] and consoled for thirteen years' lack of preferment [since 1794], thanks to the same blockheads who, despite the victories of Archduke Charles in the Swiss cantons [in 1799], nonetheless made him lose Italy three times, Belgium twice, including four French fortresses, the Austrian capital – and the Hungarian –, the left bank of the Rhine and the right of the Danube [in 1798-1806].
    Your interest, Sir, is more honorable for me than winning a battle. I am reminded that one of the fruits of your excellent work, assuring you of my enthusiasm, is your rapid and eloquent description of the Russian victory at Torgau [3 November 1760].[2]
    [You say] you died with Frederick the Great [1786]. I with Loudhon [1790] and Lascy [1801]. We are therefore in paradise and can consult together. Having been to such a good school, you've been reborn in your writings. Bellona has made you do fine things, whilst Minerva has made you a fine person.
    I'll try to acquire your admirable *Reflections* on this awful campaign[3] when our French publisher will have more freedom and be more industrious. I'm already flattered to own a few of your [other] tomes. We are familiar with the Thirty Years' War [1610-48], but not that of thirty days, counting from the disaster at Ulm [20 October 1805] to that of Vienna [16 November 1805], or else from the Seven Years' War [1756-63] culminating in the battle of Austerlitz [2 December 1805].
    With rage in my heart, I've seen ceded to the enemy this city that has twice escaped from the Turks, once from the Swedes, once from the Hungarian rebels, once from the French of yesteryear and twice from those of today.[4]
    I've seen in an impious phrase that our country, "a monarchy imagined by ignorant people,"[5] should abandon more than

two thousand men whom the enemy had been unable to dislodge from the Riedenberg[6] and were then forced to debouch on the plain [the Spinnerin am Kreuz] where the extensive flatland would have facilitated their encirclement.

I've seen an alliance without allies, without strategy, without tactics, without accords, without marching orders, without battles – except for the Archduke Charles (1771-1847) who waged a fine campaign.

I've seen how, instead of the success he deserved in using the Adige [as his line of defense], he was never -- even in the case of reverses – overcome by the enemy. [The French] would have occupied the Tyrol in his rear or on his flank and did not expect the first columns of Russians behind the Inn nor the last of them before Vienna and its suburbs. I've seen a peasant[7] sow revolt on both banks of the Inn to prevent a phalanx of the enemy from crossing.

I've seen the French unfrenched by ["valor"][8] by the thrust of the drive that has kept them going, metamorphosed from likeable Athenians into rigid and indefatigable Spartans who'll die like the Theban legion.[9]

I've seen on walls a word ["surrender!"] that used not to be part of our vocabulary , just as the village of Blindheim [Blenheim] was introduced into German, where it was not recognized.

I've seen with each campaign my vanquished Viennese begging for me to be employed [as a commanding general].

Finally, M Archenholtz, I've seen my master [Francis I of Austria] soothe the wounds in my heart with his salutary balm. I'd have wished that those on the body of my military corps included a few more men, following the conclusion of three campaigns against the Turks and the pitiful Treaty of Reichenbach that forced me to return all I had helped to conquer.[10]

You're not at all like Feuquières,[11] and your opinions are more reasonable. Keep teaching and interesting [your readers], dear Master, especially with your kind estimation of me, who owe [so much] to your indulgence, the twin of genius.

You'll certainly not regret believing in my admiration for you and the highest and most perfect devotion with which I've the honor to be, Sir,

> Your most humble and obedient servant,
> Charles, Prince de Ligne.

> Source: NLRussia (With permission)

Notes

1. Given Ligne's anti-Revolutionary sentiments, it is curious to find him dating this letter of thanks for the gift of one of Archenholtz's books using the Revolutionary calendar.
2. Torgau, the site of a Prussian victory over the Allies, 3 November 1760; see Archenholtz's *Geschichte des 7 Jährigen Krieges in Deutschland*, 2 vol. (Berlin, 1793).
3. These *Reflections* were never published; how did Ligne know they were "admirable"?
4. While there is frequent punning in this letter, as in much of Ligne's correspondence, the anaphora (I've seen... I've seen....), a classical rhetorical device, was also sometimes utilized by him elsewhere, e.g. *Frags. 1*, (Vercruysse ed.), 167-8, *2*, 44-5, etc.
5. Supposed to have been uttered by Napoleon on entering the Hofburg (Vienna) in 1805.
6. The text, though hard to decipher, clearly says "Riedenberg" ("vineyard on the hills"), frequently misread as "Ritterberg."
7. Russian delays in this campaign allowed the French to enter Vienna almost unopposed.

    The "peasant" was perhaps Andreas Hofer (1767-1809), guerilla leader of the Tyrolese against the French; captured and shot.
8. A sarcastic criticism of Paris mobs during the Revolution.
9. In Ancient History, the Theban Legion was massacred at Chæronea in 338 B.C.
10. Ligne's campaigns against the Turks in the Ukraine (1787), in Bessarabia (1788), and at Belgrade (1789-90); see his letters to Ségur. As FZM (General of Artillery), Ligne had played an important role in the fall of Belgrade, for which he was awarded the rank of Commander in the military Order of Maria Theresa, but was constrained to return the city to the Turks at Reichenbach, 31 January 1790.
11. Isaac Manassès de Pas de Feuquières, Marquis (1590 - 1640), French diplomat remembered for his atrabilious nature.

18

1768 – Friedrich [von] Gentz – 1832

Prussian publicist; served Austria as an Aulic Councillor to the emperor; rabidly anti- Napoleon; Secretary to the Congress in Vienna (1814-1815), as also, later, to Metternich; one of the best stylists in German for the time and cause; friend of Ligne.

See: Golo Mann, *Friedrich von Gentz* (Fischer Taschenbuch Verlag: Frankfurt am Main 2010).

Ligne to Gentz
4 June 1806 [1808?][1]   Vienna

I greatly wish to see you, M. Gentz, now that I've read some of your works; they are so clear and eloquent. Do you truly believe that all Europe is so blind, so degraded, as not to rally behind you and to feel again as you and I do? Is it possible? What rulers, what ministers?

There is no more soul in Vienna, no right thinking. I've sounded out all those whom I assembled at home; it was of no use. All I was able to do was to sponsor a course on the theater, against France, by M. Schlegel, whom I was honored to introduce to you.[2] Everyone's opinion confirms my own: he is a man who knows everything—twelve languages, and is the first European critic to scorn M. de La Harpe, amongst others.[3]

How can one fall under the yoke of a man who charms only idiots and has "attractions" not to be found elsewhere? There's only one way to bear up under this life,[4] and that is to consider it as the forerunner of one that might bring another, more dear, and more virtuous, to our ken. Those who will be good in this world shall attain to that perfection allowing us to enjoy it in advance. Nature is all mystery; but a purer morality shall rend the veil that covers her. It shall be as a scrim for those who enjoy the happiness of mystery, yet is but a cloud for those not seeking to rise above vagueness where they will remain for want of the resilience necessary to rise above it.

Can you imagine a Creator who desires to unite with His creation while not revealing [at least] traces of the flame He instills in every soul? What is the reason we've not been able to discover them until now? One is that we have to wish it to be so. Without that impulse what progress could be made by the spirit of man? We cannot believe that we've been put on earth merely as bodies and plants without a soul to grow on, leading an aimless life, and die. Such a plan would be unworthy of the Sublime Architect of the Universe who displays His omnipotence before us here below in order to raise us up to Him. This vivifying warmth will make us proceed from the mundane world toward the other. Everywhere there is enthusiasm, delirium, and harmony from heavenly bodies to the one that is a feeble sheath for our soul allowing it to break out and ascend to heaven.

All of which proves that Nature is prepared to reveal her innermost secrets to us in order for us not to regard her like scholars from Northern Germany where, at present, there are the most remarkable men, and she would become merely a sniveler, ever offering us the same placebos. As we conform to her presumed inhuman laws, we sink deeper and deeper into the primæval mire. Ignorance, stupidity and laziness create ungodliness; immorality, politics; uncertainty, war; and fear, peace.[5] That frame of mind can never be changed until vulgarity is forfeited. Medicine, politics, metaphysics must be reformed by a new school necessitating the abandon, especially of mathematical proofs that limit genius. We all know that two plus two equals four and proves nothing, after which the human spirit can make [great] progress. Nonetheless, we must accept what has gone before. We can admire Racine, Corneille and La Fontaine because they were fine [writers]; but we can no longer judge like them. I might as well be a machine.

Bonaparte is one tyrant too many. But there is no such person for a mind that must be untrammeled, even if Europe doesn't want it. What, for instance, does it mean to believe we must conform to unities of time, place and action in the theater? Can you understand why we must constrain genius in a suit of armor? So, what does unregulated passion mean to me, so long as it be Love? Must it too be snuffed out by cold reason, which is always applauded?

France lost Europe long before she subdued her. French culture denationalized every subject nation. [French] literature, theater, and fashionable imitations take away the poetry of peoples who otherwise would have it [in abundance], just as the influence of Francis II [of Austria] has rendered them especially prosaic.[6] The lack of religion he found in the good works he read, and afterwards sowed in the bad ones he circulated, earned for him chastisement by the hand of God as well as for those who misunderstood him. He was made to be serious, but he took away that spirit from his countrymen. Can you imagine doing anything without seriousness of purpose? What is a German without that?[7] He is worse off than the most stupid Frenchman. Thereafter, by demoralizing his subjects, he prevented them from finding an intellectual home in Germany while he destroyed the one he might have created there. If Italy were not so corrupt you might come upon men who in their appreciation of the ever-enchanting fine arts may still be met with there. Who doesn't weep at the sight of the Apollo Belvedere? Yet there is still hope for Germany: her people are musical, and there is not a tone in German music that is not religious. What does it matter if the language is not harmonious? Don't let the words get in the way, for it's the musicality that counts as it goes from the ear to the soul, and the soul becomes religious. The only way to construct a dike against French despotism is to banish the language and ideas that everywhere go by the name of "civilization," destroying Vienna, Berlin, and all that does not possess one-half the [seriousness and] depth of Northern Germany. "Kultur" alone can rescue us from the gulf of ignominy by giving birth to a new spirit that will resurrect the downhearted heart of the Continent. This transcendent and emotional belief is also active in England. You don't know what it is to be loved if you've not been loved by an Englishman. There's not a single man in that island without character, piquancy, grace, and who doesn't know Greek.[8] This is the only nation with energy, powerful, to be sure, but where even the powerlessness of the Papacy is admired along with the feverish activity but feeble results of the King of Sweden.[9] Have you ever read a finer Manifesto? It's the most superb diplomatic document I know. Bonaparte would surely tremble if he saw similar documents coming from other governments. Yet each one [that does condemn him] is amazed at a few paltry successes contributing [unwittingly] one more stone to a monument to his immortality, a pyramid to his glory that, thanks to cowardly souls, will be taller than those of Egypt where his overweening ambition made him seek victories that were but defeats.[10]

Unimaginative works have nonetheless made of Louis XIV a character poetic enough to dupe people. The gossip of Mme de Sévigné, a handbook in Northern lands,[11] successfully helped to emasculate him. Racine weakened him at a time when Shakespeare continues to praise his [own] courageous country, though we don't know which one. We know the mistresses of Francis I, the mignons of Henry III,[12] we vaunt the quiet grace of misery that is no less miserable. Since it is easy enough to possess what goes by the name of Taste, unfamiliar to powerful men, we sacrifice Genius to Taste. Rather, we have none, cannot have any, and our prosaic century will forever dishonor those who don't think like you and me, as I've already told you, M. Gentz. Yet can you imagine that there may still be some who think, speak, and see differently? Can you imagine that?

Christianity, poetic in its origins, took the first steps toward honor, intelligence, and the fine arts.[13] Those who remain unconvinced will bring all to a halt and will come to lead us by the hand in order to have us jump with two feet over the obstacles that French literature and the spirit of Frederic the Second have placed between Jesus and ourselves.

Read about Hagar in the Desert[14] [illegible] which is full of it, even though it's never mentioned directly. He organized a crusade against Taste, Reason and Bonaparte.

PS—Baron Le Roy d'Origone[15] has just informed me, Sir, that you sent me several works of yours that, unfortunately, haven't reached me. I should still like very much to read them. Please find another, more secure way, to send them to me. I've a very high opinion of them, judging by what I've heard about you, whose name is precious to me.

Receive the assurance of my thankfulness and the feelings with which I ask you to believe me, Sir,

Your very humble and obedient servant,
Prince de Ligne

Source: *APL xii* (1932), 57-62, (incl. mis-identified PS, 62)

Notes

1. Because of internal contradictions in this letter, "1808" seems the more plausible date.
2. August-Wilhelm Schlegel (1767-1845), learned critic, delivered famous anti-French lectures on theater, esp. Racine's *Phèdre* in Vienna in 1807-8; friend of Mme de Staël's who was also in Vienna from December 1807 through March 1808.
3. Jean-Francois de La Harpe (1739-1803), literary critic about whom Ligne had written very severely in *Mél. 12*, (1804). The "others" Ligne alludes to were probably Joseph Fiévée, Jean-Francois Marmontel, Elie Fréron, Jules Feller, et al.
4. For Ligne on religion, see his *Fragments*, passim, and his "Ecrits sur la religion" *in Ecrits sur la société* (Vercruysse ed), (Paris: Champion, 2010), 13-164.
5. Sentiments adapted from Mme de Staël's *De l'Allemagne* (1811), pt II.
6. Francis I of Austria (1768-1835), reactionary leader against Napoleon.
7. Adapted from *De l'Allemagne*, pt IV.
8. Fatuous, but derived perhaps from Ligne's acquaintance in Russia (1787-89) with the British Ambassador, James Harris, Earl Malmesbury (1746-1820). Ligne was not so fatuous as this statement may seem. Cf. Leslie Stephen (ca 1870): The authentic Englishman is one whose delight is to wander all day among rocks and snow and to come as near breaking his neck as his conscience will allow." But see also Matthew Arnold, *Culture and Anarchy* (1869), where Britons are classed as " barbarians"
9. Gustavus IV Adolphus of Sweden (1778-1837), King until 1814, deposed, circulated a manifesto to European courts (1 June 1807) demanding a restoration of the Bourbons in France.
10. See *Napoleon in Egypt*, by P. Strathern (London: Cape, 2007).
11. Marie de Rabutin-Chantal, Marquise de Sévigné (1626-96), celebrated letter writer.
12. Jean Racine (1639-99), French classical dramatist; Francis I, King of France from 1515 (1494-1547); Henry III, King of France (1551-89), reigned from 1574, a notorious homosexual.
13. Reflections inspired by pt II of Chateaubriand's *Génie du Christianisme* (1802).

14. Playlet based on *Genesis* 21 by Mme de Staël (1805, though not printed until 1826); in it she acted in Vienna (1807-08) to great amusement. The following sentence should then ostensibly read "she," etc, and applies to the philosophical-cultural background of *De l'Allemagne*.

15. Baron Le Roy d'Origone (dates?), native of Brabant (Belgium), minor official of the Hapsburg court; sometime acquaintance of Ligne's.

19

**1753 – Auguste, Duke d'Arenberg,
Count de Lamarck – 1833**

Distant relative and good friend of Ligne's.

In this text we have capitalized HE, HIS and HIM (His Imperial Majesty), etc. to underline Ligne's animus against Napoleon.

See: *Napoleon, etc.* (Vercruysse ed.), (Paris: Champion 2013), 170-173.

Ligne to d'Arenberg
July 20, 1807   Toeplitz

Well, here I am! I've seen HIM[1] and for fear of being partial, having perhaps been well treated by HIM (though HE doesn't appear too endearing), I am the last ruler or ex-ruler who [was not] introduced. I was amused by all those confederated Princes with whom I [dined] every day[2] and whom HE had come [to Dresden] to meet, except for Prosper [d'Arenberg], who's away fighting and the regent of Lichtenstein who's teething.[3] I told them they seemed to be there as if they were in the Valley of Jehoshaphat for the last judgment.[4] They replied to me in chorus with a hearty imperial laugh, while repeating "Touchours aimaple." I cannot say of HIM what Ali says of Azor,[5] nor what was the expression on HIS face, the timbre of HIS voice, nor HIS choice of words, for I was listening to what HE said from the gallery when HE was surrounded by the crowd. HE has indeed the appearance of a warrior, determined and calculating, rather than of a genius without the failings. A Saxon lieutenant colonel[6] who didn't leave HIS side at Friedland,[7] told me that HE was standing on a rise under cannonfire where HE could see the field so well that, crayon in hand, HE gave HIS orders on maps that HE instructed HIS aides de camp to take to HIS generals. All of a sudden, noticing a movement the Russians were attempting to make, HE said "Aha! I think they want to maneuver. I'll teach them [a lesson in] tactics." And instantly HE gave the orders to profit by the opening. On arriving [in Dresden] HE bathed and sent off several couriers while speaking with some ministers; the next morning HE was in the saddle from 5 AM without any retinue except for aides de camp (HE doesn't even have a bodyguard), [and went to] the hospital to speak with all HIS wounded from the Prussian campaign, then to see the fortifications, and afterwards to the cadets HE had gathered together without any forewarning to question them and to review the most difficult problems of mathematics.

I met Talleyrand[8] who was just arriving. I went up the stairs more quickly than he who had not stopped a minute since leaving Koenigsberg.[9] Imagine his pleasure at being greeted by me, for there are no more Frenchmen in the world except him, [and] you and me who are not.[10] He would also have liked to see you in Dresden. We had a fine meal with thirty places where he supped tête-à-tête, and out of discretion I left him despite his reluctance and returned here.

He told me that never had the Emperor Napoleon (I believe it's permissible to call HIM that) been greater than at Oesterode,[11] where eating only miserable crayfish in a hideous house, surrounded by cadavers of men and horses covered with dung with everything going against HIM, even the army, although no one dared say so. HE swore to endure anything in order to humiliate Russia.

They were extremely satisfied with the conduct of Poniatowsky, who could not be believed.[12] If things had turned out differently, Poniatowski is supposed to arrive in Dresden today, along with Malachowski, Stanislas Potocki,[13] et al to organize [a government for] Poland where they'll include a bit of the constitution of the third of May [1791][14] with sovereignty vested in the King of Saxony as the Duke of Warsaw.[15] This title made me laugh; I asked Talleyrand if it would be like the "Duke of Danzig".[16] He replied that they had chosen it out of delicacy for us [Austrians], so that a few hotheads from Galicia might not think that they [the French] wanted to reestablish the kingdom of Poland as it used to be and that we would not be asked about it.

Jerome[17] is King of Westphalia including the [territory there] of the King of Prussia, Hesse, Fulda, and Brunswick.[18] These three Princes will be granted pensions. Talleyrand was expecting [Baron] Vincent[19] in order to deal with the problem of Braunau and a few other similar topics. He claims that they [the French] are most obligated to him [Vincent] because of his prudence and the way he avoided bitterness and the reports of proposals (or demiproposals) to declare war that could have almost spoiled everything. At Tilsit, the King of Prussia, blustering and stammering, with the Legion of Honor and a mustache, had the look of an aide de camp to Alexander. The latter said on the day of signing [the treaty] "today is the anniversary of Pultava[20] and also a fortunate day for the Russian Empire." Napoleon, who prefers the appearance of greatness to being rich and conquering to acquiring, liked the interview better than marching on Riga from one direction and on Grodno from the other.

I don't know what HE has in mind or not for the Turks, but HE has said "I wished much good for Selim,[21] because he was an intimate friend." Alexander had embraced Oubril[22] on arriving, and when the latter had been disgraced by the British cabal, Alexander gave him a pension of twenty thousand rubles for good luck. After that, let coalitions be formed! If we had stirred, the French would have made peace with the Russians.

I don't understand how pretended zealots can be sorry for their exhaustion and the humbling and insignificance [of the Prussians] who will only be ranked fourth after this among European powers.[23] Moreover, I don't believe this mockery of Europe is very dangerous since we are able to outlast its author. It has been fashioned by the pen, the pen will destroy it, if we know how to use it. They've had the Spaniards declare war on the King of Sweden,[24] who has just asked for the reestablishment of Louis the XVIII on the throne [of France]. They are not even thinking of England, she will do whatever she wants.

When you want to finish a letter, people always say, "the post is leaving."[25] I don't wish [to finish], but this time it's true, and I'll not say, my dear contemporary, how dear you are to me for your taste and your good taste and mine, with thankfulness for a friendship I am very sure of and loving and lasting affection.

Notes

1. Napoleon Bonaparte (1769-1821), Emperor of the French, with whom Ligne always refused to treat. See Ligne's *Ma Napoléonide* (partially published, Brussels 1921), now edited by our friend J. Vercruysse. Paris: Champion, (2013).

2. German Princes of the Confederation of the Rhine (1806-13).
3. Prosper, Prince d'Arenberg (1785-1861), relative of Auguste's and Ligne's; collaborated with Napoleon and married a sister of Empress Josephine. The "Prince of Lichtenstein", though not head of the family, was Jean-Népomucène (1760-1836). An ironic reference.
4. Josaphat (Valley of the Cedron in Israel), where God will bring together the Gentiles at the time of the Last Judgment; see *Joel*, iii:2.
5. Characters in *Zémire et Azor*, opera by Grétry and Marmontel (Paris, 1770): reference is to Azor "who comes when called by whistling."
6. The Saxon Lt-Col. is difficult to identify; perhaps Baron Karl v. Stuttersheim (1774-1811).
7. Friedland: remarkable victory of Napoleon over the Russians (14.vi.1807).
8. Charles-Maurice de Tallyrand-Périgord, Prince of Benevento (1754-1838), former bishop of Autun, ambassador and foreign minister. He had a clubfoot, which is why Ligne was able to climb the stairs faster than he.
9. Königsberg: capital of East Prussia, where Napoleon made his headquarters during the campaign of 1807.
10. Ligne is referring to the French nobility under the Old Regime.
11. Österode: village of E. Prussia, some fifty kms SW of Eylau, where Napoleon stayed after the battle of Eylau (8.ii.1804) under miserable conditions.
12. Joseph, Prince Poniatowski (1762-1813), Polish soldier, friend of both Ligne and his son Charles-Antoine. Marshall of France, died at Leipzig; "the Polish Bayard."
13. Stanislaus, Count Malachowski (1736-1809), Polish politician, signatory to the constitution of 1791, and Stanislaus – Kostka, Count Potocki (1755-1821), Polish soldier and politician, also a signatory to the constitution of 1791, minister in 1807.
14. A relatively liberal solution to problems of the eighteenth century, but opposed by Russia, which led to the second partition of the country (23.i.1793).
15. Duke of Warsaw is Frederick-August I of Saxony (1750-1837), King, by the grace of Napoleon, from 1807-13.
16. Duke of Danzig is François-Joseph Lefèbvre (1755-1820), Marshall of France, whose vulgar wife is known as Madame Sans-Gêne.
17. Jérôme Bonaparte (1784-1860), younger brother of Napoleon, Marshall of France, King of Westphalia (1807-13); his early

marriage in the U.S. (1803) was annulled by Napoleon; married (1807) Catherine of Wurttemberg (1783-1835).

18. Frederick-William III (1770-1840), King of Prussia, reigned from 1786; nephew of Frederick the Great; reference is to the foundation of the Kingdom of Westphalia by Napoleon (9.viii.1807) similar to that with which *War and Peace* (Tolstoy) begins.
19. Charles, Baron Vincent (1757-1834), Austrian cavalry commander in 1807, well known as a diplomat and negotiator.
20. Pultava: victory of Russia over Sweden (8.vii.1709).
21. Selim III (1761-1808), Ottoman Sultan, assassinated because of overtures to Napoleon after Eylau (1807).
22. Peter, Count Oubril (?-1848), Russian diplomat, opened negotiations with Napoleon in 1806; disavowed by his government, but rewarded nonetheless by the Tsar.
23. After Austria, Brittan and Russia, Prussia would be considered fourth-rate.
24. Gustavus IV Adolphus (1778-1837), declared war on Spain (1.ii.1805) and circulated a letter to European courts (1.vi.1807) demanding a restoration of the Bourbons in France.
25. See e.g., Goethe's *Sorrows of Werther* (1778) and Laclos's *Liaisons Dangereuses* (1782).

1775 – Ferdinand Paër – 1839

Italian musician. Began as *maestro di capella* in Parma, his home. Composed the opera *Leonora* in 1804, adapted by Beethoven as *Fidelio* in 1805. While Kapellmeister in Dresden (1805-06), he knew Ligne. Greatly admired by Napoleon who called him to Paris in 1806. Director of the Opéra Italien in 1812; resigned in 1824 because of rivalry with Rossini. Composed over fifty operas, some of which still hold the stage. Influenced by the Italians, and by Mozart-Beethoven. In 1832, director of music for Louis-Philippe's private chapel. Died in Paris where he was widely mourned.

Ligne to Päer
[1800?][1]   [Toeplitz? Vienna?]
                          [In verse]
Instead of a great number of my works,[2]
I want to offer you a few choice texts.
Tis the fault of our times, when, scarce alive,
I found it pleasant to write and sell books.
I sought not so much honor as success,
Printing good and bad, while the butt of jokes.
Thus, the Walthers whom you know in Dresden,[3]
Obligingly defrayed all costs at first.
I laughed at my readers, or at myself,
So you may note grammatical errors
And sometimes even that I've changed my mind.[4]

Source: *Mel. 31,* (1808), 141

Notes

1. Probably written in 1805 from Vienna, because of the disasters of that year.
2. Ligne's *Mélanges,* 34 volumes (1795-1811), Dresden: Walther.
3. Several generations of a family of printers in Dresden; Hofbuchhändler from 1737 to 1805, publishing Voltaire as well as Ligne. See Jerome Vercruysse *Dictionnaire général de Voltaire.* Paris: Champion. 2003. 1225-27.
4. Cf. the following, for a similar sense from Ligne's correspondence with Cassanova:

17 December, 1794 [Toeplitz?]

Do as I do, and sell your [work] while you're still alive; take your manuscripts to the Walther Brothers in Dresden; have them allow you a life annuity worth 100 Ducats, or less (if absolutely necessary). And when, twenty years from now, you leave us, your charming memoirs will be worth four or five thousand to them. . . . then, receive two hundred copies of what they print. As for what they'll print after my demise which will apparently occur just about the same time as yours, and perhaps, wherever we may be, we'll laugh at the [funny] faces of those who'll be reading us.

21

1766 – Germaine, Baronne de Staël - Holstein – 1817

Daughter of the financier Jacques Neker; a modern "public intellectual"; renowned for her sexual adventures and opposition to Napoleon; but especially important for an anthology of Ligne's work (her most profitable publication) in 1809 which gained for Ligne admission to the Republic of Letters.

Letters from Ligne:
    ✉ a - 28 December, 1807, from Vienna
    ✉ b - [23 September, 1808?], from Toeplitz
    ✉ c - July [1809], from Toeplitz
    ✉ d - [1809/10], from Vienna
    ✉ e - 24 June 1810 [?], from Vienna
    ✉ f - 08 July 1811, from the Kahlenberg

See: Christopher Herold, *Mistress to an Age*. (Indianapolis: Bobbs-Merrill, 1958.)
Simone Balayé, *Madame de Staël: lumières et liberté*. (Paris: Klinksieck, 1979).
Ibid. *Madame de Staël: Écrire, lutter, vivre*. (Geneva: Droz, 1994.)

Ligne to de Staël - a
28 December 1807[1] (Vienna)

I've seen, read, and turned inside out, doubting every trait of the finest writer in the world and the nicest temperament, and after a small thrill of pleasure and pride, I'll tell you, Madame, that one and the other are going to reveal more than expected.

You [may] change your mind, but you'll be carried away. Say goodbye to my poor family where you'll find, I promise, three or four enthusiasts. Hurry and come; then when you're sated with the flattery and the zeal of the ladies, you'll find a home away from home.

My happiness will be interrupted. To guarantee me a day [in your presence], get plenty of rest today so I may go and throw myself at your feet at noon and give or receive orders.

The first is to consider yourself one of my family and come by any day toward ten o'clock in the evening until you tire of us.

The second is to disobey the first when you cannot do otherwise, for I know three or four houses who are jealous of me; I'd like you to be as present in my salon as you are in my heart. For the first time in my life I'm going to despise [certain] people, but I still hope that the meanest of my suppers and the poor caning of my chairs will deter the curious and disappoint your fans.[2] In the end, we shall see. At least there's excitement here in Vienna. For example, I who normally stay in bed until three in the afternoon reading Madame de Staël or Rousseau, Racine, LaFontaine, or Horace, or Tacitus. I spent yesterday morning going twice to the Inn of the White Swan [to greet you].[3]

To add to our exchange of credentials, I've just received more from our excellent friend Frossard.[4] In the same way, I wish we might have an exchange of feelings. Rest assured that I lack none of those inspired by you.

Monday, while awaking most pleasantly, I swear.

Source: *Lettres inédites[du Prince de Ligne]*
à *Mme de Staël* (Balayé ed.)
Bruxelles: Acad. Royale: 1966, 226-89

Notes

1. The date of this letter, mentioning Ligne's visit to the White Swan the day before, attests to Madame de Staël's arrival in Vienna only hours earlier. [From S. Balayé's edition, with permission.]
2. For details of Ligne's abode on the Mölkerbastei, see his *Fragments*.
3. The name of the Inn where de Staël was staying on the Neumarkt is given in a police report of 13 January, 1808. [From S. Balayé's edition, with permission.]
4. Marc-Etienne Frossard (1757-1815), Swiss general, serving Austria.

Ligne to de Staël - b
[23 September, 1808(?)][1]   Toeplitz

Great man, good woman,[2] luxury of heart and mind, Greetings!

If you were familiar with the portrait – private and public, sentimental and almost lifelike – that the amiable General Frossard[3] has just made of your father for us, you'd like him even more [than you do]. He spoke wonderfully about [Necker]. And about you.

I suspect that Europe is too small for you; but, so is America.[4] Therefore, we'd have to enlarge the world for your soul, greater even than your wisdom and more elevated than the Firmament. It's because you find the world too small that you wish absolutely to conquer Heaven.

You believe that all roads lead there, just as they do to Rome; but you have to pass through Rome. Didn't Fr. Matthew teach you that?[5] And I'd not want you to incur needless expenses on the journey. I, who believe everything for fear of making a mistake, I've faith (if you wish) in Werner, though his hero [Luther] doesn't strike me as being dramatic.[6] But I'd wager that Calvin was jealous of him[7] and there might be a grand finale – the burning at the stake of Dr. Michael Servetus for the enlightenment he was seeking on the Trinity.[8] Thus did Calvin preach tolerance and was known as being gentle, subtle and polite, uttering [curses like] "dog," "horse," "bull," and "swine" at whoever did not think like him. He was more chaste and sober than Luther and, as a Frenchman, should have known better.

At least your Zwingli was killed in battle.[9] Something could have been made of him. In 1523 he had already said everything Luther completed only in 1532 at Nuremberg [where freedom of conscience was granted]. John Hus and poor Wycliff had merely asked for the same,[10] but these gentlemen are no longer in fashion. I understand how important this attitude was for the more spirited and Germanic of them both – Luther: he enriched his sovereigns and loved women.

Don't go stoking a volcano in the most apathetic and peaceful country on earth. Don't upset the world. Don't disturb America; leave her as she is. The people there are poor imitations of Britain. And since you want to speak English, we have here a few bores from that [so-called] "wise" nation.

When there'll no longer be a wall of paper, more difficult to penetrate than the one in China, our affairs will gradually improve, and my 36,000 florins, essential to my small household will perhaps be worth 30,000 francs.[11] I'll spend 3,000 for the trip to Coppet[12] where, once I've worshipped my goddess in her temple, she'll feed me *sautés, suprêmes, pâtés chauds*, and mincemeat with ambrosia. I shall quit the cloud of incense that should always burn on her altar to observe in anticipation the smoke rising [into the air] from her cuisine.

You may find me unnatural, but never gross. You've made me rather witty beneath the protection of an advertisement that is wittier still. But [I am] truly grateful for what you and dear Elzéar have said about my [Free-thinker and my Capuchin] monk.[13]

[Unsigned]

P.S. I must beg your indulgence for my genealogy, chronology and pedantry concerning the heresiarchs on another page. Villiers is the man who made Luther antipathetic to me, as Christ was to Voltaire, and Voltaire to Fréron.[14] I'm brave only from a distance, and at your feet. Beneath the gaze of the most fetching eyes I know,[15] I'll abjure everything you wish and will swear to everything I feel.

Source:*Lettres inédites de Mme de Staël, etc.* (Ulrichová ed.) Prague: Akademia, 1959: 56-9.

Notes

1. Uncertain date; there are several versions, the most reliable is Ullrichová (page 56), who places this letter in the context of the correspondence with Staël from the end of 1808.

2. Part of a late-mediaeval superstition meaning "a male genius in a female body"; see Ligne's *Nouveau Recueil* (ed. Lebasteur), (Paris, 1927), 171.
3. Marc Frossard (1757-1815), Swiss general officer, friend of Stael, used here as a cat's paw to defuse any anxiety on her part regarding Ligne's unfavorable view of her father, Jacques Necker (1732-1804), to whose memory she was fanatically devoted.
4. Allusion to Staël's projected departure for America.
5. Ligne, a good Catholic, seems to think Staël was toying with the idea of converting to Catholicism, hence his joking reference to Viscount Mathieu de Montmorency (1762-1826), Staël's reputed lover around 1790-2, later a priest
6. Zacharias Werner (1768-1823), dramatist, for a time in 1808 Staël's guru; author of *Luther, or, The Consecration of Power* (1806). A study of Martin Luther (1483-1546), leader of the Protestant Reformation, in 1519.
7. John Calvin (1509-64), French Protestant theologian; "pope" in Geneva from 1541.
8. Michael Servetus (1511-53), Spanish theologian, burned at the stake in Geneva as a heretic for his work on the Trinity.
9. Ulrich Zwingli (1484-1531), Swiss Protestant theologian, died in battle at Zurich.
10. John Hus (1369-1415) and John Wycliff (1328-84), Protestant reformers, condemned respectively in 1414 and 1382.
11. Allusion to financial difficulties of the time when Austrian paper money had fallen by 9/10 of its original value.
12. Coppet: Staël's family seat on Lake Geneva.
13. [Louis] Elzéar de Sabran (1774-1846), friend of both Staël and Ligne. Staël's anthology of Ligne included the *Dialogue entre un esprit fort et un capucin* (1801), where the latter frequently has the more telling role.
14. Charles de Villiers (1765-1815), French man of letters, émigré, founded an influential literary review in Goettingen where his ideas on Luther conflicted with Ligne's, as did those of Voltaire (1694-1778) on literature and became anathema to Elie Fréron (1719-76), Voltaire's sworn enemy.
15. Staël's "Spanish eyes" were probably her most attractive and expressive physical feature.

Ligne to Staël - c
July [1809][1]   Toeplitz

My dear protectress!
No man is a hero to his valet. People used to see me writing, but no one read me; they understood me very little. A single one of your phrases, your name, have made my fortune.

If you had merely organized a promotional campaign and a little preface for my 15 or 16 volumes on warfare, I'd have been given the command of armies.

There are also two gentlemen[2] to whom I'm obliged for having put together in imitation of yourself a few scattered pieces from the less mediocre of my voluminous works.

"But without pleasure, honor is only a malady."[3] Four lines by your hand each morning from your house to mine, in reply to my four pages, were more precious to me than the fame you have brought me.

I don't like long letters any more than languid ones. Mediocre even in heart and mind, I'm worth more at two hundred paces from you than at two thousand leagues from the ladies I love and from "so many witty gents who've not said everything."[4]

If you were an amiable Frenchwoman, I'd say to you: Heavens! How stupid was that man last night, and how Madame What's-her-name bored me! How limited the conversation! I was exhausted, which is simply the truth, while you found it difficult to recover your wits, yet at the end of the evening you remained sublime and amiable – as usual.

If you were a stern Englishwoman, I should scold you for having found Mme de Sévigné's writing in poor taste when she mentioned the Duchess of Burgundy's enema.[5]

And if you were a German by adoption, I'd send you an Austrian poem to translate, or a comedy with Kasperle.[6]

If you were Swiss, I'd compliment you for keeping a witch at Uri, instead of burning the others.[7]

You understand that if I could see you for even a half an hour after writing all that, I'd not be so unlikable a jokester or, placing my hands together [to plead my case] as you know I always do after some piece of stupidity.

Several times since you left us, I showed my sober side, as frequently happens when I'm bored. But how can I be serious when I think I'm talking to you? The joy of this illusion reminds me of the good moments when, alone and confident, holding your prodigious imagination in check, my happiness was your friendship.

I trust the German post will pass letters from us other dethroned men who do not belong to the Confederation of the Rhine.[8] Here, my feelings are all excited by the charming Princess of Solms-Braunfels (Frederica, 1778-1841), who has an additional entitlement by reason of her pleasure in reading you and in talking about you. Vienna tells me that your letters are pouring down like rain; while I've had only one, so I'd like to make four or five superior women out of you; I'd say, give a little salt to one, honey to the other, and in exchange, they'd give you a little peace.

O! That you might resemble your Lake of Geneva, since you don't stop to consider and prefer it to the storm-tossed sea [of politics]![9] At least when by chance there's a small storm, one can see its limits. But you, you don't like to be limited. You ought never to take a step without consulting me who would guide you with a light when you hoist sail. Say: Rome is no longer Rome, and Rome is where I am.[10]

Be coquettish, Madame, not for yourself, but for me and Monsieur Benjamin (though I don't know him). I'm really constant for his family, who, brave in war and witty in peace, have always liked me.[11]

Adieu, good and excellent Lady, for you'll permit me [won't you?] to speak of your inimitable kindness that inspires my adoration more than all your engaging and sublime qualities.

[Unsigned]

Source: Ullrichová, 34-5., *Lettres inédites de Mme de Staël*, etc. (1959)

Notes

1. There is some question about dating this letter; but, on the basis of internal evidence, especially regarding publication of Mme de Staël's anthology, the date we have chosen seems to be correct.
2. The two gentlemen are Propiac (*Oeuvres choisies du Maréchal-Prince de Ligne*, 1809) and "M. B[oufflers]" (*Oeuvres littéraires, historiques, et militaries*, 1809), responsible for sequels to Mme de Staël's anthology.
3. Parody of "Petit-Jean" in *Les Plaideurs*, i:6, Racine's only comedy (1668).
4. Allusion to Boileau, *Epître*, vii (1677).
5. See the *Mémoires* of St-Simon for 11 Feb. 1712.
6. In the popular Viennese puppet-show, the equivalent of *Punch and Judy*.
7. Not a witch, but certifiably mad, Zacharias Werner (1768-1823), met Staël in 1808 at a commemoration of the oath on the Grütli (August, 1291 in Uri, Switzerland), and became for a time her guru. Ligne is here teasing her.
8. A confederation of German states formed by Napoleon in 1806, with certain territorial accommodations – not including Ligne. This also explains the "censors" mentioned above.
9. Allusion to Staël's plan to leave for America.
10. Allusion to Corneille's play *Sertorius*, iii:936 (1662).
11. Benjamin Constant de Rebecque (1767-1830), politician, intimate friend of Staël and probable father of her daughter, Albertine (1797-1838), Duchess de Broglie. His family were friendly with Ligne.

Ligne to Madame de Staël - d
Late 1809/ early 1810   Vienna

    If your handsome eyes were not present to my memory, if I didn't immediately see my punishment in them, I'd say you were ready for another *Colombiade*,[1] different from the one you're going to undertake. You're going to make North America as fashionable as you've made Germany.[2] When shall I get to hear all you have to say about it? What does Goethe, before whom we all kneel, have to say, and Wieland the great? Long live Weimar in every genre![3] Aside from a few good poets elsewhere, there are excellent romances whose details make them better than French ones, even than British ones. There are clever persons, great mechanics, physicians, geometers, chemists and good historians. But neither in France, in Britain nor in Italy do we find any more lyrical than David [in the Bible], Pindar, nor Jean-Baptiste Rousseau, more dramatic than Corneille, more somber than Shakespeare, more tender than Racine, more erotic than Anacreon, more poetic and amusing than Voltaire, more profound than Montesquieu, more philosophic than Montaigne, nor more natural than LaFontaine.[4]

    O dear Madame Vespucci,[5] don't let your discoveries disgust me with this petty Europe that should be proud to have given you birth. If your search for perpetual adoration and friendship costs you an eloquent and sensible preface for a mediocre American, you're going to praise him to the skies, as you did me.[6] Your sense of justice sleeps only when you are patronizing. Although all your quills are golden, I use the one you gave me in order to write my "posthumes" whose fortune you shall make.[7]

    Thus, I shall be avenged of my compatriots who want, as is right, to read me through you, while their heirs will be obliged to go through all the volumes my "too fertile quills" will have been able to fill without difficulty each month.[8]

    Many a comparison, which only a man who gets out of bed at four o'clock to perform on several stages and then be a spectator in the best boxes can see what will perhaps be rather piquant.

So, are there not enough passable Europeans to make you disgusted with the savages, or people too civilized whom the police force into exile?[9] You mistreat the whites to do good to the blacks whom you'll not treat as slaves.[10] I'm more saddened, naughty lady, by your overseas mania, since I might have been one of your acolytes on the flowery shores of Lake Geneva.[11]

I should like to know what has become of dear Albert and that beginning of an illustrious man, his elder brother, Auguste.[12] How grievous for the crowd of your idolaters, of whom I'm one. Let the others take pity on me, and I'll pity them, by which time we'll all be orphans. One of us will place his sorrow at the foot of the cross; I'm not big enough to look on sorrow as a good thing. My family, relatives, friends, Irishmen,[13] ministers, grand officers of the army, doctors, artists, artisans – we all love and will miss you. But for the first time in my life that I've become ambitious, I give you notice, dear Baroness, that I shall outdo them all.

Source: *Nouveau Recueil* ii (1812) 64-7.

Notes

1. *La Colombiade* (Lyon, 1762), epic poem by Anne - Marie du Bocage (1710-1802), retracing Columbus's first voyage.
2. *De l'Allemagne*, iii vol. (London: Murray, 1814) and Countess de Pange, *Mme de Staël et "De l'Allemagne"* (Paris:Malfère, 1929).
3. Weimar became known as "the Athens of Modern Germany" under Duke Charles-Augustus (1757-1828), reigned 1758-1828. Johann v. Goethe (1749-1832) and Martin Wieland (1733-1813), pre-eminent writers of their time, active at the court of Weimar.
4. David (1010-975 BC?), King of Israel; Pindar (521-441 BC?), Greek lyric poet; Jean-Baptiste Rousseau (1670-1741), French lyric poet; Pierre Corneille (1606-84), French dramatist; William Shakespeare (1564-1616), English poet and dramatist; Jean Racine (1639-1699), French tragic dramatist; Aacreon (560-478 BC?), Greek lyric poet; Voltaire (1694-1778), French writer and critic; Charles de Montesquieu (1689-1755), French political philosopher; Michel de Montaigne (1539-92), French moralist; Jean de LaFontaine (1621-95), French fabulist.

5. Amerigo Vespucci (1451-1512), Florentine navigator for whom "America" is named.
6. Allusion to Staël's edition of Ligne's *Lettres et pensées* (Paris/Genève, 1809).
7. On Ligne's "Posthumes" see J. Vercruysse in *NAPL xii* (1998), 7-91.
8. Cf. Nicolas Boileau, *Satires ii* (1664), v. 77.
9. On Staël and the police, see *De l'Allemagne*, 2 vol. (Balayé ed.), (Paris: Garnier-Flammarion, 1968), i:13-31.
10. See Staël's "Appel aux souverains réunis... pour obtenir l'abolition de la traite des Nègres" (mai/juin, 1814), brochure of 15 pages.
11. Staël's home on the shores of Lake Geneva.
12. Albert (1792-1813) and Auguste (1790-1827), Staël's sons.
13. "Irish," probably an allusion to Staël's intimacy with count Maurice O'Donnel de Tyrconnel (1750-1843), Ligne's future son-in-law, during 1805-8.

Ligne to Madame de Staël - e
24 June 1810 [?]   Vienna

Perhaps you're asking yourself "Am I in France? Am I in Asia? In Golconda, or in my native land? Or even in Coppet or Philadelphia?"[1] Where are you finally, dear and adorable woman? I know that Europe is too petty for you. But, if truth be told, so is America.

Tell me then, you who have me so nicely printed in Paris and who have Lausannes and Genevas at your feet, why are you taking your *Germany* (1811) to Blois [in France]?[2]

I've been asked to answer for you. It seems I'm the surety for your actions. And this Europe that you want to abandon requests of me, through some four or five hundred deputies taking the waters here, where you are and what do you count on doing? I'd like to be able to tell them, "Gentlemen, something very reasonable. She'll come here.[3] But do reasonableness and sublimity sometimes agree with one another? Yet sublimity and a good heart, great heart and great, good nature do, according to what I've heard and witnessed – and which has been proved – they go ever so well together.[4]

O prodigy of soulfulness and wit, how much I need you for me to be moral and others to be human, you to be Christian and Mme de... to be Catholic.[5]

A very nice lady[6] from a warm climate whom I listen to willingly since she, like you, has just talked to me for two hours about the immortality of the soul, making me tremble while assuring [me] that hers and mine will meet one of these days for all eternity.[7] Do come here to get over your open-handedness.

I don't understand rates-of-exchange as well as changes [variables], but I know that your francs are worth more than Banco-Zettel. You know, Baroness, that even though you understand prose, the word means "bank note".[8] Alas! Would that I could write from my house to your Jewish [?] home![9] Yours has become hateful to me for being unable to go there any more since you left. I, how I miss mornings with you: two hours of confidences are worth more than your brilliant evenings the rest of the week filled with [an audience of] Poles and people, few of whom know how to listen carefully.

And then there are your fits of anger when my stupidity makes your eyes flash, fully armed against my puns! Either hide or show yourself for a long time to come on the horizon! You cannot have been more admired or adored than amongst us, especially by me, I mean. Come, lovely lady, for my sake. Read on the other side of the page, says Christine.[10]

Have I not already told you how unfortunate it is that you're not a warrior, because of extracts [you've published] from my militaria, where, encouraged by your judgment and your fiery or pink style, you would have given me a command twenty years ago, and I'd not have been beaten at Ulm, Raab, Wagram, etc.?[11] I'd not have relied on allies, nor on insurrection, when, thanks to the carelessness of [an incompetent] minister, with less than the half the cavalry of the enemy [and] a stupid notion of economy. That's what caused a levy en mass to face the attacks of the enemy [while] the cavalry performed a brilliant movement; there was nothing to be gained by these last two wars and everything to be lost. We would have had the advantage for less five years ago at Boulogne [as at] Olomouc and Madrid this past year which would have taken us to the gates of Buda.

Our armies fought bravely, but as in a duel. No maneuvering nor any deployment in a column of divisions that I mention could be victorious, even though victory was in sight, and the isle of Lobau[12] in enemy hands protecting his passage [to the mainland] and preventing ours. Ten detached corps without a single general [commanding] on the Marckfeld. Difficulties we encountered. Our right on the Adriatic, the center on the Vistula, the left on the Danube, and me, crying in the wilderness.[13] There's Spanish and British tittle-tattle going from the cafes on the Graben[14] to salons and cabinets, [plus] a few schemers seeking advancement. Such is our history which, without the treaty [of Schonbrunn, 14 October, 1809], would have taken us to the gates of the Orient.

"Military reflections and campaigns of the Prince de Ligne, collected by General de Staël" would have caused men and women who, before your kind edition would take me for an idiot to say, "It's charming, to be sure."[15] Your friendship, which is their true title to glory is worth more than others' and takes its modest place rightfully. You don't depend on evil conquests nor on terrain that produces evil practitioners. Thus, dear and adorable lady, always reward those who consider you to be their godhead.

Source: *Lettres inédites....* (Balayé ed.) (Brussels: Academie royale, 1966), 275-79).

Notes

1. Allusion to Staël's projected trip to America.
2. Allusion to Staël's anthology *Letters and Reflexions of Field-Marshal Prince de Ligne* (Paris: Propiac, 1809).

   Her great work, *De l'Allemagne* was to be published in Blois because of implicit criticisms of Napoleon and his regime; nonetheless, the edition was confiscated and destroyed.
3. Add: "here", meaning "Toeplitz."

4. The following lines until "Prodigy" (dictated by Ligne?) are in the hand of Princess Clary, Ligne's eldest daughter (Christine, 1757-1830).

   If only you understood practical feeling, along with theory, you'd thank me very much for the bearer of this letter of credit. He's as pretty inside as out and is called Count Henri von Schonfeld (1791-1828) whom his father, the ambassador [Count Johann, 1784-1820] whom you saw in Vienna, has sent traveling to divert him from a beautiful, passionate attachment he had in Leipzig. "That he had?" you'll ask. No, but one he has and will have for a while. Isn't that how you'd phrase it?

5. Thought to be an allusion to one of Ligne's last "flames", Rosalie, Countess Rzewuska (1788-1835), omitted out of courtesy.
6. Elisa von der Recke (1756-1833), who had been living since 1801 with the poet Tiedge; Staël had met them in the summer of 1808 in Toeplitz.
7. Here begins another insertion, also in the hand of Princess Clary, as far as "courier:"

   Day before yesterday she lost one of her four professors (therefore a chatterbox) from North Germany (therefore learned) whom she brought here. What sort of man was he, she asked, who didn't allow me to speak and showed no gratitude, no sensitivity yet was nonetheless a superior being? But let's rejoice: his soul has taken wing for heaven.

   If, instead of the brick wall that prevents the Chinese from quitting their empire, we had only a paper one, more difficult to penetrate, I'd go and visit adorable Coppet [Staël's home on Lake Geneva] that you don't appreciate enough. But this same paper wall must encourage you to enter [Austria]. Break through by courier.

8. Allusions to the financial difficulties of the time when Austrian currency had lost ninety percent of its value.
9. Allusion to Staël's play *Hagar dans le désert* (1806), performed while she was in Vienna in 1808 and living not far from Ligne.
10. Another interpolation by Princess Clary, as far as "Have I not":

    This naughty father of mine [Ligne himself] has not said anything to you for me, Madame, [and] I've just scolded him. I should like to be remembered to you. You've promised us to come to Toeplitz; it would be a real pleasure for me to receive you here; is there absolutely no hope of seeing you? Please accept, Madame, the expression of my ever-faithful devotion to you.

11. Mistrusted by the political authorities (especially by Baron Johann Amédée Thugut, 1786-1810) since the Brabantine Revolution of 1787-90, but nonetheless named Field-Marshal in 1808, Ligne

was constrained to develop his ideas on strategy far from the field of battle. The Austro-French wars of 1805-09 pre-empted all in his mind, whence this sardonic re-capitulation.

12. A large island in the Danube, opposite Vienna, important for the outcome of the battle of Wagram (1809).
13. Another allusion to Staël's play *Hagar*, plus Mattew ii:3.
14. An important commercial thoroughfare in central Vienna.
15. Proverbial sarcasm: see Offenbach's *Les Contes d'Hoffman* (1880), ii:7-8.

Ligne to Madame de Staël - f
8 July, 1811   From the Kahlenberg

"You must indeed be stupid, Sir," as the Chevalier de Lisle wrote to Voltaire[1] for having acted, I know not how "incorrectly" on an errand involving watches, I believe. That made him laugh 'til he cried. "Since, he said, I'm used to insipid compliments like "Divinity of letters", "Patriarch," "Idol of the world," etc., I reply, "You must be a real monster, Madam, to believe that I am." Me! Forget you! I'd rather others forgot you, but it seems to me that they don't; for it's too much a question of you – and us, in consequence.[2]

O! what a shame! A real shame! But don't say a word. He [Napoleon] seems noble. Don't give [Him] the opportunity, dear Baroness, even when under close observation; it's one more title to fame.

You are an enchantress, but not a witch. I challenge you to guess what I'm doing right now? I'm writing letters to you that you'll not receive, or else I erase what I have written. Here's how it is: the two Christines,[3] my "jockeys" of the writing-desk, would like to make a small collection of letters they copied when, by chance, I wrote in their presence. As mine to you are a homage from my heart rather more than from my head, those letters appear in a projected volume, along with a few others to illustrious personages.[4] I remove everything which might compromise us, and I insert many things I may – or may not – have written, perhaps the originals. You'll certainly note some that [the censors at] the post will have prevented from reaching you.

If you were here, I'd no longer make the presses nor the readers groan. But I've nothing nor say, [except] you must give a more illustrious title to your *Delphines* (1802) and *Corrines* (1807) than that of "novel" which turns me aside from reading them.

The *Journey to Jerusalem*[5] takes away my desire to go there: Chateaubriand speaks too ill of the Turks. The seriousness your work instilled in me and which has flattered me all the more, since you're the only one to inveigle me into sampling the collection of

Diplomatic pieces from Clovis to Louis XIV[6] that others have read completely; yet, by adding an idea of the knowledge of people and passions that move us, you help me to find the causes of events even more in conversations and secret dispatches between war and peace, and ample matter for reflection.

I wept over some and laughed at others while realizing or guessing at the reasons for their brevity. I've done neither the one nor the other regarding our last two wars [1805-1809], nor the unfortunate treaties that were their inevitable result,[7] for I was indignant at seeing that there had been everything to lose, nothing to gain, no talent, no forethought, [but] stupidity, presumption, partisanship, idiotic proclamations, with a wisp of intrigue to bring down the monarchy.

As for conversations, there were only three all winter long. The first turned on a charitable foundation of the nobility, at whose head (as you will have read in the national *Gazette*) was Baroness Arnstein,[8] with, among other causes, schools for swimming, raising honeybees, and training oculists. The second was about a masked ball that gossip and petty spitefulness and jealousy caused to be canceled. The third, which is still going on concerns finances. "How much, Madame, did you pay for this percale? -- According to the exchange [rate]? - No, no, Madame, according to the cours. – How much are ducats worth today? - Madame, I know nothing about that, but my coachman wanted fifteen florins to drive me to *Punch and Judy* ..."[9] Then I intervened – very wittily – with, "You should talk to her about the rates and not the price [cours]."

This letter, for instance, will not be published. But in others I have written – or not – I take my revenge by naming your illustrious forebears and those to whom you've given birth.

So, take up your plan for Toeplitz.[10] The Emperor [Francis II] will not make a solemn entry into Pressburg for the stormy Diet that will assemble there; as a result, he'll not be accompanied by the Guard, and I'll go to Bohemia.

Come, do come. I need you to recover. People have too high an opinion of you not to love you. *Someone*[11] spoke well of you to *someone* who told me so. *Someone* who knows everything also knew that you had said to Moritz Liechtenstein[12] who said to you in speaking to him of your master, "Qui que tu sois, etc."[13] Always make friends, if possible. And if you prefer an armchair in Paris to a throne on the shore of the Lake of Geneva, you shall reign forever over every sensitive soul and virtuous heart.

I leave you to take this letter to Schlegel[14] to give him a hug, for the atmosphere surrounding him is precious to me and will bring me one of your contagious atoms as well as a heavenly emanation from the woman I admire and will adore my whole lifelong.

I thank you once again a thousand times over for having raised me from the dust of Dresden and the world, who, without you, would never have known I exist.[15] Kings may be made, but you alone can make a reputation from a phrase or a line [Ligne].

Source: Lettres Inédites... (ed. Balayé),
(Bruxelles, Académie royale, 1966), 279-83.

Notes

1. Chev. Nicolas de Lisle (1735-83), *Lettres intimes* (ed. Leuridant), Paris: Champion, 1924.
2. This letter is a reply to one from Staël dated 18 June, 1811. It is also interesting for the details it reveals about Ligne's habits of writing and publishing.
3. Marie-Christine de Ligne (1757-1830), Princess Clary, Ligne's daughter; and Fanny-Christine de Ligne (1786-1867), Countess O'Donnell de Tyrconnel, Ligne's granddaughter by adoption.
4. Correspondents named in the *NRL* (Weimar, 1812).
5. Francois, Viscount de Chateaubriand (1768-1848), *Itinéraire de Paris à Jérusalem*, 3 vols. (Paris: Le Normant, 1811).
6. *Recueil de pièces diplomatiques et politiques depuis Clovis* (Paris, 1697).
7. Treaties ending the war of 1805 (Pressburg, modern Bratislava, 26 December 1805), and that of 1809 (Schönbrun, 15 October 1809).
8. Fanny Arnstein, née Itzig (1757-1813); salonnière in Vienna, wife of a very wealthy banker, the first Austrian Jew to be ennobled.

9. In the text: *Kasperle*, the equivalent of *Punch and Judy*.
10. Since 1808, Staël had been planning on a visit to Toeplitz, the Bohemian spa.
11. Perhaps Count Maurice O'Donnell de Tyrconnel (1780-1834), the intimate of Staël from 1805, the husband of Ligne's granddaughter by adoption.
12. Prince Maurice Liechtenstein (1775-1819), nephew of Ligne through his wife.
13. Æneis, i: 387.
14. August-Wilhelm Schlegel (1767-1848), important translator and intermediary between French and German literature, a figurehead of German romanticism and an intimate of Staël.

    Also an allusion to Napoleon at the Treaty of Pressburg, where he created kings of Bavaria, Wurttenburg, Saxony, etc.
15. Reference to the great international and financial success of Staël's anthology, *Lettres et pensées du Maréchl Prince de Ligne* in 1809; texts originally published in London; see J. Vercruysse. *Bibliographie descriptive,* (Paris, 2008), 255-68.

22

1775 – Flore de Ligne, Baroness Spiegel – 1851

Ligne's third daughter, whose sharp tongue regarding any and every topic was probably inherited from both her parents. Devoted to her father and his friends, attaining considerable appreciation of her faithfulness, as well as for her wit; married (1812) Raban, Baron Spiegel (1775-1836).

Ligne to Flore
[26 March 1808]   [Vienna]

To Princess Flore de Ligne,
  requesting a ticket for the Creation–concert[1] of 27 March 1808 in Vienna honoring Franz-Joseph Haydn.

(Air: La Lumière la plus pure.)

Dear Goddess of rare harmony,
  Endowed with voice celestial
  (Inheritance familial)
And talent in abundance,
  I beg your filial devotion
To intercede with an admittance
  To the Creation of this generation
For the pleasure of your own Creator - *moi*.[2]

Source: *Mél. 12*, (1804),21.

Notes

1. A concert of Haydn's Creation to celebrate the composer's 76th birthday (his last public appearance) on 27 March 1808 in the New University, under the patronage of Marie-Ermengilde Esterházy (1768-1843), Ligne's niece, and conducted by Salieri (Antonio, 1750-1825). Among those in attendance, in addition to Ligne, were Beethoven, the director Iffland (August, 1759-1814), and the music critic Reichardt (Johann, 1752-1814), commemorated in a painting on the cover of a snuff-box by Balthazar Wiegand (?, now destroyed), reproduced in H-C. Robbins-Landon, *Haydn: a Documentary Study* (N.Y.:Rizzoli, 1983), 168, where Ligne is supposedly represented.

See: D. Heartz, *Mozart, Haydn, and Early Beethoven* (N.Y.:Norton, 2009), 670-72.

2. The original French is as follows:

A la Princesse Flore de Ligne
Pour lui demander un
Billet pour le concert de la
   Création.
Air: La lumière la plus pure.

Déesse de l'harmonie/ Si célèbre, et céleste voix/ A qui j'ai donné la vie/ Et les talents à la fois,/ C'est à vous que je m'adresse/ Pour l'autre Création;/ J'implore votre tendresse/ Pour votre intercession. / Et le plaisir de votre créateur.//

23

1773 – Prince Clement von Metternich – 1859

Clement, Prince Metternich, in French *le Cocher* (coachman) *de l'Europe*, as he became known at the Congress of Vienna in 1814-15, descended from a noble family in the Rhineland. He served in the diplomatic corps from a young age (1797) representing Austria in Dresden, Berlin and Paris, where he became Ambassador in 1809 at the same time as he was named Foreign Minister for Austria. In this capacity his primary objective was to overthrow Napoleon and restore peace to Europe. In pursuing this course of action he was undoubtedly encouraged by Napoleon's greatest blunder (see Talleyrand's quip), the murder of the Duke d'Enghien (1804), just as in a more positive vein he negotiated the marriage of the Usurper with Marie-Louise of Hapsburg-Lorraine (1810). Forced into retirement after the Revolution of 1848.

In youth, he had been a friend and "crony' of the Prince de Ligne who, forever after, played upon this relationship to attain the personal designs of his life – but not always successfully (see our selection of three brief missives, filled with typical cajolery and punning).

Letters from Ligne:
- ✉ a - [beginning of 1809], from [Vienna?]
- ✉ b - [1810], from Vienna
- ✉ c - Thursday [October/November] 1814, from Vienna

See: G. de Berthier de Sauvigny, *Metternich* (Paris, 1958)

Ligne to Metternich - a
[Beginning of 1809][1]   [Vienna?]

Bon voyage, dear invisible ambassador whom I wanted to embrace so warmly [before you left]!

Would you be so kind as to deliver the enclosed to the address of Roumiantsov [the younger],[2] while, à *propos* of "address", you could save me from a small unpleasantness that worries me.

Mme de Staël has printed some of my works[3] in which I'm afraid there may be a few ill-conceived remarks, especially in my letters to the Emperor Joseph II,[4] where I complained of Marshal Roumiantsov [the father] in the Empress's Second Turkish War.[5]

If perhaps the son were to read them, I beg that you forestall any criticism by saying I didn't know they were there and, if the work is being marketed, I wish all sales to stop until the publisher[6] receives further word from Mme de Staël, to whom I'm presently writing about this matter.

Kindly accept, dear ambassador, the expression of my deepest and everlasting devotion.

Source:Lettres inédites de Mme de Staël, etc.
(Ulrichová ed) Prague:Akademia, 1959: 59-60

Notes

1. For the uncertain date, refer to Ullrichová, 59.
2. Nicholas, Count Roumiantsov (1750-1826), son of a famous Russian marshal, Minister for Foreign Affairs under Alexander I, in Paris in 1809.
3. Germaine de Staël (1766-1817), cosmopolitan writer whose anthology of Ligne's work (*Lettres et Pensés*) had appeared in February, 1809.
4. Joseph II, Emperor (1741-90), intimate of Ligne's.
5. Pierre, Count Roumiantsov-Zadoumaski (1730?-1801), Russian Field-Marshal, commanded the Eastern front in Catherine II's (1732-96) Second Turkish War, where Ligne served under him, criticizing him to Joseph II in his anthology, 124.
6. J-J. Paschoud, Genève.

Ligne to Metternich - b
[1810]   Vienna

Clementissime et Amabilissime Minister,[1]

If you need a compliment-bearing commissioner, a diplomatic courier or "jockey,"[2] I am not afraid to meet the Savage[3] whom I would tame better than anyone else, since he has said several times that he would have liked to know me and much regretted that I had not wanted to see him in Dresden and twice in Vienna.[4]

He is still admiring your fine bearing in appearance and intelligence, *dixit*.[5] Good day, dear and very dear Count to whom I am very tenderly attached.

PS—If he has learned that what I most desired in the world was to command [an army] against him—even with a sort of confidence in myself that can only increase his consideration for me. All of this, together, will make him put more trust in my words than in those of another.[6]

Source: Mansel, 238.

Notes

1. Ligne is here playing on Metternich's first name "Clement" (most kind and likeable).
2. "Jockey" is one way Ligne liked to refer to himself; see the first *Lettre sur la dernière Guerre de Turcs*; etc. *Mél.* 7, (1796), 155.
3. I.e., Napoleon Bonaparte.
4. Dresden in 1807 (see letter to d'Arenberg, no. 19) and twice in Vienna in 1809.
5. Sarcastic, "or so he said."
6. Linge's sincere desire, but cloaked in his irrepressible vanity.

Ligne to Metternich - c
Thursday [October/November] 1814   Vienna

What are Europe's affairs in comparison with those of my heart? As I no longer count on being appreciated in this part of the world, and since Asia has preempted that part of America that I lost, please, dear Count, I beg of you, slip the enclosed memoir into the pocket of some Prince or Duke on behalf of the one whose console-ship I love in the person of his very lovely wife.[1]

To conclude our conversation, so rudely interrupted the other day by the Mistress of the House in her ill humor.[2] I'll say that I'm certain our attitude is correct and proper and that, after having maintained the existence of our monarchy, you'll surely find a way to improve it.

You know, excellent Excellency, how I appreciate your success and your most amiable person.

Source: *NAPL vi* (1991) 42[3]

Notes

1. Allusion to Pauline Panam ("la Belle Grecque") (1789-1840), who captured Ligne's enthusiasm after the death of Catherine II of Russia ("Asia") in 1796 and after Mme de Staël had renounced her plans for going to America (1808/10). The "memoir" is perhaps the very long letter-preface Ligne is supposed to have written for Mme Panam's *Mémoires d'une jeune Grecque*, two volumes (Paris: Brissot, 1823); see Stendhal, *NAPL* xv (2002).

    The "Prince or Duke" is Mme Panam's morganatic husband (or merely her seducer), Duke Ernest I of Saxe-Coburg-Gotha (1784-1844), a cruel cad and quasi-criminal, father of Prince Albert of Great Britain and uncle of Queen Victoria, and, so, the ancestor of both Queen Elizabeth II and the Duke of Edinburgh.

    Metternich's first wife, Marie-Eleanor de Kaunitz (1775-1825) and his position as *consul*.
2. Probably Dorothea, Princess Lieven (1785-1857), known for her sharp tongue and imperious manner, one of Metternich's lovers during the Congress of Vienna.
3. Ph. Mansel has published (*NAPL vi* (1991) 7-46), 32 letters from Ligne to Metternich.

24

1757 – Karl August von Saxe-Weimar – 1828

Karl August von Saxe-Weimar, Duke from his birth, reigned from 1758 to his death, "enlightened" patron of Goethe and Ligne, under whom Weimar became "the Athens of modern Germany".

Letters from Ligne:
- ✉ a - 12 June 1810, from Toeplitz
- ✉ b - [Autumn 1810] from Baden bei Wien

See: Ph. Mansel, *Prince of Europe* (London: Weidenfeld and Nicolson, 2003) 284 - 5

Ligne to Saxe-Weimar - a
12 June 1810   Toeplitz

Monseigneur,

Your letter on blue stationery[1] has been going the round of Vienna society this summer and has given me great pleasure. The baths at Toeplitz help to maintain my health, [also] because Your Serene Highness has come to support me, and I always need to see you. Since, Monseigneur, you are the best errand boy there may be for bookshops, I'm taking the liberty of forwarding to you five volumes in order to have them printed as I've marked. The representatives of Your Serene Highness, my old Brigadier Müffling and Mr. von Rühle,[2] may be of help. As the book is [entitled] *Fragments Militaires*,[3] they should each begin a new line as in, for example, the first volume: "The 18th of June, 1757, we passed, etc." and then up to and including the last words "*pas accoutumés*" (page 9), followed by [another entry] "The 16th of August, our noble [regiment of] guards," and so forth (page 14), in order to show that these are unconnected fragments.

The gentlemen to whom I entrust this chore will see clearly from the start what has to be done by the sense and then by the capitalization (at the beginning of each entry), as well as by the context. What has decided me to ask you, Monseigneur, to oversee everything is your expertise in counterfeits, hoaxes, signatures, etc.

I trust that the dog-eared pages will not disturb Your Serene Highness [with their suggestion of cuckoldry] and that they'll not be a bad omen for the wedding [of your daughter].[4] I might have wished for the fiancé to be Austrian, for they're the only [worthwhile] ones. You are familiar with all the Princess's good points. I'm merely concerned for her virtue because of the Catholic usurper and head of your house, whose life-style, formed in Paris and Warsaw, encourages him, according to what people say, to have designs on all his female relatives.[5] You then have to avenge yourself (and your family) on his wife when she's not wearing a shift.

We have legitimized Titine[6] who, instead of the name of her mother, has had two or three,[7] is known as Mlle de Ligne, but always "Titine" to those who have a soft spot in their heart for her.

If your printer earns too much money from my story, Monseigneur, I'd also like the small profit from this publication to be set aside for the widows and children of the Weimar heroes who fought in Spain,[8] although their Lutheran fathers will no doubt keep me from Paradise and not let me in.[9] There's no Brotherhood for heretics there. HRH of Constance, Erfurt, Mainz, and Frankfurt has not [yet] signed a Concordat with St. Peter.[10] It's better to be beaten and run away.

With my two other protectors, Messrs Müffling and von Rühle, please pay attention, Monseigneur, to the text at the beginning of this letter. Marry off (whomever you may wish), then come to the English grotto[11] and receive the tender respects of him who from your feet will throw himself into the arms of Your Serene Highness, the man whom he most loves.

PS – The little lady lawyer[12] is arriving and would [also] like to throw herself at your feet in order to form an opinion of you. We've already discussed Your Serene Highness.

Source: Mansel 284 - 5

Notes

1. Blue was the normal color of writing paper until the French Revolution; see *Les Liaisons dangereuses* (1783).
2. Friederich Weiss, Baron Müffling (1780-1843), State Councilor in Vienna (1808), commanding at Waterloo and Paris in 1814; and Major Johann von Rühle und Lilienstern (1788-1847), Chief of the Austrian General Staff against Napoleon; two friends of Ligne.

3. *Fragments Militaires*: thanks to the learned researches of Professor Jeroom Vercruysse, we now know that this is the work referred to with many important details. See his *Bibliographie descriptive* (Paris, 2008), 313-7.
4. Princess Caroline of Saxe-Weimar (1786-1816), married on 1 July 1810 Frederick - Louis, Duke of Mecklenburg - Schwerin (1778-1819).
5. Frederich-August, King of Saxony (1750-1827) and Grand Duke of Warsaw, in 1807, thanks to Napoleon; his wife, Marie-Amélie von Zweibrücken (1752-1828). The Dukes of Saxony had changed religion from Catholic to Protestant in 1536, and back to Catholic in 1807.
6. "Titine" was Fanny-Christine de Ligne (1786-1867), married Maurice, Count O'Donnell in 1811; hence the need for legitimation.
7. Titine's mother, Hélène (1763-1815), was born a Massalska; married (1779) Charles-Antoine de Ligne (1759-1792); then, in 1794 married a cousin, Vincent, Count Potocki (1755-1825), divorced in 1805.
8. Troops from Weimar were sent by the Duke to fight in Spain on the side of the French, as their forbears had been sent to America to fight against the British for the Colonials.
9. Ligne, nominally a Catholic but of a broad, tolerant outlook; see H. Lebasteur, "La religion du Prince de Ligne," *APL xi* (1931), 57-73. Also J. Vercruysse, "Sur la religion", Écrits sur la société, etc. Paris: Champion, 2010, 11-164.
10. The last Archbishop-Elector of Mainz, Sovereign of Erfurt and Grand Duke of Frankfurt, thanks to Napoleon (1807), was Charles-Theodore Dalberg (1744-1817).
11. "English" grotto, a prominent feature of the picturesque garden in Weimar, laid out by Goethe and the Duke around 1778.
12. Person difficult to identify, perhaps Marianne Saaling (1786-1869); see *Frags.1,* (Vercruysse ed.), 369.

Ligne to Saxe-Weimar - b
[autumn] 1810   [Baden bei Wien]

I'm not paying 100 fl for toys any more! This is the last time. Nor will I eat any more ices at the theatre, nor put anything in the hand of a soldier who lost the other at Aspern.[1]

For you see, I'm saving up to go and visit you next year. But, it's really quite difficult, while waiting, not to see you in the street nor meet with you anywhere. It's no fun stealing someone else's money-box alone, or do you have some other crime in mind?

I've returned [to Vienna] every Sunday to do my duty as a Christian or as Captain [of the Palace Guard].[2] During the week I go hunting boar in Moravia or Hungary; [for instance] the other day, I killed a hundred pheasant or hares.

Helped by a good translation, I've read with enthusiasm *The Elective Affinities* [of Goethe].[3] I'm sorry for strait-laced men—and women who are often less prudish—who have not found, instead of vices that are everywhere, the true secret of the human heart, the development of a thousand things unfelt, because people do not stop and reflect, or [because of representations of society, of nature]. There are two new and piquant characters: Ottilie is one type.[4] But what a masterpiece, even in French, especially when she is center stage![5]

How profound, how attractive, how unforeseen is this work, so far superior to those of any other nation! Beyond that, what a pleasure to know and like the sublime author, with all his excellent, gentle, simple, and sociable qualities![6] I hope, and surely you do too, that Edward and Charlotte are now somewhat consoled, and that if they each have a few minor escapades, they'll tell one another, for that's the only way to find happiness in marriage.

What has kept me from writing novels is that I find it impossible to consider suffering in any form of body or soul. If I did, I'd immediately smooth out the difficulties. On the first page—declaration of love. On the second—resistance. On the third—description of a fortuitous encounter by moonlight in a bower with nightingales. On the fourth—perfect union, happiness and pleasure. On the fifth—mutual infidelity. On the sixth—reconciliation. On the seventh—death from an excess of pleasure. I did consider, I must say, having them die laughing or from indigestion, but I think they may still be suffering a bit, and a surfeit of pleasure can produce a swoon leading to eternal sleep.[7]

What's your doctor's name? I can prove to him that three months of our Baden are necessary for you, even more than the care of our wise and gentle Ambrosi.[8] I'll grant you six months for tidying up your affairs; but for mine and those of your Lignes and Clarys,[9] they must be renewed every year. All of them have asked me to remember them to your goodness that we all deserve because of our fondness for you.

Source: *NRL 2* (Lebasteur ed.)3-5

Notes

1. This outburst involves two youthful vendors at a theater in Vienna whom Ligne had attempted to seduce; see *Frags. 1*, (Vercruysse ed), 367.
   Aspern: Site of Napoleon's victory over the Austrians in a village East of Vienna, 21 May - 6 July 1809.
2. To which Ligne had been named in 1807.
3. *Wahlverfandtschaften*, novel by Goethe (1809). Two translations available to Ligne were published in Paris by Lhuillier, 1810, and by Vve Lepetit, also 1810.
4. Despite Ligne's enthusiasm for Goethe's "Ottilie" in *Elective Affinities*, (1809) He sometimes is confusing her with "Louise Miller" in Schiller's *Love and Intrigue* (1784), as here.
5. The types Goethe has chosen are Edward, a mature gentleman who has no character; Charlotte, his wife, an experienced woman, the opposite of Edward; the Captain, an active and practical man; while Ottilie is a living enigma whose nature is extremely passionate.
6. Ligne met Goethe in Carlsbad, Bohemia, in 1810; they sometimes saw one another thereafter and exchanged verses.
7. In the same vein, see, in Jane Austen's *Juvenalia*, "The Loiterer" (1789-90), no. ix, 52:

"Let us see some nice, affecting stories, relating the misfortunes of two lovers who died suddenly, just as they were going to church. Let the lover be killed in a duel or lost at sea, or you may make him shoot himself, just as you please; and as for his mistress, she would of course... go mad; only remember, whatever you do, that your hero and heroine must possess a good deal of *feeling*, and have very pretty names.

Later, there would be Northanger Abbey (1790-1803?). At roughly the same time, there appeared under the pseudonym "Lady H. Marlow" [Wm. Beckford, 1796] the satire *Modern Novel Writing, or The Elegant Enthusiast,* while, on a more serious note, Goethe wrote "Über Wahrheit und Wahrscheinlichkeit"; for this last, see his *Schriften zur Literatur, Kunst, und Natur.* München, Goldmann 1960 [?], 25-49.

8. Dr. Wenzl Ambrosi (1757-1813), a popular doctor in Toeplitz, Bohemia.
9. Allusion to various members of Ligne's family frequenting Toeplitz: his daughters Féfé (1773-1834) and Flore (1775-1851) and the family of Marie-Christine, Princess Clary (1757-1830), and her husband, Prince Jean Clary-Aldringen (1753-1806) and their children.

1774 – Count Alexander de Laborde – 1842

Alexander, Count de Laborde, scion of a wealthy French banking family, served in both the French and the Austrian armies (1789 - 96); pactised with Bonaparte and began to publish a famous series of "voyages" including a well-received *Description des nouveaux jardins pittoresques de la France*. (Paris: Delance, 1808), later becoming prefect of Paris, publishing on Greek vases; the words to the Second Empire march, "Partant pour la Syrie;" and the beginnings of the municipal waterworks in Paris; a trusted and valuable friend to Ligne.

See: Henry Eaklund, "Alexander de Laborde et sa contribution au romantisme" (Essay for the degree of Master of Arts), U. C. Berkeley, 1976

Ligne to Laborde
1810?   Vienna? Toeplitz?

Dear Alexander,
   I hope your almost (or future) Excellency will allow me to address you by your Christian name and that of a pagan hero you tried to imitate in the ranks of the Austrian military.[1] But, since you are deserving enough, you now seem to be, rather, the latter's tutor, Aristotle: wise, knowledgeable, and perhaps as imaginative as yourself.
   Tell me, for I never know what I'm saying nor writing, whether I've already forwarded to you all I'm going to say about:
   Eisenstadt, brought back to life by Prince Esterházy and famous for its greenhouses where quantity and quality outdo all others;
   Weimar for its broad and handsome flowerbeds and lawns, laid out in the grand manner, with the Roman house and rockeries;
   Wiegnowitz, with its august castle, like Lublin in Poland, belonging to Countess Mniczeck, a niece of the last king;
   Kresowice, the property of another Countess Mniczeck in the province of Przemysl, combining a lake, coppices, and follies (a mix of both Wörlitz and Ermenonville);
   and Frain, on a cliff plunging toward the Taya (modern Dyje) in Moravia;
   the Orczy Garden close by Pesth where only water is lacking;
   Geymüller, near Vienna, that lacks almost nothing -- temples, ruins, Gothic residences, castles old and new, and a superb parkland;
   and the underground lake of Prince Lichtenstein [at Lednice][2] – all these are topics worthy to be added to the publication of which you've agreed to be the editor.
   Apropos of other letters than those selected for the volume to be printed, I believe, at Weimar,[3] I commend myself to your friendship as a survivor. For it will provide a fine framework for the Bagatelles, imprudent and mischievous that people might

want to insert when I am no more. I am too lazy to take the trouble to raise the lid of my coffin and defend myself.

Nowadays, people like unedited, posthumous stuff, frequently bastards and ill- fated children; there is scarcely an actor, musician or even a footman whose conversations are not immediately in print in order to disinter with them something spicy, revealed merely in unrecognizable names and characters. If I've chosen not to amuse myself by being nasty in this life, I don't wish to be so in the hereafter.

Yet, while still alive, I've been made to say so many witty, foolish things I've never conceived of, that it will be worse after I'm dead. Partisan spirit or gossip can imagine people and places, along with turns of phrase, embarrassing for the survivors. So, take care, Count, I beg of you. I'm quite sure I've never written anything against religion or monarchs.[4] But people do misread. They make up a name from a single initial letter, they have fantasies, they "interpret". In some stupid article I've not seen, I'm severely taken to task for absurdities. How foolish to accuse me! People should be ashamed. Have everything suppressed that might give that appearance. At the moment, posterity is a letter opener; there are no more confidential writings. You find yourself in a nightshirt and exposed.[5] There are far too many deaths "like Turenne's",[6] too much news, unbelievable battles, too many river crossings, too much festivity and too few good sermons to be preached.

I just might be credited nowadays without being able to imitate the charming naturalness of Mme de Sévigné,[7] with more piquant anecdotes than those embellished with her gracefulness that would otherwise be of no account. I myself, prefer to be nothing, but simply to be quoted. Besides which, it's not worthwhile, for what has given me the most pleasure and increases my gratitude to Mme de Staël[8] who raised me from the dust and without whom no one would ever know I'm a writer because she has noted that I have a serious turn of mind.[9] You must have it for yourself but not broadcast the fact. I'm not fooling. There's no fun in today's reflections for sharing, and I dislike fashionable melancholy or too much imagination in the little wit that is so frequently displayed. It's because there's no wit when people pretend to be thinkers and they're merely thoughtful instead of being profound. The Greeks, the French and the Italians have too much of it to be melancholy; it doesn't suit either their physiognomy or their language. In both respects, the British are better and worse than that, which is to say, they are too somber and of a sobriety that affects their poetry and other interesting compositions. Ovid was sad when writing the Tristia[10] and was of a naturally melancholy disposition. Horace, Virgil, Boileau, and Voltaire[11] would never have been so. Jean-Jacques was somber like a clutch of Britons because they don't know how to be moved. Today we see so many melancholy and bucolic poetasters. A squireen, with his manner and his orchard in a glenn surrounded by sparsely covered hillocks, can claim that the site inspires melancholy; an author abandoned by his mistress, who found him boring, can therefore, claims he, compose melancholy rhymes.

You, dear sir, didn't write melancholy verse when you were 18 and the commander of Kinsky's dragoons. Your verse was fantastic like your handsome green dragoons.[12] Oh! There, I've made a pun for you without intending. Forgive me dear Count, and please excuse me for having written such a long screed in order to request that you correct or purify my writings if you should receive them when I am no longer able to greet you with all my heart.

Source: *NRL ii*: 136-41 Lebasteur ed.

Notes

1. From 1784-96, Laborde served with the Austrians in Kinsky's squadron.
2. The mention of gardens is probably meant to follow on Laborde's *Voyage pittoresque de l'Autriche*, 3 vols (Paris: Delance, 1809).

    "Eisenstadt," property of Prince Nicolas II Esterházy (1765-1832); see *Coup dœil sur Belœil* (Guy ed.), 230-3.

"Weimar," (Central Germany), in *Coup-dœil* (Guy ed.), 251, laid out by the Duke Karl August and Goethe around 1778.

"Wiegenowicz," belonging to Countess Ursula Mnizech (1750-1808), see G. Ciołek, *Gärten in Polen* (Warsaw: Budownictvo i Architektura, 1957).

"Kresowice," property of another Countess Mnizech-Isabelle (1790-1852); See Ciołek.

"Worlitz," (Central Germany) and "Ermenonville" (Ile-de-France), see *Coup d'œil* (Guy ed.), 259-61 and 185-8.

"Frain," (mod. Vranov), near Schoenwald, (Moravia, Czech Republic).

"Orczy Park," now within the city limits of Budapest (Hungary).

"Geymüller," castle and park to NNW of Vienna near Pötzleinsdorf, formerly more extensive than at present.

"Lednice," (Czech Republic), see *Coup-d'œil* (Guy ed.), 12.

3. The *Nouveau Recueil de Lettres*, 2 vols. published at Weimar in 1812; see the critical edition of Henri Lebasteur (Paris: Champion, 1927) and J. Vercruysse, *Bibliographie descriptive* (Paris, 2008), 318-22.

4. On Ligne's religion, see Ph. Mansel, *Prince of Europe* (London: Weidenfeld-Nicolson, 2003), 199-201, and J. Vercruysse, ed. of Ligne's *Écrits sur la société,etc.* (Paris: Champion, 2010), 11-164.

5. See "De moi pendant le jour / la nuit" in Guy ed. *Œuvres choisies du Prince de Ligne* (Stanford, CA: ANMA Libri, 1978), 3-9

6. Henri, Viscount de Turenne (1611-75), modest general of Louis XIV; died heroically in battle, the subject of great admiration. See the letter of Mme de Sévigné to her daughter, 25 August 1675.

7. Marie de Rabutin - Chantal, Marquise de Sévigné (1626-96), author of spontaneous-seeming letters to her daughter, Marie-Françoise, Countess de Grignan (1646-1715), first published in 1726.

8. Germaine, Baronne de Staël (1766-1817), compiler of *Lettres et pensées du Maréchal Prince de Ligne* (Genève: Paschoud, 1809), where, in the Preface, she calls Ligne "the only foreigner who in French has become a model, not just an imitator." See the re-edition by R. Trousson (Paris: Taillandier, 1989) and J. Vercruysse, *Bibliographie descriptive*, (Paris, 2008), 255-80.

9. Ligne's false modesty aside, it is nonetheless true that Mme de Staël's anthology (no. 8 above) saved him from oblivion.

10. Ovid's *Tristia* (10 AD) are a collection of verse complaining about his exile from Rome in modern Romania.

11. Horace wrote gentle satires, Virgil a sentimental episode in Book 4 of the Æneid; Nicolas Boileau *Satires* of Parisian society of his time, while Voltaire's "tragedies" are noticeably lacking in melancholy. Jean - Jacques Rousseau (1712-78), celebrated writer of the Enlightenment, whose *Confessions* began appearing in 1782.
12. Pun on "dragon verses" (or "fantastic verses") compared with the uniforms of Kinsky's dragoons, wearing a shade of "electric green" after a lizard found in the Indies.

26

1769 – Caroline Pichler – 1843

Viennese *salonnière* and author of *Agathokles*[1] (1808) among sixty-odd other volumes, including important memoirs (*Denkwürdigkeiten aus meinem Leben* – 1841), where Ligne is singled out for praise in volume ii *in principio*.

See: Karl Philip Moritz in *Reisen, Schriften zur Kunst*, 2 vols (Günther ed.) Frankfurt a/M: Insel, 1981
Caroline von Gunderode, *Sämtliche Werke* 3 vols. (Morgenthaler ed.). Frankfurt a/M: Strömfeld/Rotenstern, 1990.

Ligne to Caroline Pichler
June 1, 1812   Vienna

    How will you take it, Madame, if one who is so unfortunate and awkward as not to have obtained the honor of your acquaintance, ventures to take the liberty of writing to you? Worse still, if I wish to tell you what you do not know; as, for instance, the fact, which I am sure is unknown to you, that your romance, which is not in the least over-romantic is one of the best that I have ever read.[1] I should like to tell you why: it is written neither in Rosewater, nor in Gaulish, like so many others, which pall, or horrify, or make us yawn. I do not weep to order. Your Agathokles made me shed some quiet tears. There is never anything unlikely or forced: as much happiness as you can arrange. All is with chivalry, distinction, sensibility, frankness, with the exception of one or two rogues. To throw the honest and delicate characters into relief, all our [men] handsome, young, well-dressed, courageous in war, and brilliant at court: the charming, piquant, interesting, witty figures of the women seem to live; and they all differ from one another. Each character has his style and physiognomy, and each is true to himself. The plot is well sustained throughout: there are no complications beyond those necessary to interest, agitate, disturb, and torment thoroughly, when a catastrophe is required.

    Calpurnia is the most delightful thing that has ever been created: she is a masterpiece: I laughed in my mind, if I may use such an expression, until I was obliged to weep in my heart. As for you coloring, Madame, it has a freshness, a truth, a power to please, which are inexpressible. Your charming descriptive style, elegant without being labored, your accurate comparisons, the depth, novelty, and subtlety of your thought, the reflections to which you give rise, without exhausting your own, are further reasons for my admiration of you. You warm the feelings without seeking to enflame them. Do not fatigue an excess of riches and preserve a happy variety throughout.

Unfortunately, I only know the language of the camp. I can do what is required by my profession, and from time to time, when I have the good fortune to write simply, I may attain the historical narrative. But I cannot err in praise of your German. I have perhaps dared too much in speaking of your coloring, but it seemed to me that this appeared even in translation. That of Madame de Montolieu is so pure in style, so simple, and so wellwritten that I think I can judge this point by the little I can follow in the original.[2] Your prose rises so gently and so appropriately into poetry, that there is no feeling of abrupt transition when you return to the ground.

One of these days, Madame, I shall descend from my refuge on the Caelian Hill, now called the Kahlenberg,[3] for the privilege of paying my respects to you. If I could not profit by your acquaintance, what would Wieland and Goethe say when I see them again?[4] The friendship with which these two celebrated men have so much honored me almost gives me the right to merit your own. They say you are kind: your heart is spoken of as often as your intelligence. Myself, I must believe you unkind; for your book is an epigram against the world in general which seems at present to disparage it. I have omitted to speak to you of religion: and I should ask God's pardon for this. How sublime, brilliant and inspiring yours seems to me! You are right to depict its triumph: and most adroit in not losing, for its sake, the gracious forms and beautiful names of the pagan world. You present a Christian philosophy, which affords a secure consolatory refuge against all. You elaborate it with a touch of fervor: if the purity of the earthly paradise could be restored, Fenelon[5] would return to the world and ask permission to embrace you. I myself ask that of laying at your feet the homage of these noble sentiments which you stimulate of friendship, respect and admiration inspired by you, and with which I have the honor to be, Madame,

Your very humble and obedient servant,
Marshal Prince de Ligne.

I beg of you, Madame, not to take the trouble to write me a reply. I'll go to look for it with my excuses for this too-long epistle.

> Source: *NRL ii*, no. 34,
> Lebasteur ed. 2 vols.

Notes

1. *Agathokles* (3 vols.), Berlin, 1808.
2. *Agathoclès* (4 vols.), Paris 1812. Translated into French by Mme de Montolieu (1751-1832), a prolific literary intermediary.
3. The Caelian Hill (55 m., one of seven in ancient Rome, SE of the city, now the Lateran). The Kahlenberg is a hill outside Vienna (483 m., the last spur of the alps), where Ligne had a "refuge" and where he is buried.

    These two names provoke a fanciful excursion into philology for Ligne, where Kahlenberg does not derive from the name of the plebian *gens* "Caelius", but from Germanic *kahlen* plus *berg* ("bald hill").
4. Two preeminent German writers of the time: Christoff-Martin Wieland (1733-1813), and Johan-Wolfgang von Goethe (1749-1832).
5. François de Salagnac de La Mothe-Fénelon (1651-1715), French prelate and author, known for his gentleness.

1789 – Pauline Adélaïde Alexandre Panam – 1840

Pauline Adélaïde Alexandre, reputed mistress of Duke Ernest I of Saxe-Coburg (1784- 1844) by whom she had a son; the Duke attempted to silence her by fair means or foul. He was also the father of Prince Albert of Great Britain (1819-61) and so the father-in-law of Queen Victoria (1819-1901). Ligne gave advice to her for her son's future and wrote notes on her behalf to Metternich while attempting to present her (unsuccessfully) to his family, who refused; probably Ligne's last sexual enthusiasm, for whom he caught cold waiting for an assignation that led to his fatal illness.

Letters from Ligne
    ✉ a - 2 August 1814, from Vienna
    ✉ b - 28 August 1814, from [?]
    ✉ c - [1814 ?], from [?]
    ✉ d - [Nov / Dec 1814 ?], from [?]

See: Pauline-A-A. Panam, *Mémoires, 2 vol.* (Paris: Brissot-Thivars, 1823).
Roland Mortier, "*La belle Grecque*," NAPL xv (2002), 151-77

Ligne to Panam - a
2 August 1814   Vienna

Beautiful Pauline (whom I see), dear Pauline (whom I cherish), adorable Pauline (as I believe)—

Send me your letter for Trogoff,[1] if you care to. Although a "goodbye", even if only for a few days, makes me sad, I'll go and bid you adieu this morning, but very tenderly (as one must, when one knows one of the most beautiful women in the world).

Almost without hope of seeing you, I went yesterday evening to the ramparts after the ballet,[2] it appears that I'm still in need of telling you I love you. One of my servants leaves today for Paris.[3]

Ligne

Source: *NAPL xv* (2002), 171

Ligne to Panam -b
28 August 1814   [Vienna]

I went early to see the most beautiful of beauties rather than the ballet, but came home at 10:00. May I see adorable Pauline at nine tomorrow morning? Good day to you dearest.

Ligne

Source: *NAPL xv* (2002), 172

Ligne to Panam -c
[?]   [Vienna]

I quickly sealed your letter, dear and adorable Madame Alexander - no! - dear Pauline, and it will leave in a few hours. If you'd like to see my mountain[4] and the one who goes there to think of you, say so. Or, tell the man who delivers this note (his name is Joseph) when you need a carriage. It takes an hour from the foot of my mountain, and if the coachman cannot make it, you need an extra half hour.

Good day my daughter, mother, niece—my all.[5]

Ligne

Source: *NAPL xv* (2002), 172-3

Ligne to Panam - d
[Nov / Dec 1814?]   [Vienna?]

Do you know, dear Pauline, that the Duke has arrived,[6] handsomer than ever, and better disposed toward you, I'm sure. I'm even more certain he'll be moved by your plight as soon as he glimpses his pretty little likeness.[7] I shall tell him of your good behavior, certified by Mme Argus[8] and will console myself by saying that you treat all those who worship at your feet the same, except [of course] for me. I've just spent three days on my mountain and yesterday all day at court from nine in the morning.

Your principles and your stairways prevent me from going to see you today,[9] dear Pauline, as I'm resting from one and the other in my good bed. Let me know where Mr Blumenburg is staying[10] - is this not the name of your agent at Coburg? I'll go and visit this amiable and arrogant Duke who must take care of his son and who, seeing the mother more beautiful than ever (unfortunately too virtuous for us) will guarantee her a happy future.

I shall avenge myself on Mme Argus for your principles. One of these days she should tremble at midnight.

Good day, dear and adorable!
Ligne

Source: *NAPL xv* (2002), 173

Notes

1. Trogoff was an aide-de-camp to Count d'Artois, later Charles X of France.
2. Ligne was in the habit of doing this, which led to his death of cold.
3. Apparently with this letter
4. The Kahlenberg and "Little Belœil".
5. Note by Madame Panam: This so tender friendship with the Prince de Ligne is one of the nicest memories I have to console myself.
6. Ernest III of Saxe-Coburg-Saalfeld, later Ernest I of Saxe-Coburg-Gotha (1784-1844); ancestor of both H. M. Queen Elizabeth II and the Duke of Edinburgh.
7. Mme Panam had had a son by Duke Ernest.
8. The concierge at Mme Panam's.
9. Ligne was aware of these problems. Cf. his verse: Vous êtes la dernière que j'aurai aimée au troisième [in succession/on the third - or fourth - floor].
10. Blumenburg: Mme Panam's agent at Coburg, but in Vienna for the Congress with Duke Ernest.

28

– To My Readers –

This letter is a sort of summing up of the second inspiration of Ligne's life: writing (the first was the military) – especially about women. Virtue and vice ennobles and in Ligne's own letters, ending with advice for the Walthers, his printers in Dresden, and an encomium of Duke Karl August of Saxe-Weimar, who at one time had circulated a *canard* about Ligne's early demise (Ligne was to live another two years after this letter).

For another view of this same reaction, but in English (Jane Austen), see chapter 25 above and Lady H. Marlow [pseud., William Beckford]; *Modern Novel Writing: or the Elegant Enthusiast* [London] 1796.

[1812?] [Vienna?]
To My Readers
if there are any to be found.

You will easily note that my letters are not meant for you, still less for the printer or the impression they may make. Those I wrote to men were often copied by my aides-de-camp who asked my permission before sealing them. My letters to women were copied by my confidants [usually] my children,[1] which goes to prove that they are not malicious. They are a *jeu d'esprit* or a *jeu de coeur* and a lesson in morality by a sort of conventional immorality that fools no one, since the language of love is so well-known that no one takes it seriously any more. Those [ladies] who might misjudge it (and me) will find here an antidote. Nor are there any of those scorched pages or exaggerations in lovers' points of suspension, or exclamations like "O cruel mistress! O superb goddess! O wretched misfortune!" I converse, I reason and I reasonably urge, almost always sure of being unrequited. If I were sure [of being taken seriously], I would not have written. In general, my letters were usually composed on the eve, never on the morrow. You must never admit to failure. If St-Preux had been more delicate, he would never have written, the day after his victory, "Let us meet death, my sweet."[2] I don't recall if I didn't say the same in another one of my own letters.

Perhaps there are some repetitions: likely I did say to one correspondent what I had said to others. But those remarks are proof of cruelty and beauty which could be published in a half-serious correspondence if ever it were to see the light of day. If the other half – which is to say the replies – were to appear, they would show me to be ridiculous (by being rather harsh) or fatuous (if perchance they were made public). But fear of what I might say in my posthumous writings has already set off the alarm that has served me badly. I've sworn that I would never include any of those, and the reader would never be able to guess who is "Madame or Mademoiselle ***" and who would perhaps have had the bad taste to have a taste for me.

Works about flirtation and dreaming are not the most dangerous; rather, those which, under the cover of feeling and morality, lead to a passion that people say cannot be stopped, and where family misfortunes, abductions, duels, suicides, and sorrow from disappointment are the result.

What reader doesn't feel pity in the *Liaisons dangereuses*[3] for the stupidity of Cécile by yielding [to Valmont], the little boarding-school minx, created to prevent just that? And who is not horrified by Valmont's strategy? Who does not shudder at his hypocrisy, especially in almsgiving, and his shocking tactics with the Présidente? It's all so abominable that it seems to me that this book could serve as the guardrail on a highway running atop a cliff.

I come back to my poor innocent little writings. These commonplaces of tenderness are the way to one's heart, like the post from Vienna to Paris. If the heart desires to surrender, each letter marks two leagues of the way. In return for that, while following the same order to go forward, you need one hundred fifty leagues to conclude.

How far is it from what you ask to what you might ask? Who could notice the imprint of vice in that? We delicate ones are satisfied with a simple "I love you" while awaiting an "I adore you" which would give us so much more pleasure. My family secretaries never understood more than that and would have scolded me severely if there had been more.

What's certain is that I never know what I'm writing, that I've not re-read these copies[4] that people don't mention now and which I myself have forgotten until this moment. Moreover, I think they're correct, and I don't worry about mistakes and missing words -- if there are any. I won't go back on the good I say about these persons or to these persons. I remember quite well their looks, their wit, or their amiability. I even think that there is no exaggeration at all; least of all there is no deception.

Dear readers, be indulgent for the material and the form, for maxims perhaps a bit superficial, and for the style. It seems to me that morality and also perhaps religion might redeem them.

Editors and printers - - do with me what you will. If it's at Weimar that you wish to assemble these trifles, I've already published there my *Prince Eugène* and my *Fragments militaires*[5] under the protection of Baron Müffling,[6] who has ostensibly looked after them. I've been honored by the sublime kindness of Goethe,[7] and I adore the sovereign of the Athens of modern Germany.[8] He is my ideal ruler because of his amiability and goodness toward me. I should add "because of his inestimable friendship." I'm proud of the affection of a great Prince, a good general, a good officer, a good soldier who makes his subjects happy, is easy to live with, is merry, sociable, amused by everything, and, as a result, sure to please everyone.

This homage is little enough for me who'd like to say more about him, but here is the only place where I can raise a monument to him, my garden [on the Kahlenberg] being too small and trophies and marble statues of the virtues too cold and cost too dearly.[9] I don't believe there's a letter to him in this collection;[10] it would be too light-hearted and disrespectful, or too sensitive and would border on boredom. In the first instance, I'd recall too many things that have amused us, and in the second his precious tears at the false announcement of my death. Happily, I'm unable to repay him in kind. May he live long for the honor of his country, the happiness of all those who know him (including my own), until what people had mistakenly told him has happened, does happen one day or another.

Source: *NRL* (Lebasteur ed.) Préface

Notes

1. Usually, Ligne's daughter Marie-Christine, Princess Clary (1757-1830) and his step-granddaughter "Titine," Countess O'Donnell (1786-1867).
2. In Jean-Jacques Rousseau's famous novel *La Nouvelle Héloïse* (1761), part 1, no 55.
3. A novel in letters (1782) by Choderlos de Laclos (1741-1803).

4. Despite assertions like this, it is now known that Ligne did rewrite many of his texts, taking great care with his revisions; see Mansel, *Prince of Europe* (London, 2003), 194-5.

5. *Mémoires de Prince Eugène de Savoie* (Weimar, 1809), a very successful hoax by Ligne; his *Fragments militaires* have recently been re-edited in two volumes. See, by Prof. J. Vercruysse, *Bibliographie descriptive* (Paris, 2008), 302-12 and 313-19.

6. Friederich Weiss, Baron Müffling (1775-1851). German general, commandant of occupied Paris, 1814-15.

7. Johann v. Goethe (1749-1832), illustrious German author; knew Ligne.

8. Charles-August, Duke of Saxe-Weimar (1757-1828), patron of Goethe; friend of Ligne's.

9. "Te aere perennius." reminiscence of Horace, Car. iii: 30, v.1. For details of Ligne's interest in gardens, see my translation and edition of his *Coup-d'Œil* (Berkeley, 1991).

10. There is such a letter in Ligne's *Nouveau Recueil de Lettres* (Weimar, 1812), 2 vols, part 2, no 1.

– Two Scenes from Ligne's *Fragments* –

A - Encounter at a Gala

I met a woman who looked vaguely familiar at a Gala. The Emperor[1] said to me, "She's the daughter of a Lt Col in the regiment from Licca [Austria]. I've no time to receive her." Smiling [slyly], he added, "Ask her what she wants."

She knew even less German than I. All she could say was, "Burgerspital, Morgen eine Supplik."[2]

I go there as she had asked. It would have been dishonest not to present her with my own request and leave without chatting. We [simply] didn't understand one another. Usually that creates a problem [in etiquette]. I give signs of my discomfort. "Fürst," [Prince][3] she utters. I find it hard to keep muself from taking her in my arms. She was beautiful as a summer's day. She whispers a friendlier "Fürst" that encourages me. I stifle on her lips a third "Fürst" she is on the point of delivering in anger. The more she insists, the more I attempt to discourage her. Finally, barely able to distinguish the first letter [of the word Fürst] I throw myself at her feet to ask her forgiveness. "Fürst," she then says, so moved that, not knowing whether it was from displeasure or astonishment at such lack of respect, or surprise at this great respect on my part, "I've nothing to lose," I said to myself, "Perhaps I've displeased her."

The situation absolutely demanded a shift in positions. A more satisfactory arrangement disposed of my uncertainty. Alas! It came about in a terrifying way for me. A very loud "Fürst!" floored me as she was attempting to rise from the sofa where she had been sitting. This effort, plus a slight weakness after what had just occurred, caused her to fall back immediately, uttering a "Fürst," she says, careful not to annoy me. Without affection nor haste, I take her to my breast. She returns the favor with a most tender "Fürst". I want to prove to her that I am worthy. I demand other "Fürsts". And by a sort of magnetism in getting closer to her, I hear her complete..., interrupt..., stammer..., twenty "Fürsts" in every key. After the last one that I might have taken for affection (if I'd been conceited), she gave me the prettiest little "Fürst" of gratitude and friendship that made up for all the distress I had caused her to prove my own.

Source: *Frags. 2,* (Vercruysse ed.), 366

Notes

1. Joseph II (1741-90), Emperor in 1765.
2. A large hospital and apartment building in Vienna, where Beethoven once lived.

   "A petition in the morning".
3. "Fürst" refers to "Prince" hereafter.

B - An Austrian Babel

I'm often afraid of making solecisms in one or the other languages of the Court (in Vienna). Nevertheless, I'll try to capture the tone of a performance by [Ignatz, Baron] Koch.[1] He was in the habit of greeting many guests, and, so, one evening he caught sight of [Carlo] Pellegrini.[2] "Ah!," he exclaimed, "Voilà le beau major! [Here's the handsome major!]" Then, to a General of Ordnance, he said, "Excellenz, ich bin dein gehorzamter Diener [Excellency, your obedient servant]". Pelligrini inturrpted with, "Avez-vous eu la bonté de parler de mon affaire à l'Impératrice? [Have you had the goodness to mention my affair to the Empress?]" "Oui, certainment [Yes, most assuredly]", he replied, "e sua maestà ha mi detto... [and her Majesty told me...]", immediately cut short with "Wie gehts mit ihrer Gesundheit jetzt Herr Lt. Feld Marshal? [How is your health now Lt. Field Marshall?]" while repeating his reply to Pellegrini. When a Col. of cavalry passed by he practically shouted, "Ah! Caro colonello che fanno gli cuirassiere del'Imperatrice? [Ah! Col. how are the brave cuirassiers of the Empress doing?]" Then turning again to Pellegrini "... e sua maestà ha mi detto... , [and her Majesty told me...]", before hailing a minister, "Ihr Excellenz, ich nenne mich deinen Entwurf... [Your Excellency, I myself am forwarding your project...]" Once more to Pellegrini whose had he had not released, "E sua maestà ha mi detto, [and her Majesty told me...]", before noticing a Major General of his intimate card-playing circle, "Eco il terrore del taraco [Here's the terror of card sharps]" [Pellegrini at his wit's end was unable to control himself.] exploded with "Ma CHE ha detto sua maesta? [what DID her Majesty say?] "Ah! Messieurs, je vous demande pardon, mais je vois un homme de ma chancellerie qui m'apporte des papiers à signer. [I beg your pardon, Gentlemen, but I see a man from my office coming with papers for me to sign.]"

Source: *Frags. 2,* (Vercruysse ed.), 324

Notes

1. Ignatz, Baron Koch (1771-63), private secretary to Maria-Therersa, a silly minister, a favorite of the Court, but very important.
2. Carlo Pellegrini (1720-96), Austrian Field Marshall.

A Letter on the Turks

[1795?] [Vienna?] [1]

Do you want to know about the Turks? Here they are, quite different from the idea we used to have of them.[2] They are a people of contrasts: brave and cowardly, active and lazy, pederasts and devout, sensual and hard, refined and coarse, clean and dirty, one hand carrying roses and the other a cat that has been dead for two days, sometimes one hand fondling the charming protuberances of either sex and the other on the Koran. If I were to speak of the leaders of the court, the army and the provinces, I'd say: high and low, mistrustful and ungrateful, proud and cringing, generous and cheats. All these traits, good and bad, with the first generally outweighing the second, depending on circumstance and covered with a crust of ignorance and insensitiveness that preserves them from being unhappy.

It's clear that if they weren't under the yoke of masters who strangle them[3] in order to abduct their sons and daughters while confiscating their wealth, they'd not be so accustomed to habits that make them look like barbarians.

They smile very little, answer with the head, the eyes, or the arms or the hand that never moves without a noble gracefulness. They hardly ever speak. There's nothing vulgar about them, neither in what's been explained to me nor in their manners. The little flatterer of a Janiaasry[4] (whatever he may say), very often like his master with bare feet and legs and no shirt, is stylish in his fashion and seems to be more elegant than the young lords of European courts. To be sure, the poorest of their soldiers have nothing to cover themselves with, but their damascened weapons are made of silver. I've seen them refuse two hundred piasters for them, fearing less to die from hunger than from shame.

The Turks are very touched by acts of gratitude and kindness and are always true to their word in every circumstance of life, whether in war or not. The more so, they tell me, because they don't know how to write.

The Turks are a bit like the Greeks, and even more like the Romans. They have the tastes of the first (for they make love like the Greeks) and the habits of the others. Their handwork is charming, tasteful, and shows a thoughtfulness that is very refined and delicate. Their mind is well furnished, if we may judge by the little they say. They are serious like the Romans and do not take the trouble to laugh or dance. All of their lords retain clowns. The prettiest of their little boys, prettier I'll wager than Horace's Ligurinus and perhaps even Virgil's Alexis,[5] are an object of magnificence. Ibrahim Nazir,[6] whom we drove from Moldavia, had five or six superbly dressed, who accompanied him on horseback. The Turks explained to me that independently of such "philosophic"[7] tastes, it was pleasing to them to awaken in the morning to see lovely faces who were supposed to serve them coffee, or their pipe, or their sherbet, or their aloe-wood for perfuming the air, or their attar of roses. They don't care two figs for us who have wretched masseurs or an old family servant come to set our fire or throw aside our drapes. They are forever in the prone position, like the Romans (who I don't doubt) had couches like theirs where they ate lying down and seemed to forget the livelong day that they had legs. Their tunics and slippers prove that these two peoples did not like walking. As one gets angry, as quickly as cold and phlegmatic people, the Turks, like the Romans, put their stock in revenge; aside from working, they're gentle, never having arguments or quarrels If a republican form of government didn't bring about a spirit of partisanship, intrigues, jealousy, and the crimes that follow, the Romans would have been a good people. If the opposite excesses of freedom that produced two Brutus[8] and so-called virtuous monsters when extremes are joined, if the despotism of a sultan and two or three Grand Officers of the Porte [palace] did not alarm them continually, the Turks would simply be the best people in the world.

Ignorant out of laziness, in politics, superstitious out of habit and calculation, they are guided by a natural and happy impulse. What would the nations of the Ottoman Empire become if a soap-maker were premier, a gardener Grand Admiral, or a footman commander of the armies? Where would you find these same individuals ready to fight as foot soldiers, cavalry, sailors AND clever in everything they undertook, or, individually, always daring all? Since the [various] conditions are indistinct, no one is classified, everyone has the same rights to everything and expects [no more than] the rank that destiny has assigned him.

Observers, travelers, spectators – instead of making trivial remarks on the nations of Europe, all of which more or less resemble one another, reflect on all that concerns Asia if you desire to discover novelty, beauty, grandeur, nobility and frequently reasonableness.

Source: *Mél.* vii (1798), 221-6.

Notes

1. The location and dating of this letter, the last in a series supposedly addressed to Ségur, is problematic; the last previous one in this collection was dated 10 December, 1790, as from Vienna.
2. See C.D. Rouillard, *The Turk in French Literature, Thought and Legend* (Paris: Boivin, 1941). Also B. Guy. "Le Prince de Ligne et les Turcs", *Le Gai Savoir* (Studia Humanitatis: Potomac, MD., 1983; 132-45.)
3. The normal mode of execution under the sultans.
4. The Janissaries were a corps of guards originally composed of Circassians who had been abducted when still children and formed into an elite group.
5. Ligurinus, see Horace, *Carmina:* v: 1, 10. Alexis, see Vergil, *Eclogues* 2, 5, and 7.
6. Ibrahim Nazir (died 1789) governor of the Yedisan (Moldavia).
7. "Philosophic:" a pejorative term in Ligne's vocabulary, equivalent to modern "intellectuals".
8. The two Brutus were Lucius Junius, founder of the Roman Republic, consul in 509 B.C., and Marcus Junius (85-42 B.C.), "the noblest Roman."

Acknowledgements

Bowdoin College, Brunswick, Me., Scholarship Committee,.

Fulbright Committee

J.S. Guggenheim Fellowship

Belgian-American Educational Foundation.

Faculty Committee on Research, U.C. (Berkeley)

And to the many individuals - friends and acquaintances - who, over the years, have favored me with counsel, ideas and solutions to the several problems involved in this work.

www.ingramcontent.com/pod-product-compliance
Lightning Source LLC
Chambersburg PA
CBHW020049170426
43199CB00009B/223